Foreword

When war broke out in August 1914 Australia's commitment to the Home Country was immediate: within a couple of months General William Throsby Bridges' newly raised 1st Division and 1st Light Horse Brigade were off to war, soon followed by the 4th Infantry Brigade. At that time the Western Australian goldfields and south-west forests were the homes and work places for thousands of men from other states of Australia, many of whom ultimately found their way to Blackboy Hill Camp, which was to be the main training camp for 32,000 Western Australian volunteers.

Jeff Hatwell's *No Ordinary Determination* tells the story of two of these men, Lieutenant Colonel Harry Murray VC CMG DSO DCM Croix de Guerre and Major Percy Black DSO DCM Croix de Guerre, both men in their mid-thirties, who joined the 16th Battalion as private soldiers and sailed for Gallipoli. Jeff, himself a former soldier who saw active service in South Vietnam, has crafted a wonderful story of mateship and courage and takes us on a journey through their recruitment and training, their action in the trenches of Gallipoli, and in the Hell that was to be the Australians' lot on the Western Front.

No Ordinary Determination at once describes the war experiences of Australian soldiers from enlistment to death or demob, and the personal journey of two great friends who distinguished themselves in the horror of war. It is an enthralling account of the First World War, clearly portraying the intensity of front-line battles at the unit level. Much time has passed since these battles and happily the experiences are well beyond those of contemporary generations, but this very personal story brings them to life in a vivid and very real way.

Lieutenant General John Sanderson, AC
Governor of Western Australia
Honorary Colonel, The Royal Western Australia Regiment
25 April 2005

Preface

The genesis of this book goes back some twenty-five years or more. For someone with a great interest in military history since my early teens, it is somewhat embarrassing to admit that it was only after passing thirty years of age that it occurred to me that I should know something about my own country's record in war — and this after having served in the Australian Army myself, in 1970–71, as a national serviceman. I decided to start my education with the 1914–18 war, at the obvious point of C E W Bean's classic *Official History* of Australia in that conflict, with his Volume I covering the first few days of the ANZAC landing at Gallipoli.

Reading the book with increasing wonder at both the industry of the author and the drama of the story he told, I came to Bean's account of the second day at Anzac, 26 April 1915. Here he devoted part of a long paragraph to introducing two 'men of no ordinary determination' — Lance-Corporal Percy Black and Private Harry Murray of the 16th Battalion. This introduction, along with Bean's usual biographical footnote showing the soldiers' birth dates, birthplaces and occupations and their eventual ranks and gallantry awards, made it apparent that here were two remarkable men, in their mid-thirties (Bean in fact understated their ages), of no particularly distinguished background, who each went on to reach high rank with numerous decorations.

The first questions that came to mind were, 'Who were these men? What was their story?' But almost immediately I realised that the real question was, 'Why don't I already know this?' Why wasn't it common knowledge, at least for a military history enthusiast like me? Reading the succeeding volumes of the *Official History*, I found the names of Harry Murray and Percy Black recurring frequently as Bean described the fighting of the First AIF infantry on the battlefields of Gallipoli and France.

One or both men played some part (usually outstanding) in almost every battle — from the Landing to the Armistice — in which their units were involved. Eager to discover more, I waited many years for 'someone' to write a book about them. The idea that I might write it myself did not occur to me until comparatively recently. Of course, once I had done my research and got about halfway through the first draft, such a book actually did appear — *Mad Harry*, George Franki and Clyde Slatyer's biography of Harry Murray. Although rather taken aback by the timing, I decided to continue with my own work, which took, after all, a somewhat different approach to the *Mad Harry* authors — whom I soon found to be affable, helpful gentlemen with much the same attitude as myself to our shared interest.

I have drawn on a variety of sources, mostly conventional, but some less well known. Particularly useful have been the published writings of C E W Bean. Apart from the *Official History* and Bean's various articles, I have also consulted his notes, correspondence and diaries held at the Australian War Memorial. These contain material that Bean would have found inappropriate for the *Official History*, but there were details that proved invaluable for filling in small but important gaps in the stories of my subjects. Numerous articles by Harry Murray and others in the 1920s, 30s and 40s in *Reveille*, the New South Wales RSL magazine, helped flesh out the story, as did the 'Digger's Diary' column of the Perth *Western Mail* over the same period. Generally, I have combined all relevant sources, including unit 'war diaries' and individuals' army service records, to come up with this narrative of Percy Black's and Harry Murray's military careers.

Comments on Black's or Murray's state of mind at any time are based on either their own writings or on the direct reports of others who were in close contact. On the very few occasions when I have inferred someone's feelings without a definite statement from a source, this has been based on very strong indications in the material. Where I believe that a statement or description needs further explanation, these are included in the chapter notes. Any direct speech in the book is taken unchanged from original sources.

Regrettably, there are still considerable gaps in the available information, particularly as regards Black's and Murray's lives before the 1914–18 war brought them to prominence, but one can still be optimistic that more details will come to light some day.

A perennial difficulty in writing military biographies is to reconcile admiration for the qualities shown by the people involved, with the unquestioned horror and tragedy of the events in which they achieved their prominence — speechmakers at Anzac Day ceremonies are often at pains to resolve this conflict. Such a reconciliation was, I believe, best expressed by Siegfried Sassoon, the British soldier/poet who developed an intense anti-war attitude through his experiences on the Western Front in 1914–18 (the authorities naturally decided that he must have taken leave of his senses). In his *Memoirs of an Infantry Officer*, Sassoon contemplated the comrades with whom he had shared the trenches:

> *... men whose courage had shown me the power of the human spirit — that spirit which could withstand the utmost assault ... against the background of the War and its brutal stupidity, these men had stood glorified by the thing which sought to destroy them.*

Perhaps that thought can be borne in mind when considering the story of Harry Murray and Percy Black, and of all the millions who fought on both sides of the 'war to end all wars'.

Jeff Hatwell, April 2005

Chapter 1

COLONISTS AND CONVICTS

In the first days of August 1914, the young nation of Australia was electrified to find itself, with the rest of the British Empire, at war with Germany. The thousands of Australian men who rushed to enlist in the armed services in the first weeks of the war included a few individuals who were destined to make special marks on their country's history. In Western Australia, two rural working men would emerge from obscurity to place themselves among Australia's greatest soldiers: Percy Black, a prospector from the Yilgarn goldfields, and Henry (Harry) Murray, a timber contractor from the forests of the south-west.

Percy Black's family had been established in Australia since the mid-nineteenth century. His parents, William John Black and Ann Longmore, were both from County Antrim, Ulster, and were almost certainly members of the extensive Scottish Presbyterian culture in Ulster.[1] The horror of the Potato Famine had struck Ireland in the 1840s with around a million deaths from starvation and related diseases. Another two million Irish people emigrated during and after the famine period. Although the Ulster counties suffered slightly less from the famine than the nation as a whole, their loss through emigration was just as high. The majority made their way to America, but William Black and Anne Longmore chose the Australian colony of Victoria as their destination.

It is not clear whether William and Anne had married (or even met) at the time they embarked for the Antipodes, and the details of their voyage and arrival are also not known. It was as a married couple, however, that they made their way to rural Victoria. The district around Ballan, roughly seventy kilometres west of Melbourne, had been opened up by the von Stieglitz family (of Irish extraction despite their Teutonic name) in the late 1830s. The area was rich farming country, particularly suitable for sheep; the Blacks obtained a property in the locality of Beremboke, a little south of the Ballan town site, and set about establishing their farm and raising a family.

The Blacks raised fourteen children,[2] the eleventh of these being a boy born on 12 December 1877 and given the names Percy Charles Herbert. The Black children grew up in the outdoor life of the sparsely populated district. By 1870 there were enough people around Beremboke for the Victorian government to approve the establishment of a tiny one-classroom school, of which the four eldest Black siblings were original pupils. The youngest son Percy attended the school in his turn, receiving the solid basic education that was becoming available to most children in the Australian colonies. As they reached adulthood, several of the young Blacks moved away from the farm and took on other occupations. No less than four of Percy's older brothers (Hugh, Samuel, Robert and Joseph) joined the Victorian police force, although Hugh later left under some sort of cloud. Percy himself seems to have become a carpenter after leaving school, but where he plied his trade is not known. Not far from Beremboke was the locality of Mount Egerton, where gold had been discovered in the 1850s. Although Ballarat, thirty kilometres further west, was far better known as one of the focal points of the Victorian gold rushes, the Mount Egerton deposit proved to be quite lucrative. The original strike evolved into a mechanised underground operation (the shaft eventually went to a depth of over 600 metres) and it is possible that the young Percy Black developed an interest in goldmining from his proximity to the mine.

William John Black and Anne (Longmore) Black.
(Courtesy Ballan Shire Historical Society)

Certainly it was gold that took him to the other side of the continent to seek his fortune. The economies of the eastern colonies sank into depression during the 1890s, coinciding with a remarkable series of gold discoveries in Western Australia. The western colony was inundated with a huge rush of gold seekers from overseas and from the east of the continent. From Victoria alone, 75,000 people made their way west between 1895 and 1900, and by 1901 it was estimated that two-thirds of the West Australian population had been born elsewhere.[3] Some time around the turn of the century Percy Black, in his mid-twenties, decided to join the exodus. With a friend named John Hughes,[4] he set off westwards.

Established in 1829, the Western Australian colony, comprising a third of the continent, made only slow progress in its first sixty years. The first discoveries of gold in the 1880s changed all that: as the immigrants began flooding in and the sluggish economy boomed. The initial rushes had subsided by the time the young carpenter from Beremboke arrived, but there was still money to be made in many of the diggings. Percy Black probably travelled by ship from Victoria — the trans-Australia railway was not completed until 1917 — although a few remarkable characters actually walked across the continent to join the search for gold. Travellers by ship usually landed at Albany in the south of the state (the Fremantle harbour improvements were only completed in the early 1900s), and from there made their way inland to reach the goldfields. Railways were being extended from Perth to the closer gold diggings at about this time, but a variety of other means were used — horses, camels, bicycles or simply walking, perhaps pushing a wheelbarrow with one's belongings.

Percy Black initially headed for the coincidentally named Black Range area of the East Murchison goldfield, about 600 kilometres north-east of Perth. This area was prospected in the late 1890s, but significant finds were not reported until 1903, and it was probably then that Black and Hughes made their way to the area. No details can be found of their activities at Black Range but presumably they led the normal life of small prospectors. Having pegged out and registered a lease, they would have established a camp and set about trying to extract the elusive metal by a variety of methods. Most common for the arid goldfields of the west was 'dryblowing' — in the non-mechanical version, small quantities of dirt and crushed rock were allowed to fall between two dishes so that the breeze blew away the lighter particles, leaving the heavier gold (if there was any) to collect in the lower container. More sophisticated methods included mechanical 'batteries' to crush the ore and extract the gold. Although these were expensive, small fossickers could have their ore treated by paying a fee to the battery owner. Some groups could finance shaft mining, and a few people had the capital to establish large operations. Life on the diggings was hard and primitive, although supplies, drink and a few luxuries were usually available in the townships that sprang up almost overnight near the diggings, such as Nungarra and Sandstone at Black Range.

The level of Percy Black's success on the Murchison can only be guessed at. Certainly he didn't make his fortune, but it is reasonable to assume that he was able to get some sort of living from his various claims. In any event, as the emphasis shifted from the small prospectors to a few big operations, he decided it was time to move on. Whatever the results of his first venture into prospecting, he was sufficiently encouraged to continue the search for gold. He took up a number of leases in various districts, including several at Mount Margaret, and in about 1908 moved further south to the Yilgarn goldfields. There he established a claim at Mount Jackson, about a hundred kilometres north of Southern Cross, the main town of the area. He seems to have had several partners in the venture (including Hughes), probably operating a shaft mine rather than dryblowing — in 1914 he was quoted as saying that the mine had its own battery for ore-crushing, so the partners seem to have had access to some capital. It appears that Black found it necessary, however, to work for wages as well: a photograph from 1912 shows him as a member of an underground shift at the big 'company' mine at Bullfinch, thirty-five kilometres from Southern Cross.

The township of Bullfinch formed a centre for the sparse population of the area to the north of Southern Cross, and Black played a part in the civic life of the community. He became an official of the Bullfinch Sports Committee, with the duties of Starter, and he was a member of the Bullfinch

Rifle Club — later he would be recognised as a superb shot. He was also a member of the Bullfinch Miners' Union. Although he was no teetotaller, the indications are that Black was a man of moderate habits, quiet and unassuming but with an underlying toughness that was suited to the hard life of the goldfields. Percy Black remained a bachelor all his life, but at some point he established a relationship with a woman, of whom all that is known comes from a couple of surviving letters, signed only with her initial and surname, M Cassidy. In one letter she stated that she had never seen Bullfinch, so they may have met at one of the larger towns, or perhaps on one of Black's trips to Perth — she was certainly living in Perth in 1915.

By 1914 then, Percy Black was established as a fairly typical citizen of the Western Australian goldfields, not overly distinguished perhaps, but (in C E W Bean's phrase) 'known from Yilgarn to the Murchison'. He was in his thirty-seventh year when he filled out his enlistment papers, five feet nine inches tall and a trim 150 pounds in weight, measuring 41 inches around the chest. Although not much more than medium size, he had a reputation for great physical strength, and his only health problem seems to have been poor teeth — examined by army doctors in September 1914, his fitness was endorsed as 'subject to extraction of stumps'. With his blue eyes and dark hair, and a luxuriant drooping moustache, he was thought to bear a superficial resemblance to General Lord Kitchener, Britain's hero of the Battle of Omdurman and soon the face of the 'Your Country Needs You' poster — 'with the same weather-beaten complexion, strong brows, heavy dark moustache, square jaw, but not quite so full in the face, and with lines more sensitive.'[5]

Harry Murray, the other protagonist of this story, was also of Scottish extraction, although his antecedents followed a somewhat different path to become established in Australia. In September 1786, a young Scotsman named Kennedy Murray was arrested in Glasgow on a charge of petty theft. Characterised as 'a person of bad fame and character', he was sentenced to transportation to the colonies. After some time in local prison, the twenty-five-year-old Murray embarked in 1791 on a convict ship bound for the penal

Bullfinch Sports Committee, 1912. Percy Black is second from the right at the rear.
Bert Longmore is third from the right in the front row.
(Courtesy Battye Library, Item 005662D)

colony of New South Wales, established only three years earlier. Arriving at Port Jackson early the next year, Murray remained in the colony until 1796, when he was one of a draft of convicts transferred to Norfolk Island, the beautiful speck in the Pacific claimed by Britain at about the same time as the Port Jackson landings. Norfolk Island did not yet have its reputation as a convict hell-hole ('the worst place in the English-speaking world', in Robert Hughes' phrase)[6] but conditions were arduous and primitive for both convicts and guards, and the discipline was certainly brutal.

Here Kennedy Murray encountered Anne White, another transported convict who had also been convicted of theft. At the age of seventeen she had been sent out with the Second Fleet in 1790, and had been on Norfolk Island since November 1791. The two soon formed a relationship, and in August 1799 Anne gave birth to their son, also named Kennedy. By 1802, their sentences had expired and their relationship had broken down. Kennedy Murray Senior returned to the mainland, but Anne White stayed on Norfolk Island until 1813 with her son, by which time she had taken up with another former convict and borne more children. With the closing down of the Norfolk Island colony in 1813, she and her blended family moved to the new colony of Van Diemen's Land, the future Tasmania.

The younger Kennedy Murray came to exemplify the phenomenon of Australian convict settlement — the transformation of the convicts' usually illegitimate 'currency' children into solid, law-abiding industrious pioneers within a single generation. Kennedy Murray Junior, with two convicted petty thieves as parents, plus another convict for a stepfather, founded an extensive family of respectable citizens — including a grandson who would become one of the great heroes of the British Empire. In 1820, Kennedy was granted a tract of farmland in the Evandale district, a little south of Launceston in northern Van Diemen's Land.[7] He steadily expanded his property and built a fine residence that he named, with justifiable pride in his success, Prosperous House. Kennedy Murray Junior married twice and fathered no less than seventeen children. His first child by his second wife, Hannah Goodall, was a son, Edward Kennedy Murray, born in 1840.

When Kennedy Murray Junior died in 1860, an obituary described him as a man of 'most industrious habits' and 'of a generous and obliging disposition'. His son Edward Kennedy Murray, apparently a man of less affable personality than his father, also became a farmer, acquiring another Evandale property that he named Woodstock. Portraits show Edward as a man of impressive appearance, with a strong face and a luxuriant beard. He married the dignified, intelligent Clarissa Littler, and the couple had nine children. Their eighth child and youngest son was born on 1 December 1880, and christened Henry William, although he would be best known by his nickname 'Harry'.

Growing up in northern Tasmania, as Van Diemen's Land was called after 1855, the young farm boy attended the government school at Evandale with his siblings. There is a story that he would often frighten his sisters when crossing a bridge on the way to school by walking along the handrail. Young Murray left school at thirteen or fourteen, apparently against his preference, under pressure from his father to help out on the farm. His older brothers had been allowed to continue their education, and this seems to have been one of several sources of an ongoing resentment against his father. He appears to have been a keen learner, and many of the references in his later writings point to a far wider reading than would be expected from a basic schooling. His clever, erudite mother no doubt contributed to his education also.

At some point the family took up another property, known as Northcote, near St Leonards. On New Year's Day 1901, the six separate colonies became a single nation, the federated states of the Commonwealth of Australia. The following year, the 22-year-old Harry Murray had his first taste of military life, joining the part-time militia of the Launceston Volunteer Artillery. He remained with this unit for six years, establishing a reputation as a crack rifle shot — he would have had plenty of practice on the farm — and experiencing what he later described as a very strict standard of discipline. By 1908, he was looking for a change of scene and a fresh start. His father had died in 1904, and the viability of the family farm was declining. Two of his older brothers, Albert and Charles (and later a sister, Marion), had already moved to Western Australia, and now he decided to follow them.

At about the same time as Percy Black was relocating from the Murchison goldfields to Mount Jackson, Harry Murray arrived in Western Australia, probably also by ship at Fremantle or Albany. His brother Charles, ten years Harry's senior, had established himself in the west some years earlier.[8] The oldest Murray brother, Albert, was also in Western Australia, where he had followed several occupations, including running the Kanowna hotel on the goldfields and later managing Meeberrie station on the Murchison River. Charles Murray originally came west in 1890 or 1891 with the intention of taking up work in a sawmill, but the lure of the goldfields took over. He was among those who walked from Albany to the goldfields, in his case to Southern Cross before following the railway line further east. With some prospecting, Charles Murray accumulated enough funds to start a cartage contracting business, transporting supplies by horse-drawn wagon to outlying diggings in the north-eastern goldfields between Leonora and Laverton, such places as Mount Morgans, Red Flag and Hawk's Nest.

When his younger brother Harry showed up looking for a job, Charles took him on in the cartage business, where he seems to have worked for some time. Harry Murray's private memoirs include an account of an incident that occurred when he was carting stores to an isolated gold mine, and a 1917 newspaper article mentioned that he had worked at Morgans and Hawk's Nest, although without saying what he was doing there. At some point also — it is not clear whether this was before or after joining his brother's business — Murray set himself up as a courier, carrying gold and mail by bicycle between outer diggings and the railheads. Bicycles were used extensively for personal transport and communications on the goldfields at this time, and although the heyday of the famous cycle mail service had ceased by about 1900 with the coming of the railways, there were apparently some niches where a demand still existed. Murray contracted for the run from Kookynie (about 160 kilometres north of Kalgoorlie) to a mine at Linden, on the edge of Lake Carey, a round trip of about 330 kilometres.[9] The back areas were crisscrossed with camel pads, the firm trails formed by the plodding camel caravans that carried the heavier loads from the railway to the outer camps, and these made fine cycle tracks. Many years later, Murray wrote of his regular trips on the lonely tracks, and the danger from hostile Aborigines and

Edward Kennedy Murray and Clarissa (Littler) Murray.
(Courtesy R Murray)

'bad lads with white hides', as he put it. He discouraged interference by '[letting] loungers see what I could do with the .32 carbine I carried.'

The work did not have a long-term future, although it may well have been quite profitable while it lasted — expenses would have been low, and the bicycle couriers charged substantial fees; a shilling per mile per item was not unusual. It was probably a decline in the diggings on his route that caused Murray to take up work with his brother Charles again.[10] Charles had moved his business to Comet Vale, about ninety-five kilometres north of Kalgoorlie and thirty kilometres south of Menzies. There were a couple of mines operating at Comet Vale, but Charles Murray's interest in the region was in wood rather than gold. The gold rushes had created an enormous demand for timber. Apart from domestic requirements for cooking and heating, structural timbers were used for propping the mine shafts and passageways, and as fuel for the steam engines powering the mine machinery, the winches and ore-processing furnaces. Wood also provided charcoal for gas-producer engines running the small prospectors' batteries. The remarkable goldfields pipeline, completed in 1903 to bring water 600 kilometres from Perth, used wood-fuelled steam pumps to keep the water flowing. Charles Murray, among many others, took up the business of supplying this insatiable demand.

Despite its sparse rainfall, the goldfields region was quite thickly forested at the beginning of the gold rush period. Scores of different species of eucalypts and acacias are native to the region, but the voracious appetite of the towns and mines resulted in huge areas being cut over, to an extent that is horrifying to present-day environmental thinking (later conservation policies have resulted in a recovery of the vegetation). The woodcutters worked outwards from the numerous sidings along the railway lines around Kalgoorlie, building private narrow-gauge tramways out to fresh areas as the nearer trees were cleared. Joining his brother's operation based at Comet Vale, Harry Murray was put to work cutting timber, and had to quickly adjust to life on the 'woodlines', living in isolated camps and working from dawn to dusk in the heat and dust.

It was hard, exhausting work with axe and crosscut saw, attacking some of the toughest tree species on earth. An old hand commented that he had seen 'quite a few cases of the "new chum" coming onto the woodline and losing the use of his axe on the first day. Unless an old hand had warned him, the newcomer could easily sharpen his axe to a fine point, swing it at a salmon gum and take out a sizeable chunk — not from the tree he was cutting, but from the axe head itself.'[11] Tools had to be purchased and replaced by the woodcutters themselves, usually on credit from the wood company's store. Purchases of clothing, small food items, personal effects and so forth were also debited against their meagre pay, and the workers often found themselves working for not much more than their keep. Harry Murray seems to have stuck with this for a year or two — he was registered on the electoral roll for 1911 as 'woodcutter, Comet Vale', and wrote to his sister from there in 1912 — but eventually he decided that he was getting nowhere, and began to look around for something else.

He travelled back to Tasmania to spend Christmas of 1912 with his family, returning to Western Australia in the new year to work in the great forests of the south-west. Here the local economy revolved around the timber industry, and a particularly important part of this was the production of railway sleepers. These were in high demand for both export and local railways, including the Trans Australia then under construction. The wood of the huge jarrah trees around the townships of Dwellingup and neighbouring Holyoake was ideal for sleepers, and the industry supported several thousand people in the region. Various sawmills were engaged in sleeper production, but those of the best quality came from hewers working with manual tools deep in the bush. Harry Murray was able to set himself up as a carting contractor in the area, collecting the sleepers produced by a team of those tough bushmen, for transport to the railway siding and sale to the users; it appears that he employed the hewers as subcontractors. The seven-foot long sleepers were cut from felled trees with a broadaxe, and it took great skill trimming them into perfect shape for the approval of the government inspectors. It was hard work, more so than working in the local sawmills, and the pay was not as good, but the sleeper hewers were the type of men who preferred the freedom and independence of the forest life.[12] In later years, after he had achieved distinction, Murray was often described as a sleeper cutter, but is unlikely that he did much hewing himself — he gave his occupation as sleeper *carter* on the local electoral roll. As an experienced bushman and a former goldfields woodcutter however, he would have been a handy man with an axe.[13]

The hewers would spend several weeks working through an area before taking a break at one or another of the small townships to let off steam, usually involving some hard drinking (although Murray himself did not drink at this time in his life). Home for the sleeper cutters and the various contractors was usually a large tented camp set up near the railway line, and a number of these were established at different locations as the cutters moved on to fresh patches. In 1914 Murray was living at Smith's Camp near Holyoake, at the twenty-six mile mark of the local railway. He was probably a member of the South-West Timber Hewers Co-operative Society (the 'Teddy Bears') and an article in the *Westralian Worker* of March 1917 says that he was also a member of the Timber Workers' Union, which may date from his woodcutting days at Comet Vale.

Possessed of a great inner strength and a quiet self-confidence in practical matters, Murray was also a very reticent man. Although known and respected in the district, he does not seem to have achieved any particular distinction or taken much of a part in the lively social life of the community, which tended to revolve around the frequent dances held in the local halls. As well as his shyness, Murray had the misfortune to be tone-deaf, and was, not surprisingly, a non-dancer. He would thus have been at a considerable disadvantage in meeting eligible women. Harry Murray was approaching thirty-four years old in August 1914; he was yet to find his true path in life, no doubt becoming increasingly restless and discontented. This would all change with the arrival of the news from Europe that his country was at war.

Australia was reasonably well informed about international events. Recently completed undersea cables allowed transmission of telegraphed news stories from Europe, and the capital city daily newspapers could have up to date information within a day or so of its appearance overseas. Scores of local newspapers in the bush towns, avidly read in the absence of other

A typical sleeper-hewers' camp in south-west Western Australia, c. 1914.
(Courtesy H McMeekin and R Richards)

communication media, picked up such stories as well. Most Australians were therefore aware of the international tensions that had been building in Europe in previous years, and of the bellicose attitudes of Germany and Austria towards their neighbours. They had noted the crisis resulting from the assassination of Archduke Franz Ferdinand of Austria by a Serbian extremist on 28 June 1914. Nevertheless, it was only in the last few days before these events reached their climax that it began to dawn on the British peoples that they were about to become involved in a major war.[14] On 4 August, faithful to her formal and informal alliances, Great Britain declared war on Germany, and the announcement struck Australia like a thunderbolt.

The Australian reaction was astonishing, with an instant outpouring of enthusiasm and almost hysterical patriotism. The leader of the Federal Opposition, Andrew Fisher, promised Australian support for the mother country 'to the last man and the last shilling.' Newspapers generally welcomed the war as an opportunity for the new nation to prove its worth, and editorialised against the brutal aggression of the Central Powers. Recruiting for an Australian force commenced almost immediately, and men from all over the country rushed to enlist. Their motivation is difficult to be sure of at this distance in time: a young man's desire for adventure was certainly part of it, to share in the glories of war that many of them had read about at school, in particular British glories. The desire for their new nation to take its place as a full member of the British Empire, proving itself in blood, was surely present in many, as was the simpler inclination to help a friend in need. Economic conditions were of some importance also. In Western Australia, the effects of drought and increasing unemployment were beginning to bite, and the guarantee of 'six bob a day' was a factor (the daily rate of pay for a private soldier was set at six shillings, far in excess of what a British 'Tommy' was paid). These were some of the more obvious reasons for the rush to enlist, but no doubt there were many more affecting each man who came forward, not least of which was the strong underlying patriotism — felt for both Australia and the Empire — of most of the citizens.

Army recruiting offices in the capital cities were soon swamped, and more than enough recruits were obtained to fill the initial quotas. Volunteers continued to make their way to the capitals from the bush areas, many delayed by distance but determined to make their mark. From Bullfinch in the Yilgarn came Percy Black, one of more than a hundred men from that tiny community who enlisted. He left his partners to manage their mine, and headed off with a quiet determination to play his part in what was to come. Down in the south-west forests, Harry Murray wound up his sleeper business and set off to enlist also, following hundreds of other timber workers, many of whom literally downed tools and jumped on the first train for Perth — their rusting broadaxes could be found lying in the bush after the war. The motives of Murray and Black were probably much the same as those of their contemporaries, although they were older by ten years than most of the first volunteers. Percy Black also felt that it was his place to represent his family in the Empire's struggle — he was the youngest of the brothers (even he was approaching the maximum enlistment age) and had fewer commitments. It is difficult not to speculate also that both men instinctively recognised the opportunity to discover their own untapped capacities. These first began to emerge at the army's Blackboy Hill training camp in September 1914.

Chapter 2

BLACKBOY HILL TO CAIRO

They come from the distant stations, bushmen bold and free,
The silent men of our silent land, knights of the saddle-tree;
They come from the rush of the goldmines, steady and strong and true —
Sons of the Southland, one and all, ready to see it through.
They leave the desk in the city, they come from the survey camp;
The pearling boat on the north coast, the garden by the swamp;
From every part of the country, from every sphere of life,
Eager they come to the training camps, longing to join the strife.[1]

Volunteers were quickly accumulating for the Australian force to join the mother country on the anticipated battlefields of Europe. The government had promised 20,000 men, and it was decided that these would be formed into an infantry division and a mounted brigade, the whole to be known by a name which would become legendary — the Australian Imperial Force. Western Australia's quota was 1400, but thousands more joined the initial rush to enlist in the AIF when men from all over the state converged on Perth.

The first recruits accepted for the infantry were sent by railway to a newly designated training area at Blackboy Hill, an expanse of bush twenty kilometres or so east of the city (in the modern suburb of Greenmount). Their first task was to set up the tented camp that would become the main army training site in the west throughout the war, and Blackboy Hill was officially established on 17 August 1914. These early recruits were to form the 11th Infantry Battalion and part of the 12th, but there were many more volunteers than were needed to fill those units. Men continued to pour in over the next few weeks, including many like Harry Murray and Percy Black who had been delayed by the necessity of winding up their civilian businesses. Each state of the Commonwealth found itself with an excess of volunteers, and the decision was soon taken to form these into extra units.

The infantry of the AIF was to be structured in accordance with the British Army's standard pattern, for ease of integration when they came under British command.

The infantry's basic unit of organisation was the battalion; at full strength a battalion consisted of approximately one thousand men (officers, non-commissioned officers and 'other ranks'), although in practice, casualties meant that battalions were rarely at full strength after they first went into action. A battalion was subdivided into companies identified by letters of the alphabet; initially each battalion had eight such companies, but these would shortly be grouped by twos to make four companies, each of which was further subdivided into four platoons. Each battalion was commanded by an officer of the rank of lieutenant-colonel; company commanders were majors or captains, and platoon commanders were lieutenants or second-lieutenants. In addition to the riflemen who formed the vast majority of a battalion's personnel, each included a few small specialist groups, including a machine-gun section.

Working upwards from the battalion level, an infantry brigade was a grouping of four battalions, roughly 4000 men at full strength. In the AIF, a brigade was at first commanded by a colonel, later raised to brigadier-general. An infantry division was made up of three brigades (therefore twelve battalions) and with other units, such as artillery and engineers, amounted to about 18,000 men, under the command of a major-general. These groupings of units were generally known as 'formations'.

The AIF battalions were identified by a simple numerical designation, and were recruited on a geographical basis. Thus the 1st, 2nd, 3rd and 4th Battalions (forming the 1st Brigade) came from New South Wales; the 5th to 8th (the 2nd Brigade) were from Victoria, and the 9th to 12th (the 3rd Brigade) came from the other, less populated, states. These three brigades made up the 1st Australian Division. The different battalions quickly built up a remarkably strong *esprit de corps*; the individual soldier's first loyalty (after his mates) was always to his battalion, then to his brigade.

When Percy Black officially enlisted on 8 September 1914, excess recruits were intended to make up additional reinforcements for the 11th Battalion, but a few days later it was announced that a further infantry brigade would be formed, made up of battalions from all the states. This new 4th Brigade would comprise the 13th (New South Wales), 14th (Victoria), 15th (Queensland and Tasmania) and 16th (Western Australia and South Australia) Battalions. The reinforcements at Blackboy Hill would form the greater part of the 16th Battalion: five of the eight (at that time) rifle companies; headquarters and signals; and the machine-gun section.

The battalion history describes in detail how Private Percy Black found his niche: the recruits were paraded by Major Mansbridge (commander of 'A' Company) for allocation to the various sub-units; 'as far as possible men from the same districts were allotted to the one company … while the specialists were drawn from those whose civil occupations were thought to fit them for particular military work.'[2] Mansbridge was marching the men off when he noticed Black standing to one side. He asked Black where he came from.

'The Goldfields,' Black replied, and continued, 'Look here, Mister, I don't know anything about this soldiering game. What crowd would you recommend me to join up with?'

The major then quizzed him about his occupation, and found that he operated a mine, with its own ore battery.

'What motive power?'

'A gas engine.'

'Can you drive it?'

'Yes, and I can drive a gas producer engine.'

'Very well,' said Mansbridge. 'Wait here, and I'll place you with the machine-gunners.'[3]

Harry Murray arrived at Blackboy Hill some time during the next two weeks, enlisting officially on 30 September. Perhaps fearing rejection because of his age (although he was not yet 34, and the maximum age was 38), he stated that he was 30 years 9 months old.[4] Fit and strong from years of physical outdoor work, he was a compact 5 feet 8 inches and 152 pounds, measuring 36 inches around the chest. Murray was a fine-looking man, with grey-green eyes and thick brown hair; clean-shaven in 1914, he would later grow the small neatly trimmed moustache familiar from his wartime photographs. He had wanted to enlist in the artillery (his militia experience being in that arm) or the dashing Light Horse, but lack of vacancies saw him sent to the 16th Battalion and allotted to a rifle company.

Murray, however, had already developed a strong interest in the battalion's machine-guns, and he was determined to get himself into that section. Cyril 'Syd' Longmore would in later life become a journalist,[5] war correspondent, and author of the 16th Battalion's history, but in September 1914 he was a regular soldier on the permanent training staff at Blackboy Hill, a sergeant-major in charge of machine-gun instruction. One evening Private Murray presented himself at Longmore's tent and made his case for transfer to the machine-guns. Impressed by the manner and bearing of the square-jawed Tasmanian, Longmore had little hesitation in agreeing, and Murray 'was a happy man when he was told to take his kit down to the section's tents.'[6]

In common with all British and Empire infantry battalions, the 16th was equipped with two .303 calibre Maxim machine-guns. Black and Murray were part of a section of seventeen 'other ranks' (ORs) led by the battalion machine-gun officer, Lieutenant A E Carse, and the section began its training under the supervision of Sergeant-Major Longmore. (Longmore and Black may have already known something of each other; Longmore's brother Bert had worked with Black at Bullfinch. Bert Longmore had already enlisted with

Private Harry Murray, Blackboy Hill, 1914.
(Courtesy R Murray)

the 11th Battalion and was later killed at Gallipoli. It was probably only a coincidence that the maiden name of Black's mother was also Longmore.) The 16th Battalion Machine Gun Section trained hard for the next two months, taking part in normal infantry drill and exercises with their Lee-Enfield rifles as well as their main duty of learning the operation of their Maxim guns.

The Maxim (and its development, the Vickers gun) was a sound design that would still be in use in the 1950s. It was a reliable, accurate weapon, firing belts of .303 ammunition at up to 600 rounds per minute. The gun was water-cooled, the tubular water-jacket around the barrel giving it its distinctive appearance. Although this system was very effective in keeping the gun cool during firing, it was something of a disadvantage in that it needed regular water supplies (the water began to boil away after about 600 rounds had been fired), and the gun could be put out of action by damage to the water-jacket. It was very heavy, weighing about 18 kilos (plus 3 kilos of water), with a sturdy tripod mount weighing another 23 kilos. The men chosen for the machine-gun section obviously needed considerable physical strength to move the guns and their heavy ammunition boxes on the battlefield. Black and Murray certainly qualified in that respect, and their other qualities were apparent from the beginning, even in that outstanding small group of men that their instructor would remember as the best he had ever handled.

Longmore later wrote of Black's 'strength, steadiness and reliability', and remembered Murray as 'quick in mind and body ... as keen as mustard' and having a 'wonderful eye for ground' — the instinctive assessment of the importance of terrain which marks the natural soldier. The two men were allotted to the same gun team and quickly became close friends. Somewhat older than most of their colleagues, that extra maturity gave them something in common, as did their quiet resolve to succeed at the task that they had set themselves. Their personalities were perhaps complementary, the phlegmatic Black and the rather more mercurial Murray (he once described himself as 'nervy and highly strung' at this time of his life), each unobtrusively self-reliant, and possessed of what C E W Bean called, 'that easy confidence in tackling men and situations that seems to be more easily acquired in the Australian bush than in most environments.'[7] The bush life meant also that they were accustomed to a very basic lifestyle (as were many of their fellow recruits), often living for long periods under canvas; they were familiar with firearms and used to hard physical work. To this background Murray, among others in the group, added several years of militia experience. Both men were fascinated by the power and efficiency of the machine-guns.

Each of the two Maxim guns was crewed by a team of six. Number One in each team was the leader and fired the gun, with his Number Two feeding the ammunition belts into the gun during firing. Number Three had the main responsibility for ammunition supply, and the other three carried ammunition and formed the reserves. The remaining men in the section had miscellaneous duties including looking after the horse-drawn transport used to carry the equipment on the march. Although the men were soon allocated to particular positions in each team, all the members of the section were trained in each of the various duties on the guns. The battalion history recorded that the men had mastered the techniques of the guns within the first few weeks, then began to work on improving their speed at regulation machine-gun drills.

The basic exercise in the manual was 'Action', performed by a three-man team. On a starting signal, Number One dashed forward for five metres carrying the bulky tripod and set it up in position to receive the gun itself, carried up by the Number Two. The latter placed the gun on the tripod, with Number One locking it in place with two metal pins. Number Three had meanwhile brought up a 250-round ammunition box; Number Two inserted the end of the ammunition belt into the breech, and Number One completed the loading and signalled that he was ready to open fire. On the firing range, this would be followed by setting the sights and loosing off a burst at a target. The manual laid down a time of 45 seconds for efficient performance of this exercise,[8] but the 16th Battalion's machine-gun section was beating this by large margins within six weeks of starting their training. Black was Number One in a team which recorded a time of 13.4 seconds, and even that was later improved upon by another team from the 16th. Black was soon established as the regular Number One on one of the guns, and on 16 October he was promoted to lance-corporal, after a mere five weeks in the army. Black's shooting with the Maxim was described by another section member as 'deadly': he was able to 'drop on the target [with] split-second accuracy',[9] and was one of the three best shots in the section (the others being the section sergeant, George Demel, and Private 'Tiny' Hatcher).

The 16th continued its training at a strenuous pace through October and November, combining physical exercise with military drills, weapons training and field battle practice, under the watchful eyes and sharp tongues of the instructors. At the end of October, the original 11th Battalion marched out of Blackboy Hill en route for Fremantle; from there they would sail to join the fleet transporting the main body of the 1st Division. The intention at the time was that this first Australian contingent would complete its training in England before crossing to France and joining the Allied armies in the bloody struggle on the Western Front. The 16th Battalion had shaped up well by the end of its two months of basic training, to the satisfaction of its commanding officer, Lieutenant-Colonel Pope, and his second-in-command Major Tilney, and it was assumed that they would take a similar route to France in due course.

First, however, the 16th would join with the other battalions of the 4th Brigade, which was to assemble at Broadmeadows in Victoria to complete its organisation and do further training as a brigade. The 16th left Blackboy Hill on 21 November 1914, and embarked at Fremantle in two troopships for the week-long journey to Melbourne, where they were joined by the battalion's three South Australian companies, completing the unit's establishment. Broadmeadows was not a popular spot with the troops; when it was not teeming with rain, it was hot and dusty, and rain turned the ground into particularly sticky mud. (One battalion history claimed that some of its men's uniforms still carried Broadmeadows mud-stains at Gallipoli six months later.) Training continued in spite of the weather, and the troops spent the next few weeks improving their military skills, and learning to work together as a brigade. The heavy work was relieved by a sports meeting and various contests of military drills. It was during the brigade machine-gun competition

Lance-Corporal Percy Black with a Maxim gun, Blackboy Hill, 1914.
(Courtesy West Australian Newspapers)

that a three-man team from the 16th's section completed 'Action' in 12.5 seconds to win the championship.

The 4th Brigade was an interesting formation in many ways, not least in the person of its inaugural commander, Colonel John Monash, at this time better known as a civil engineer than as a soldier. It differed from the first three infantry brigades of the AIF in that it was composed of battalions from all the Australian states; there were eventually fifteen brigades formed, and only two others were structured like the 4th — the 8th Brigade, which was also raised as a one-off (and did not include a Tasmanian element), and the 12th, which was 'cloned' from the 4th in 1916. The mixture of defined groups from the various states seemed to produce differences in characteristics between the four battalions, which everyone was aware of but no-one was able to identify. These differences persisted throughout the war; Murray was later quoted as saying, to general agreement, 'I can't just say what the differences really are, or why, but march a section of each battalion of the brigade before me with their [identifying] colour patches off, and I'll guarantee to tell the battalion they belong to.'[10] Another characteristic of the 4th Brigade, also unusual in the AIF, was a tendency for sudden frictions and feuds to arise between different battalions, conflicts which were mostly (although not always) forgotten when the units went into action. One is reminded of a volatile family, often squabbling among themselves but firmly united in a crisis.

The brigade's training period culminated on 17 December in a march from Broadmeadows to Melbourne, marching through the city to be reviewed by the Governor-General at the federal Parliament House (this was before the establishment of Canberra as the national capital). By all accounts the brigade put on a fine show, and the troops regarded themselves as at least the equals of the 1st Division in soldierly virtues. The troops expected that they would soon be following the senior formation overseas, which proved to be the case within a few days. The brigade marched out of Broadmeadows in the inevitable downpour on 21 December and entrained for Port Melbourne, to board a convoy of troopships. The 16th Battalion embarked the next day on the 18,500 ton *Ceramic*, which they shared with the 15th. A week's travel saw them back in West Australian waters, anchoring in the harbour at Albany (the troops were not permitted shore leave). Here the full convoy of nineteen transports assembled, the 4th Brigade being joined by a Light Horse Brigade and various other troops, as well as 2000 New Zealanders. The convoy headed for the open sea on 31 December. For too many of the 10,500 Australians on the ships (described by the official historian as 'one of the finest contingents that ever left Australia'), the coastline around Albany would be their last sight of their homeland.

The first contingent had sailed two months earlier, headed (as far as the troops knew) for England to complete their training, but the situation had changed while they were at sea. In the first place, German diplomacy had encouraged Turkey to enter the war against the Allies. At the same time, the Allied authorities realised that the existing training camps in England would be inadequate to accommodate the troops from Australasia; an alternative had to be found. The convoy was scheduled to pass through the Suez Canal on its way to England, and a hurried decision was taken to disembark the force in Egypt and conduct its final training in camps around Cairo, under the overall command of General William Birdwood, an experienced British officer. Once they had heard of Turkey's entry into the war, the troops had half-expected to be diverted to Egypt, in order to defend it against the Turks, but this was apparently not the original intention: at this stage it was still planned that the Dominion troops would eventually proceed to the Western Front to fight the Germans. A new Allied strategy, however, would soon change this.

In the first few weeks of the war in Europe, the German master-plan to crush the Allied armies with a huge sweeping movement through Belgium had almost succeeded. Delayed by Belgian resistance and then stopped by counterattacks when on the brink of success, the Germans had entrenched themselves in defensive positions and repulsed further Franco-British attacks in their turn. The Allies attempted to get around the western flank of these defences, only to find the Germans extending their trench lines further and further westwards. The Allies dug their own trench systems facing the German line, and by October 1914 the huge armies of the combatants each occupied a continuous line of trenches stretching from Switzerland to the sea.

Attempts by both sides to break through the enemy's lines by frontal assault failed in a series of bloody disasters. This was the first conflict in which machine-guns were used in significant numbers (the Germans in particular had adopted the weapon with great enthusiasm, using the same basic Maxim design as the British) and their scything hails of bullets mowed down line after line of advancing infantry. Prevented by the opposing machine-guns and thick barbed-wire entanglements from achieving any kind of significant advance, the dug-in troops made a fixed target for the enemy's artillery. The leaders on both sides, faced with appalling casualty lists, cast about for some means of breaking the deadlock.

Britain's First Lord of the Admiralty, the young Winston Churchill, had turned his mind to the problem, and it was largely his influence which would decide the future movements of the Australian Imperial Force. Turkey's entry into the war, while increasing the resources ranged against the Allies, had also opened up what Churchill saw as a great opportunity. In January 1915, Turkish military pressure on Russia had resulted in an appeal by the Russians for British forces to create some sort of diversion to draw off Turkish forces. The British war minister, Lord Kitchener, conceived a plan for a feint attack on the Dardanelles, the long narrow strait forming part of the waterways joining the Mediterranean to the Black Sea, and leading to the Turkish capital, Constantinople. A threat in this region, he felt, would tie down a large proportion of Turkish forces in defence of the capital. Kitchener was reluctant to release ground troops from France however, and he approached Churchill at the Admiralty to suggest that the navy should carry out the proposed diversion by bombarding the forts on the coasts of the Dardanelles.

The First Lord had already been considering several radical schemes for winning the war in a hurry, and he immediately seized on the Dardanelles project and carried it much further. The original suggestion swiftly became a full-scale naval attack on the straits: a fleet of battleships would use their heavy guns to pulverise the Turkish coastal defences and force their way up the channel, to drop anchor off Constantinople and accept the surrender of the enemy capital. Churchill wasted no time in presenting the plan to the government's War Council (choosing to ignore the reservations of senior navy officers, several of whom doubted the plan could succeed), and gained authority to proceed. The attitude taken was that success would have decisive effects on the outcome of the war, and that the operation could easily be called off in the event of setbacks. Orders were issued to the Royal Navy's Mediterranean Squadron to begin the bombardment as soon as possible. The only requirement for ground troops would be to form an army of occupation, and it had occurred to the high command that the Australian and New Zealand contingent then assembling in Egypt would be suitable for these duties. The force had by then been designated as an army corps (it was during these early days in Egypt that the term ANZAC was first used), and the Englishman General William Birdwood was appointed as its commander.

The story of these deliberations is familiar enough today, but was of course unknown to the AIF contingents already in Egypt and the men of the 4th Brigade, arriving in the Middle East at the end of January 1915. The voyage of the 4th Brigade from Albany lasted about three weeks, the convoy reaching Aden at the mouth of the Red Sea on 20 January. As in any army in history, idleness was not tolerated, and the troops had spent the otherwise monotonous voyage in a continuing round of training exercises and lectures, as far as could be accomplished in the cramped shipboard conditions. The men were kept busy and continued to improve their military skills, with the junior officers receiving a program of theoretical instruction as well. As the troopships moved through the Red Sea and into the Suez Canal, the level of excitement rose with sightings of various warlike preparations along the canal, and with news of recent minor fighting in response to Turkish raiding parties. The brigade was greeted by cheering groups of Allies as the convoy passed along the waterway to its final anchorage at Alexandria.

The 16th Battalion disembarked at Alexandria on 3 February, and set off in two contingents on the 200-kilometre train journey to Cairo. A short march then took them to the 4th Brigade's designated training camp at Heliopolis, a few kilometres outside Cairo. As the 1st Division had done before them, the brigade now began to undergo an advanced training program, along with an exploration of the wonders of Egypt ranging from the astonishing relics of the country's ancient history to the squalor of the worst segments of Cairo. Most of the troops who were Australian-born (a large proportion had actually emigrated from Britain and Europe before enlisting) would have never travelled overseas before. Many would have been as well read as Murray was, and would have known something about the ancient monuments and been delighted to see the Pyramids and the Sphinx, but as many others of these boisterous young men were more interested in the sordid entertainments of the back alleys. It is unlikely that Murray and Black, both rather more mature than the majority, and by all accounts men of restrained habits, would have joined in the wilder behaviour. Some months later, one of Murray's letters to his family mentioned that he detested Cairo, and that 'it has been a curse on our men from the first.'[11]

The majority of the men's time, however, was spent in advanced training in the desert. Here they further honed their skills, and gained some practice in working together in larger groups. On arrival in Egypt, the 4th Brigade had joined with the New Zealand Infantry Brigade, the Australian 1st Light Horse Brigade and the New Zealand Mounted Rifles to form a new Division, designated the New Zealand and Australian (NZ & A) Division. In another administrative change at this time, each battalion's original eight rifle companies were regrouped to make four, designated A, B, C and D companies (the machine-gun sections remained separate, attached directly to each battalion's headquarters). The training continued through February and March 1915, the NZ & A Division starting to conduct manoeuvres with the whole division relatively early in the period, when the 1st Division was still training in brigade-size groups. Each day the men marched several miles through the sand to their designated training areas to spend at least eight hours in various military exercises. 'All day long, in every valley of the Sahara for miles around the Pyramids, were groups or lines of men advancing, retiring, drilling, or squatted near their piled arms listening to their officer.'[12] Monotonous and exhausting as the exercises were for the rank and file, they enabled the unit commanders and their staffs to gain some experience of handling large bodies of men in the field. For the machine-gunners, it was an opportunity for plenty of live firing on the shooting ranges and in field exercises.

The tedium of training was relieved late in February by the exciting news of the beginning of the naval attack on the Dardanelles. A British and French squadron, comprised mostly of older-type battleships, had commenced bombarding the Turkish forts on 19 February; hopes were high for swift success, but weeks went by without any news of major progress being made. The powerful naval guns proved to be comparatively ineffective against the forts, their flat trajectory often sending the shells far beyond the target. Minefields had been laid in the waters of the Dardanelles, and the Turkish gun batteries (including mobile guns which the battleships had no chance of hitting) prevented the Allied minesweepers from eliminating this hazard. On 18 March, the fleet made a determined effort to force its way through the straits, but lost three major vessels sunk by mines and had another badly damaged. The attack had failed, and the high command now began to reconsider the whole Dardanelles operation, in particular the role of ground troops.

Already at the end of February, a brigade of the 1st Division had received unexpected orders to depart Egypt for an unknown destination. This proved to be the island of Lemnos in the Aegean Sea, about eighty kilometres from the mouth of the Dardanelles. Their original purpose was to form an advance guard for the forces that were intended to occupy Turkish territory after the navy had gained victory, but a much different task was now being planned. The repulse of the fleet had convinced the high command that the navy could only get through with the support of an army fighting on the enemy's territory. General Sir Ian Hamilton, military commander in the region, informed Lord Kitchener that the army would have to undertake a major operation if the Dardanelles scheme was to succeed. The only alternative was withdrawal, and Kitchener (supported by the undeterred Churchill) felt that he could not order this without serious damage to British prestige. A large army force would be assembled to land on Turkish territory and secure the passage of the fleet. The landing areas chosen were on the long narrow Gallipoli Peninsula, which formed the northern or European shore of the Dardanelles. The troops allocated for the task were the British regulars of the 29th Division, a French Division, and the raw colonials of the Australian and

New Zealand corps, with General Hamilton in overall command of this Mediterranean Expeditionary Force.

Although the troops in Egypt knew little of this, the level of excitement rose steadily and rumours abounded. The volunteers had joined up to see glorious action in battle, and all signs were that they would not have much longer to wait. The men of the 4th Brigade, after six months solid training in Australia and Egypt, felt themselves to be ready for anything; few of them would have been aware that their routine British Army training was already outdated by the realities of the war. Suddenly orders came out on 2 April to prepare for movement within the next few days. Just before this, the Australian battalions had received a boost to their *esprit de corps* by the adoption of a system of colour patches sewn onto the upper sleeves of their uniform jackets, identifying the different units. For the 1st Division and the 4th Brigade, the patches were rectangular, divided horizontally into two colours; the lower band identified the brigade, and the upper the battalion within the brigade. The 4th Brigade's lower colour was navy blue, and members of the 16th Battalion were soon sporting their white-over-navy patches on each shoulder. This seemingly trivial decoration quickly became a symbol of the intense pride in their units felt by all AIF members.

The organised training programs had been ordered to cease on 2 April, and all leave was stopped, but this did not deter small groups of soldiers from making their way to Cairo where they staged the infamous 'Wozzer' riot, burning down several buildings in the squalid Haret el Wasser area in retaliation for what was perceived as sharp practice by some of the businesses in the district. The 1st Division began to leave its camps in the next few days, to be transported by train to the port of Alexandria, there to take ship for a destination still unknown to the troops. The NZ & A Division moved out next, and the 16th arrived in Alexandria early on 11 April. Here most of the battalion, including the machine-gunners, embarked on an old steamer hastily converted to a troopship, the *Haida Pascha*. Their immediate destination was the island of Lemnos, where the 3rd Brigade had preceded them a month earlier. The final objective was still officially a secret, but there were plenty of shrewd guesses that they were headed for the Dardanelles.

The *Haida Pascha* arrived at Lemnos on 15 April, after a voyage which Murray later described as 'wonderfully pleasant'; he must have been thinking of the scenery (he had a keen interest in ancient history) and the sea air, for the vessel was verminous and badly overcrowded, according to the 16th Battalion's history. The next morning, the ship moved into the vast Mudros harbour, and the troops saw for the first time the awesome sight of the expedition's assembled fleet of 150 transports and warships. Among them was the battleship HMS *Agamemnon*, her upperworks a mass of twisted metal from hits by the Turkish shore batteries in the straits; the men of the 16th gave her crew a cheer as they passed. The troops spent the next few days practising boat drill, clambering down rope ladders into the ships' boats with their full equipment and extra loads of supplies. They managed to attain some degree of proficiency in this exercise which was, of course, a further hint that they were about to undertake an amphibious landing. Details were still scarce, however; George Mitchell of the 12th Battalion later recalled that 'through an excess of secrecy the junior officers … knew little, and the men nothing of what was wanted of them. We found brave men … floundering about, seeking for a task, a plan on which to work.'[13]

At last, on 23 April, after a delay of two days owing to bad weather, a series of orders was issued, heralding what was to become both a disaster and a legend. An inspirational letter from the corps commander, General Birdwood, gave a general outline of the mission, as well as a few practical hints on what to do in action. In the 4th Brigade, Colonel Monash's operation order gave more detailed instructions ('3500 rounds with each machine-gun') and was specific about the geography of the mission: finally the troops knew for certain that they were about to land on the Gallipoli Peninsula to fight the Turkish army.

Chapter 3

DISTINGUISHED CONDUCT

The fleet began to depart Lemnos on the night of 24 April. The British and French forces would make the main landing at Cape Helles, the southern tip of the peninsula, and advance northwards; the Anzac troops would land on the coast some twenty kilometres further north, near the promontory of Gaba Tepe, then push inland across the peninsula to reach the straits. In countless later assessments of the campaign, the objectives set for the Allied force have been rightly judged as absurdly optimistic, but the Australian and New Zealand troops knew little of the grand strategy. They were only aware that they were about to risk their lives in battle; through them, their young nations would face the test of war for the first time.

In the Anzac part of the operation, the 1st Division would land before dawn on Sunday 25 April, to secure the high ground towards the centre of the peninsula. Several of Murray's Tasmanian relatives were in this first wave, including his cousin C H Littler, an eccentric adventurer who would later take charge of supplies on Anzac Beach, becoming known as the Duke of Anzac. The NZ & A Division would land later in the day and begin the advance across country to the opposite shore.

From sunrise on the morning of that first Anzac Day, the men of the 16th, waiting on their uncomfortable vessel, could hear the faint sounds of naval gunfire drifting over the eighty kilometres of sea separating them from Gallipoli. Late in the morning, the *Haida Pascha* got under way, together with the ships carrying the rest of the 4th Brigade. The flotilla chugged slowly across the calm sea, the level of tension rising as the sound of the guns grew louder, the men impatient for the waiting to be over and the great adventure (as many of them still saw it) to begin.

Harry Murray was mentally preparing himself for his first battle. He had no doubts about his technical ability as a soldier; he had gained a solid grounding from his earlier militia service and the previous six months of training with the 16th, and he was quietly confident about his skills with weapons — particularly with the machine-guns, but he also knew he was a good shot with a rifle and effective with a bayonet. Now he saw in his imagination the terrible wounds and mutilations which he knew must happen in battle, and formed an iron resolve to do his duty regardless of the danger. At the same time he found himself hoping, paradoxically, that he would not have to kill a man. At some time during the morning, Black and Murray found an opportunity for a quiet talk about what was to come. The two friends made a pact with each other that (as Murray later put it) 'we would never let the enemy prevent us from carrying out what we set out to do … that we would never take an order from … the enemy.'[1]

In this mood, they settled down to wait for their arrival at the beaches. Murray filled in time by playing cards with some of the other machine-gunners, but as the afternoon wore on and they came closer to the drama ahead, that prospect soon occupied all their attention. As they passed the site of the British landing at Cape Helles on the right, signs of the distant battle were clearly visible. As they neared the Gaba Tepe beaches, the supporting warships came into view, firing their roaring broadsides at the Turkish positions on the shore. The concussion from their guns, transmitted through the water, began to shake the *Haida Pascha*. Fast destroyers could be seen shuttling to and from the beach, towing lines of boats to land the last elements of the 1st Division. Amid the excitement, it occurred to some of the

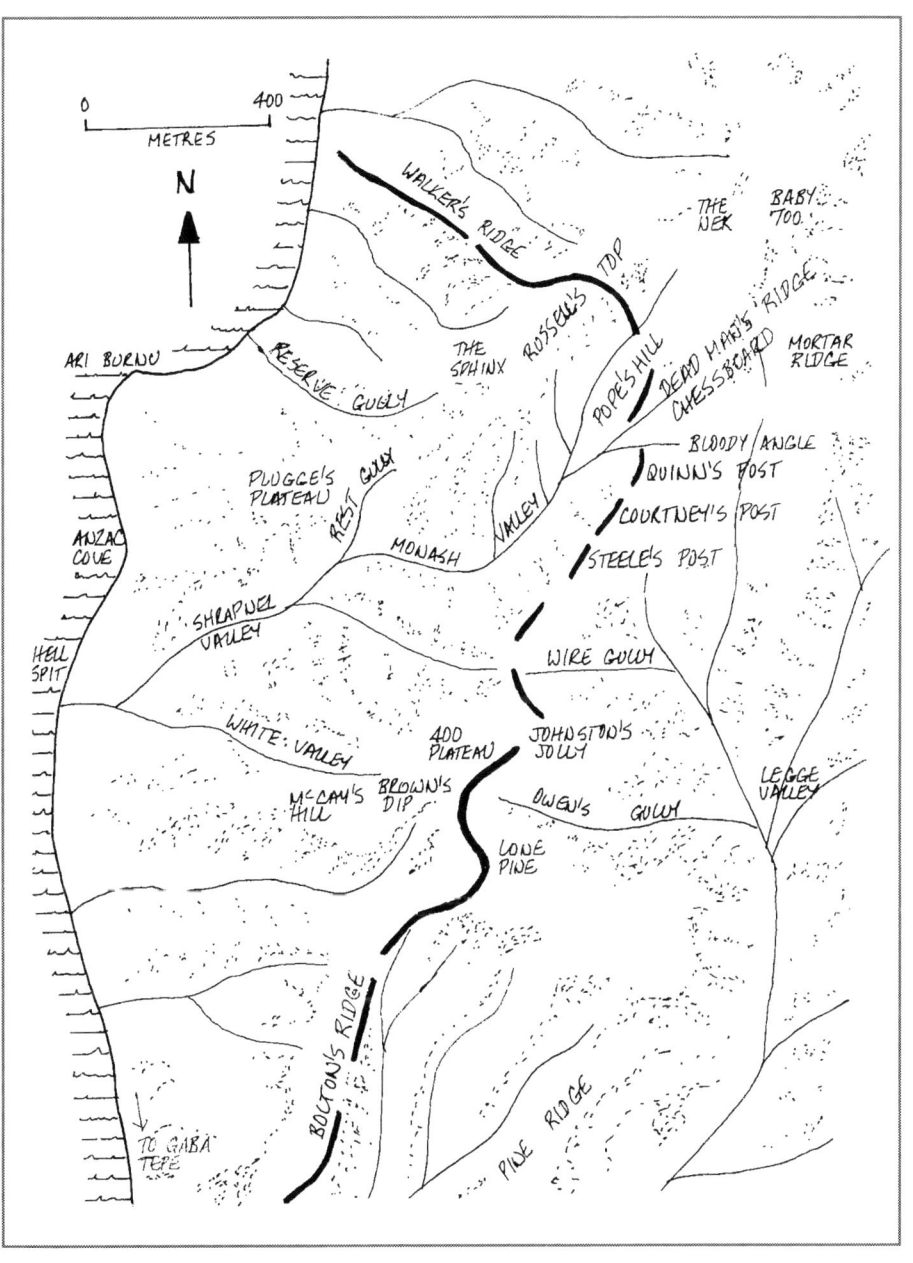

Gallipoli — The Anzac Line, May 1915.
The 4th Brigade occupied the positions from Pope's Hill to Courtney's Post.

men that the naval shells were bursting much closer to the beach than might be expected, indicating that the first waves had not penetrated anything like as far as planned. They were not yet aware that the initial landing force had lost direction in the dark and had landed a mile north of the intended position. Instead of facing comparatively open country, the men of the 1st Division found themselves trying to scramble up precipitous slopes, running almost straight up from the narrow beach into a tangled mass of steep ridges and gullies, all the while under increasingly heavy fire as more and more Turkish reinforcements arrived. Heavy casualties, exhaustion and disorganisation had left the landing force clinging to a precarious foothold on the heights, with great gaps in their line. Among those who had waded ashore that morning was a civilian journalist, Charles Bean, the Australian official war correspondent and later official historian, who was beginning his life's work of recording the Australian experience of the war.

The landing had been made in the wrong place, but the die was now cast and the 4th Brigade was to be landed at the same point. Instead of being the spearhead of a victorious advance however, they were now desperately needed to fill the breaks in the firing line. The 16th Battalion landed at about 5.30 in the evening, the men clambering down from their troopship to the decks of the destroyer *Ribble* which took them closer in to shore, then transferring to rowboats for the last few hundred metres. Turkish artillery on shore was firing at the boats with shrapnel shells, their fuses timed to burst the shells in the air and spray hundreds of metal pellets downwards. Murray, the old artilleryman, could tell that the white smoke puffs and cracking explosions overhead were not close enough to be dangerous, but even he was puzzled at first by a continuous low whistling noise in the air. The cause of the sound soon became apparent as men in the boats began to be hit by rifle and machine-gun bullets.

At last the boat carrying the machine-gunners reached the shore. Murray went over the side as soon as he felt the boat touch ground, but it had just scraped a rock and he found himself completely under water. Soaked to the skin, he struggled up to the beach to join the rest of the section. Black had immediately set up his machine-gun, and the men started on digging a trench, in strict obedience to their training. The digging had scarcely been completed when they were ordered to move off again, then to wait once more for further orders. For the first time they experienced the deafening din of mechanised war: the continuous rattle of rifle and machine-gun fire from up ahead, the ships' guns firing from the sea behind them and the shells roaring above them to explode on the hills, the Turkish shrapnel still cracking overhead. Murray's earlier wish that he would not have to kill a man had vanished at the sight of dead and wounded Australians in the boats and on the beach, and looking around he could see in the set faces of his comrades that they too were ready to kill.

Most sources state that Murray was 'Number Two' on Black's machine-gun at the time of the landing. Murray himself wrote later, however, that he was the 'scout' for the team, and this term was also used by Cyril Longmore in a post-war article, in which he referred to Murray's 'wonderful eye for ground'.[2] Murray also wrote that Private Harold George was Number Two on the gun at the time of his death on 27 April. The section suffered heavy casualties in the first few days and the survivors would no doubt have had to take on extra duties. As mentioned before, each man in the section was trained in all the duties. It seems most likely that Murray took over as Number Two when George was killed but also continued to act as scout. The Number Two normally carried the gun itself; in his account of his experiences at the landing, Murray clearly remembered being submerged over his head when he left the boat — had he been carrying a twenty-kilo Maxim gun as well as the rest of his gear, he would almost certainly have mentioned it.

It was nearly dark before orders arrived to move further inland, and Colonel Pope led the machine-gunners and two rifle companies of the 16th up a small gully in the direction of the firing. This was later called Shrapnel Gully — the names given to various geographical features over the next few weeks have become famous in Australian tradition, and soon the whole area of the landing became known as Anzac. The gully led into muddy Monash Valley, leading further upwards into the heights, and the column dumped its heavy packs and struggled up this channel to reach a steep, razor-backed hill at the point where the valley forked. This was Pope's Hill. The 16th positioned itself on the hilltop, plugging a gap in the firing line. In the darkness and confusion it was impossible to tell exactly where they were in relation to the rest of the Anzac force and to the Turks — Colonel Pope himself came within a hair's-breadth of being captured by a Turkish patrol as he attempted to reconnoitre the position. The darkness all around was lit up with myriad flashes and the air was filled with an almost continuous roar of rifle-fire as both sides blazed away incessantly. The 16th placed its firing line along the crest of the hill, and some of the men relieved the tension by firing their rifles in the direction of the invisible enemy while others dug furiously to establish trenches.

After a sleepless night, dawn on 26 April showed that the 16th on Pope's Hill was in an awkward position. Their entrenched front line faced eastwards across a branch of the valley and was reasonably well protected, but the next hill (Russell's Top) to the north-west was unoccupied and the Turks began to move on to it, to positions from which they could fire into the supporting troops at the rear of Pope's Hill. The 16th's two machine-guns had been placed in this area. Shortly after sunrise, Black had used his rifle (the machine-gunners carried rifles as well) to pick off a single Turk at ninety metres range, but more and more of the enemy were making their way on to Russell's Top, and their fire began to cause casualties among the Australians.

The machine-guns went into action, firing across the western fork of Monash Valley. Black's accurate shooting took a heavy toll of the Turks; he fired at any target he could see, with the rest of the gun team keeping him supplied with ammunition and using their rifles whenever they could. At one point he caught several lines of Turks from the flank ('in enfilade') and mowed them down; another group made the mistake of huddling together, and his fire cut them to pieces also. The Turks made a concerted effort to knock out the machine-guns. The surviving enemy riflemen on Russell's Top concentrated their fire on the guns and their crews, and a Turkish artillery piece opened up, bursting its shrapnel shells over the rear of Pope's.

We can imagine the scene on the hill that day, although only those who were there would know what it was really like. The noise must have been deafening, with the constant roar of rifle fire, the cracks of the shells overhead, each accompanied by a flash and a cloud of white smoke, the pellets whizzing down into the men crouched on the slope. Through all this rose the screams and cries of the wounded, and the shouted orders of officers and NCOs. The machine-guns hammered away, Black's at one end of the line and Bert Sykes' at the other, ejecting puffs of steam as the coolant started to boil. There would have been constant activity among the gun teams to keep their weapons operating, oiling the moving parts, perhaps changing the barrel if they had the opportunity — constant firing wore away the rifling, and a supply of spare barrels was part of the gun team's equipment. There were only limited numbers of the canvas cartridge belts, and a few men would have been detailed to refill the emptied belts from a stock of loose rounds.

The vulnerable water-jackets of the Maxims were holed again and again by bullets and shrapnel, the gun teams desperately plugging the holes with pieces of ammunition boxes: if too much water leaked out, the barrels would quickly overheat and render the guns useless.

The Turkish fire killed or wounded many of the machine-gunners. Black was hit by a shrapnel ball through the right hand, and other shots tore his tunic. The painful wound should have put him out of action, but he refused to leave the gun. Murray was wounded in the left arm at about the same time, and he too insisted on staying in the firing line. At one point a squad of about seventy Turks emerged from a small depression and charged at Black's position; firing with one hand, he swept the attack away, none of the Turks getting closer than 40 metres. Operating a Maxim gun normally required both hands, but Black evidently had the strength and technique to traverse the weapon and control his aim with only one. Tradition has him responding to Colonel Pope's concerns with the comment, 'That's the beauty of these guns — you can work 'em with one hand.' The long day at last faded into dusk; by then both guns had been too badly damaged to be used, and it was fortunate that the Turkish attacks subsided, although the fusillade of rifle fire went on all night. The Turks, however, continued to move on to Russell's Top during the night, and the next morning found them strongly entrenched.

Two replacement machine-guns were obtained from the navy during the night (many of the naval small craft carried Maxims), and these were sent up the valley at daybreak. On this or another morning — the guns were disabled at least once more during this first week — Black collected one of the replacement weapons himself and carried it up the valley on his shoulder. Murray later remembered the inspiring sight Black made striding up the valley, the unpainted brass water-jacket of the navy gun shining in the sunlight: 'a splendid physical specimen, afraid of nothing on earth, and glorying in his strength and power ... his eyes beaming with joy.'[3] The Turks kept up the pressure on the 16th's line, and the gunners were again in action throughout the day. Black's Number Two, the twenty-year-old Harold George, was killed by a sniper during the day ('just a boy' wrote the recording officer on his casualty document), and Murray took over his duties. Casualties continued to mount; Lieutenant Carse, the battalion Machine Gun Officer, was badly wounded during this period. Evacuated back to Egypt, he died in hospital on 2 May. Command of the machine-gunners fell to the senior NCO, Sergeant Demel, a twenty-one-year-old former militiaman, highly regarded by the troops.

The Turks launched attacks at many points of the Anzac line in the afternoon of 27 April, in a determined effort to drive the invaders back into the sea. A massed assault by six lines of infantry was shattered by shells from the navy's battleships. Towards the end of the day, a small force of Turks tried a local attack on the 16th's line at Pope's Hill, but they were almost wiped out by fire from the battalion's machine-guns and rifles, supported by a small party from the 3rd Battalion. By evening, the weary troops were still holding their positions. Black later estimated that he had fired 35,000 rounds in 36 hours of almost constant fighting. After another sleepless night the troops stood-to again to face another day under fire, although there was now some protection at the rear of Pope's Hill after a concerted effort of trench digging. Communication from the beach to Pope's remained highly dangerous, constant Turkish sniping adding to the difficulties of the terrain for the carrying parties bringing up food and ammunition. Water was in particularly short supply, not only for drinking but also, almost equally important, for keeping the machine-guns' cooling jackets filled. The gunners resorted to the expedient of mixing kerosene with water to stretch the supply for their weapons. Colonel Pope made an entry in his notebook on 28 April that he was intending to put Black up to sergeant and Murray to lance-corporal, noting also that the two were not included in the casualty figures because they had remained on duty after being wounded.

In his unpublished reminiscences written many years later, Murray recalled some personal incidents and observations from these first days.[4] On that Wednesday morning he was almost nodding off from lack of sleep, and Black offered him a drink of rum to wake him up. The teetotal Murray refused at first, but Black insisted. This was a mistake: the drink went straight to Murray's head and a few minutes later he decided to climb out of the trench to watch for a Turkish sniper who had been particularly troublesome. Somehow the Turks failed to notice him before Black realised what his friend was doing and hauled him back into the trench by the collar. Although Murray later became a moderate drinker, he avoided alcohol in front-line situations from then on. In another incident, Murray was cautiously scouting through the scrub, looking for a better position for the gun, when a Turk emerged from hiding and engaged him in a bayonet duel (perhaps a sniper not wanting to give away his position by firing prematurely). Murray soon realised he was getting the worst of the fight, and took the unsporting but practical action of shooting the enemy soldier.

Also on the Wednesday, the 16th's left wing was reinforced by troops from the 13th Battalion, the New South Wales unit of the brigade, which had experienced its own baptism of fire in another sector of Pope's Hill. Observing the platoon taking up position near his gun, Murray was struck by the efficiency and leadership of its very young commander, Lieutenant Douglas Marks. Another of the 13th's officers who made an impression on him was the lively, cheerful Captain James Durrant. Both these men would play a significant part in Murray's later career, and became his close friends.

A somewhat quieter day followed on 29 April, and the next day the 16th Battalion was relieved by the 15th. The surviving troops made their way back down Monash Valley to the reserve position called Rest Gully. The battalion had lost perhaps 250 men killed and wounded in these first five days, and the losses continued, even though they were now out of the line. Rest Gully provided some protection from shellfire, but the ever-active Turkish snipers caused fifty more casualties in the next two days of 'rest'. There was no such thing as a safe location at Gallipoli.

The 16th was sent back into action after their short break. The Anzac commanders had decided that the precarious position around the head of Monash Valley had to be improved. An offensive was planned to capture the hill known as Baby 700 (to the north of Pope's) and the ridges to its south, clearing the Turks from their positions overlooking the Anzac line. The 16th and 13th Battalions and a New Zealand battalion would be used in a night operation, the 16th's task being to seize the crest of the ridge to the east of the valley. The jumping-off point for their attack was to be a short steep gully branching off Monash Valley; this gully would soon be named, with good reason, the Bloody Angle. At nightfall on 2 May, the troops moved back up the valley from their 'rest' area, the battalion now a little over 600 strong after incorporating a few reinforcements. A heavy covering bombardment was provided by the warships and the few field guns that had been landed, and the 16th reached their position in the Bloody Angle, turned right to form a line and clambered up the side of the valley.

As soon as they emerged onto the crest of the ridge, they ran into a storm of gunfire from Turks positioned to their left rear. Scores of men were cut down as the 16th returned the enemy fire and made frantic efforts to dig in for protection. Their position was more or less on the objective, but something was clearly wrong far to the left, from where the Turkish fire continued unabated. The 13th Battalion had managed to approach its planned position, but the New Zealanders had been delayed on their march to attack the Baby 700 hill itself. Throughout the campaign, the command staff at Anzac seemed unable to adjust the timing of their plans to allow for the extreme difficulties of the terrain. By the time the New Zealand unit was in a position to attack, the Turks were fully alert and opened up a withering fire, which the New Zealanders could not penetrate. The left of the 16th's position remained open to flanking fire from the Turks entrenched on Baby 700 and in the system called the Chessboard. The rear slope of the ridge became a death-trap for the carrying parties attempting to bring ammunition up to the line on the crest; most of the volunteers for this task were killed or wounded and the line became increasingly isolated.

The 16th's machine-guns had moved up with the rest of the battalion, and were in action to repulse the probing Turkish counterattacks which began late in the night. Black carried his gun well forward in advance of the main firing line, but Murray had suffered a slight wound and Sergeant Demel would not allow him to go forward.[5] Murray had to watch what he later described as 'a sad and terrible business … excepting Bullecourt in April 1917, the worst stunt I was ever in.'[6] Going forward himself with the gun, the popular Demel was shot dead on the ridge some time before midnight. The pressure increased as the light grew on the morning of 3 May; an attempted relief by a recently landed unit of British marines failed with heavy losses, and another blow came when a salvo of shells from one of their own batteries blew away part of the bank behind the trench. The shock of being bombarded by their own side was too much for some of the overstrained men, who abandoned the position and ran for the rear. Most of them held on, however, under increasingly heavy fire, and another attempt was made to reinforce them. This also failed amid confusion and sweeping fire from the Turks, and the survivors of the 16th finally began to fall back in small groups. Black stuck with his gun, firing into the parties of Turks closing in on the 16th's position. By then the rest of the gun team had been killed or wounded, and he was operating the weapon alone. The wound to his hand had scarcely healed, and now a bullet took a chunk out of his right earlobe, but he ignored the pain and the bleeding to keep the gun firing and provide some sort of cover for the retreat. Finally the ammunition ran out and it was time to get back. Black was then under fire from three sides, but he was not prepared to abandon the precious machine-gun. He lifted the heavy overheated weapon onto his shoulder and made his way back to the shelter of the gully, somehow avoiding being hit by the bullets whistling around him.

Once under cover, he exchanged one burden for another. It seems it was only then that he became aware that Demel had been killed. Black was deeply affected by the news; the sergeant's body had been brought back to cover, and it was Black who carried him back down the gully and conducted the burial later that evening. The whole operation had been a ghastly failure; by the evening, when the last isolated elements of the 13th Battalion were withdrawn, the survivors of the attacking force were back where they had started, and the Turks were once again occupying the high ground across the head of Monash Valley. Contemporary accounts speak of the chaotic confusion in the Bloody Angle itself, jammed with wounded men, stretcher bearers and survivors of the disorganised retreat, with men from various units mixed together. Eventually some order was established, and the shattered 16th Battalion tramped back down the slope to Rest Gully.

The battalion's strength at the beginning of the fight had been 645 officers and men; the morning after, the count was 307, not much more than a full-strength company. Since the landing, casualties had totalled 688, of which 113 were dead or missing; many of the wounded, consigned to the chaotic medical system, would also not survive. The remaining men were reorganised into two half-size companies, with the machine-gun section also down to less than half of its normal complement. Both Maxims had been put out of action again by 5 May, and the surviving machine-gunners were sent to assist the 13th Battalion until replacement weapons could be obtained.

Colonel Pope managed to find some positives in the recent events when he wrote a report a few days later that identified the most outstanding efforts by men of the 16th. Black's work at the Bloody Angle was described at some length, and it was for that exploit that he was recommended later in the month for the Distinguished Conduct Medal (DCM), the second highest gallantry decoration, after the Victoria Cross, that could be awarded to rank and file soldiers.

Since 25 April, the battalion had lost twenty of its twenty-nine officers, and replacements had to be found. From the beginning of 1915, the AIF had adopted an informal policy of selecting its front-line officers from the ranks (the few regular officers joining after 1914 were mostly sent to the staffs of the higher commanders), and this was now being put into practice in all units.[7] The British Army's standards of education, family background and socio-economic class in the choosing of officers were largely ignored in the AIF once it went into action. Performance in battle and leadership qualities became virtually the only factors considered, although it is likely that a traditional 'officer' background would help in gaining promotion above the rank of captain. A few days after the Bloody Angle fight, the 16th Battalion chose six men from its ranks for promotion to officers; one of these was Percy

Black, granted his commission as a second-lieutenant on 7 May, and appropriately assigned to duty as the battalion Machine Gun Officer. He was now entitled to wear on each shoulder-strap the single lozenge-shaped rank badge which the Australians called a star, and the British a pip, although with the rapid deterioration of uniforms at Gallipoli, these were more likely to be simply drawn on the shoulder-strap with indelible pencil.

One of the myths of the Anzacs is the idea that the Diggers had no respect for the institution of commissioned officers, and that those who did become officers did not take their rank seriously. Probably there was a minority with this sort of attitude, and the Australians generally resented any distinctions based entirely on class. Once a man had proven himself in action, however, he would be given all the respect that was needed. There was no shortage of men in the ranks who aspired to commissions, and as good sons of the Empire the Diggers were aware that it was a considerable honour to be an Imperial military officer. Writing to Demel's grieving family, Black made a point of mentioning that the dead man was to have been commissioned: 'something to be proud of'.[8] Rather than continuing to socialise with their mates, new officers were encouraged to make the separation necessary for discipline in a fighting army. In 1917, when Edgar Rule was commissioned with several others, they were told by the commanding officer 'to have a night out with our pals … and after that to seek our friends among the officers.'[9] A distinguished officer of the battalion, himself promoted from the ranks, welcomed them into 'the brotherhood'.[10] In the 48th Battalion, George Mitchell was unexpectedly commissioned; he felt himself 'honoured to take up the responsibilities and added risks involved.' He was delighted with the sincere congratulations of his mates, and the warm welcome into the officers' mess. 'Men do not ask more of their officer than that he can endure equally with them, keep his head, think well and fast,' he later wrote.[11] 'Our relations with the ranks were the happiest … [our] promotion was proof to them that officers were not a class apart, but that commissioned rank was open to all.' In his quiet way, Percy Black took considerable pride in his achievement of rising to command the section he had joined as a raw recruit eight months earlier.

Murray took over as Number One on the gun team, and was promoted to lance-corporal on 13 May. By that time the 16th was back in the firing line, still only at about half-strength after incorporating more reinforcements. The weakened battalions of the 4th Brigade now faced perhaps the most harrowing assignment of the campaign, the holding of the isolated outposts at the head of Monash Valley. The failure of the Bloody Angle attack had left the brigade clinging to three positions just behind the crest of the slope — Pope's Hill itself, and the two rough trench systems called Quinn's Post and Courtney's Post; the New Zealanders held the line from the north of Pope's to the sea, with the 1st Division south of Courtney's Post. At many points of the 4th Brigade's sector, the Turks on the Baby 700 hill and other nearby heights could observe and fire at any movement, but the positions had to be held to prevent the Turks sweeping down to the beach. All three posts were extremely dangerous, but the worst of them was Quinn's Post.

The defence of Quinn's was entrusted to the 16th and 15th Battalions, rotating from front line to reserve every 48 hours in recognition of the strain of holding this particular post. There were Turkish positions on higher levels able to fire at the post from three different angles (including one from partly to the rear) and a Turkish trench on the other side of the crest which was, in places, only twenty metres away. It was certain death for any of the garrison to raise his head above ground during daylight, and when the Turks obtained supplies of crude hand grenades it became dangerous to occupy the trenches at all. The Australians had no grenades at this time, until they improvised the famous 'jam-tin bombs'. So exposed was the position that the garrison had to rely on fire from the trenches on either side to defend against attacks, but their presence meant that the place was denied to the Turks.

The fire-power of the brigade's machine-guns was vital to the defence of Monash Valley. A decision was taken early on to transfer the general control of the guns from the individual battalions to the brigade headquarters, with the intention of creating an integrated defensive system. In charge was Brigade Machine Gun Officer Captain J M Rose, a British veteran previously attached to the New Zealand force and a specialist in weapons doctrine. The guns were distributed along the brigade's frontage in positions where they could cover the area between the posts and the Turkish line with an interlocking crossfire. Exactly where in this system Black's 16th Battalion guns were first positioned was not recorded at the time. There are indications, however, that the 16th's section provided one of the four guns on Pope's Hill, firing south-east across the front of Quinn's Post (this being Murray's gun), with the second behind Steele's Post, which was actually the northernmost point of the 1st Division's area. Other guns of the brigade were positioned to produce narrow lanes of fire between the front-line posts, sweeping the area that would have to be crossed by any attackers. It appears that the exact positioning of each weapon was left up to the individual teams, and Captain Rose took particular note of Murray's skill in placing his gun in concealment.

Two weeks of bloody skirmishing at Quinn's, with each side attempting to extend its position at the expense of the other, resulted in heavy casualties but no change in the overall situation. On the Australian side, the brigade machine-guns had already proved their worth in the repulse of a strong local Turkish attack on 1 May. The enemy was so close to the 15th Battalion's trench that the stream of bullets from the Maxims skimmed the Australian parapet. The Turks, however, were planning a full-scale offensive with the intention of driving the Anzac force into the sea. The date was set for 19 May; reinforced by fresh divisions to a total of 42,000 men, the Turks intended to make a massive surprise attack all along the line. Their preparations were detected, however: changes in the pattern of the Turkish artillery and rifle fire aroused suspicion, and on 18 May a British aircraft spotted hordes of troops massing in their rear areas. Forewarned, the Australians and New Zealanders were fully prepared when the Turks launched the assault at 3.30 am on 19 May. The Turkish attacks were poorly coordinated, and the forces attacking the 1st Division's sector had already been shattered and repulsed by the defender's fire by 4 am when the Monash Valley positions were attacked. It was nearly full daylight by that time, and the 4th Brigade's machine-gunners opened a deadly crossfire at the clear targets, joined by the rapid fire of riflemen in the trenches.

In front of Quinn's Post, not a single Turk managed to cross the short space between their trenches and the Australians'; at Courtney's Post to the south, however, a squad of Turks managed to get into part of the front-line trench. Here one of the 4th Brigade's legends was born, when a tough young private of the 14th Battalion, Albert Jacka, killed seven of the intruders and recaptured the trench single-handed, thereby winning Australia's first Victoria Cross of the war. All along the line, the Turkish attacks failed with disastrous losses. With futile bravery, small groups made local attacks throughout the day, achieving nothing and suffering more casualties; most of the few Australian losses occurred during this period, many of the troops leaving the shelter of the trenches for a better shot at the enemy. The 4th Brigade machine-guns were in action again in the afternoon, when the Turks made several more assaults — perhaps as many as five more — in front of Quinn's Post; all were swept away by the 'whirlwind of fire' from the gunners and riflemen.

By the end of the day, the Anzac troops had fired 948,000 rounds of ammunition and inflicted 10,000 casualties on the Turks. Around 3000 of these had been killed, their bodies sprawled in no-man's-land between the opposing trench lines, and an all-day truce was declared on 24 May to bury the rapidly putrefying corpses. No details were recorded of individual experiences of the 16th's machine-gunners during the battle of 19 May, but they certainly played a big part in the Turkish defeat. In his only known comment on the episode, Murray wrote in a post-war letter, with typical understatement, that he had had 'an excellent view' of the attack.[12] Murray's work with his gun during the past weeks had made a great impression on Captain Rose, the Brigade Machine Gun Officer. Rose made a point of commending Murray in writing to the Brigade Commander, praising his 'initiative and energy' and describing him as an 'ideal machine-gunner and the class of man that is required to take charge of machine-gun work.'[13]

The 4th Brigade machine-guns were redeployed on several occasions over the next few months as the Australians worked on improving their defences. Within a few days of the Turkish attack, the 16th Battalion's guns were located around Courtney's Post, Murray's being on one flank of the post, and the second gun mounted in a tunnel in the front line. The *Official History* recorded that there were by then nine guns altogether around Courtney's Post under the control of Captain Rose, part of an 'overwhelming force' of machine-guns protecting the key point of Quinn's by their crossfire.

A concealed machine-gun post at Gallipoli (soldier and unit unknown).
(Australian War Memorial Neg Number P02141.002)

Life for the troops at Anzac had begun to settle into some sort of routine. When not 'standing-to' in the front-line trench, the men lived in holes scraped in the reverse slopes of the ridges. Further down the slopes, the various unit headquarters, administration and medical formations had established themselves in larger holes. Units in reserve were dug in closer to the beach, and the beach itself was jammed with crates of supplies and ammunition, with a constant throng of working parties carrying stores up to the firing line and returning for fresh loads. Stretcher-bearers brought a continuous stream of wounded men down from the heights to wait on the beach for transport to Egypt on some overcrowded hospital ship, for treatment in the army hospitals there. The Turkish artillery on the heights could reach virtually any part of the Anzac area, and nowhere was safe from shrapnel shells bursting overhead and spraying their deadly pellets downwards. Fortunately, the Turks had very little high-explosive ammunition at Gallipoli; a sustained bombardment with such shells would probably have wiped out the beachhead in short order.

Food was reasonably plentiful for the troops, but monotonous and lacking in nutritional value. The staples were very salty 'bully beef' and rock-hard biscuits, with bacon, jam and cheese for some variety. The water supply gradually improved to the point of being barely adequate for drinking and machine-gun coolant, but remained completely inadequate for washing and sanitation. The whole area was infested with flies — bad enough at the time of the landing, they found new breeding grounds in the numerous unburied bodies, and reproduced in their millions. Almost as bad were the lice, which began to appear within the two weeks of the landing, once the troops had become immobilised in trenches. More than twenty years later, Murray could still recall his disgust when he first noticed lice on his body. The Australians called them 'chats'; in the AIF, 'chatting' did not mean conversation, but rather the process of attempting to remove the lice from the seams of clothing. The combination of inadequate nutrition, fatigue, poor sanitation and the ever-present flies meant that disease began to spread in the army after the first month or so of the expedition.

Enemy action was still the main danger, of course. On 29 or 30 May, Murray was hit in the right knee by a shrapnel pellet. There was a ferocious local fight going on at Quinn's at this time, and the Turkish shell may have been part of their covering bombardment during this action. Even Murray could not ignore this wound — the shot was lodged in the joint and he could not stand up. He was carried to the beach and ferried to Lemnos, and from there evacuated to Egypt on the hospital ship *Franconia*. There were 1850 patients on the ship and seven doctors working around the clock on life-threatening cases; Murray's injury went untreated on the ship, and he spent the days of the voyage trying to avoid the swarms of lice on his blanket. He was admitted to hospital at Alexandria on 8 June, and had the pleasure of being bathed and deloused before he was operated on two days later to have the pellet removed. He remained in Alexandria for another two weeks recuperating, after which the medical officer reported that the wound was healed and 'knee movement good' (this was somewhat optimistic of the doctor as the injury was to trouble Murray for the rest of his life). He was discharged on 25 June as fit for duty, and he was back with his unit at Anzac early in July.

While in hospital, Murray had been awarded the DCM, the decoration being approved on 20 June (Black's DCM had been approved two weeks earlier; these were the only DCMs awarded to the 16th Battalion during the Gallipoli campaign). The recommendation for Murray's medal owed much to Captain Rose's earlier comments to the Brigadier, but also mentioned favourable reports by the Battalion Commanding Officer and Machine Gun Officer (presumably Black rather than his predecessor Lieutenant Carse). It was not for one particular outstanding deed, but rather for his consistent gallantry and resourcefulness throughout May 1915. This may have been the reason for Murray's somewhat ambivalent reaction to the award; although pleased with the congratulations from his colleagues and his relatives at Gallipoli, he revealed many years later that he had some doubts about whether he had really deserved the medal, and thereafter had felt the need to live up to it.[14] If that were the case, he would not lack opportunities to do so. The overall situation on the peninsula had changed little during Murray's absence, but the Allies were by then planning major undertakings which were intended to bring the campaign to a decisive climax.

Chapter 4

OFFICERS AND GENTLEMEN

The savage burst of fighting around Quinn's Post died down at the end of May, and the 4th Brigade was pulled out of the line for a rest after five weeks of constant combat. The Monash Valley posts were taken over by the New Zealanders and the troopers of the Light Horse Brigade, who had left their horses in Egypt and come to the peninsula as infantry. The 4th Brigade machine-gunners remained in position however, since their defensive fire-power was indispensable. On 22 June, Black wrote to his brother Joe: 'I have not been out of the firing line yet, the only section in the brigade that has not had a spell, we got the credit of being the best Gun Section that landed so we are getting plenty to do.'

The remainder of the battalion, together with the other units of the 4th Brigade, spent June and July 1915 away from the front, in Reserve Gully, near the rock formation known as the Sphinx. Here the troops were kept busy with 'fatigues', the constant labouring tasks of an army. Digging of trenches and tunnels took up the most time, and the men were also employed in unloading barges at the beach and carrying fresh supplies up the gullies to the men on the heights. Although the bivouacs were partly sheltered from enemy fire, intermittent shelling and the occasional sniper still caused some casualties during this 'rest' period. The 16th absorbed drafts of reinforcements and gave them as much local training as was possible, while the battalion administration tried to get their unit's sparse records into some sort of order.

In early July, the battalion second-in-command, Major Tilney, was promoted to lieutenant-colonel and posted to take command of the 13th Battalion, a circumstance that would have some influence on Harry Murray's future. It was during this period that sickness began to strike down many of the surviving veterans, with dysentery, enteric fever and diarrhoea sending increasing numbers away on the hospital ships. During these months, the majority of the Anzac force worked on extending the systems of tunnels and trenches that soon spread through the battlefield, while a concerted effort by the Anzac snipers established a superiority over their Turkish counterparts. These activities, and a much-improved supply of the makeshift jam-tin grenades, resulted in some sort of equilibrium being reached between the opposing forces.

It was to this stalemate situation that Murray returned from hospital in early July. Most of the 16th's troops were sent to the nearby island of Imbros on 5 July for a few days rest away from the peninsula, but the vital machine-gunners again stayed behind, and Murray would have rejoined his fellow gunners up on the heights. On 14 July, the Corps Commander included his name in a list of 16th Battalion soldiers who had 'performed various acts of gallantry and valuable services' in May and June. It appears that Murray was made acting-sergeant about this time: although his service record does not show this, both the *Official History* and the battalion's unit history mention him as a sergeant at the beginning of August. By that time, the Allied forces on Gallipoli had resumed the offensive in an attempt to break out of their beachheads and finish the campaign.

The British War Cabinet had decided to reinforce Sir Ian Hamilton's army with several new divisions of infantry for this effort. The tangled terrain north of the Anzac position was only lightly defended by the Turks, and it was here that the main attack was to take place. The NZ & A Division was given this task, its objective the capture of the features known as Chunuk Bair

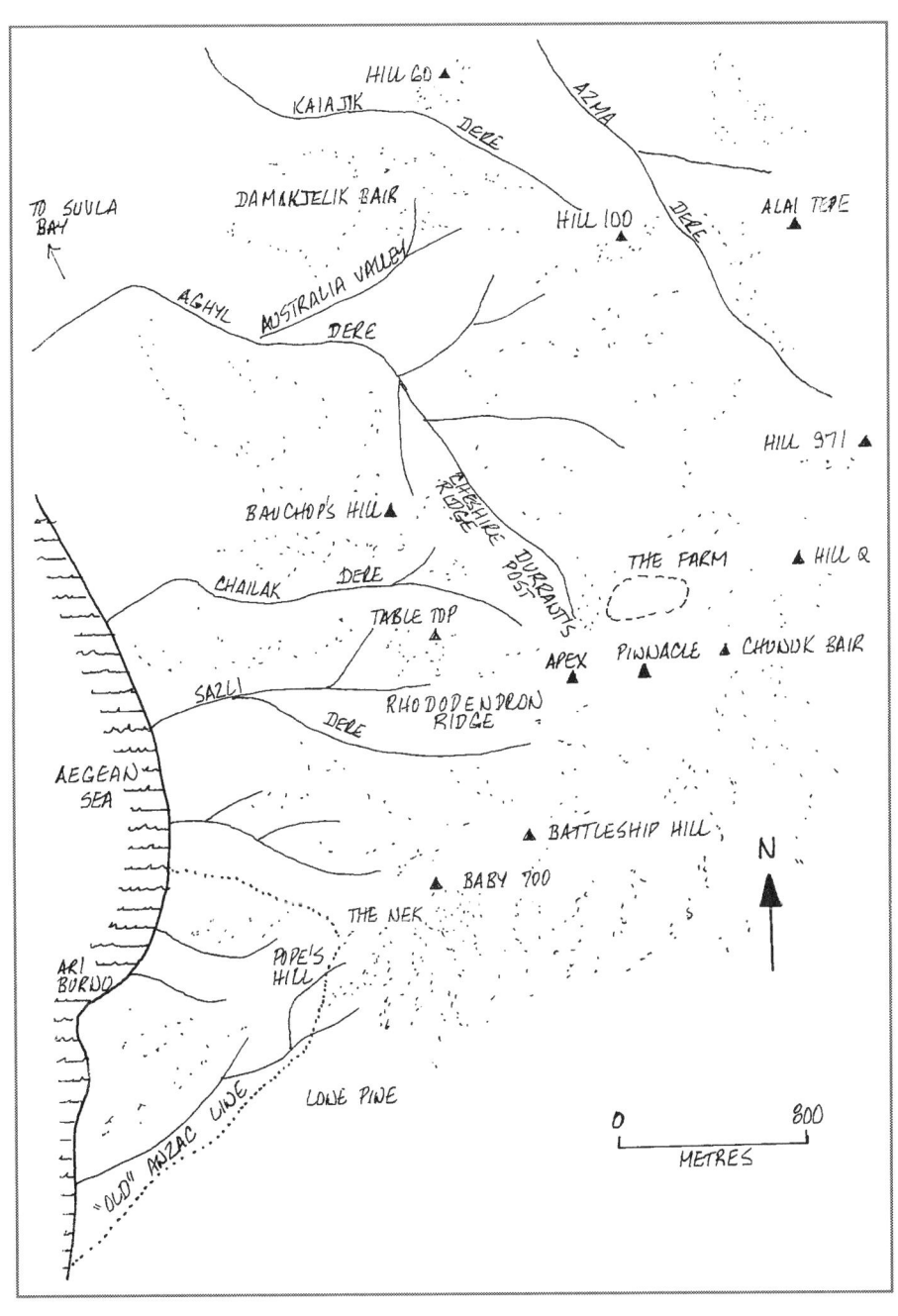

Gallipoli — area of the August battles.

and Hill 971, the high points of the northern ridges. The division's resources would be boosted by British and Indian reinforcements. Further north, a new British force would make a landing in the Suvla Bay region, supporting the Anzac thrust on the heights and putting further pressure on the Turkish northern flank. At the southern end of the Anzac line, diversionary attacks would be mounted to draw the Turkish reserves away from the decisive point. For the troops of the 4th Brigade, rumours of action after their two months of fatigues raised spirits, in spite of their deteriorating health.

The 4th Brigade, reinforced by British and Gurkha units, would form one of the northern assaulting columns. The operation was to be launched after dark on 6 August, and in the late afternoon the brigade's machine-gun sections were brought down from the firing line on the heights to join their battalions in Rest Gully. As the 16th's gunners made their way down the hill, they were greeted by one of their bandsmen playing selections on his cornet, providing a few moments of beauty for the men who would be fighting for their lives that night. The brigade moved off at around 9 pm, first down to the beach, then along the beach track for four kilometres to the point where it turned and then clambered up the steep ridges and ravines leading to the objectives. Several hours earlier, at the other end of the Anzac line, the 1st Division had captured the Turkish trenches at Lone Pine after a desperate struggle, and was now resisting savage counterattacks.

The 4th Brigade made its way into the northern hills in the pitch darkness, the machine-gun sections struggling under their extra loads of weapons and ammunition. Things began to go wrong almost from the start. A supposed short cut to the Aghyl Dere (valley), the main route to the heights, proved to be the reverse, costing the column three hours in lost time. Reduced to a shuffle for large sections of the march, the brigade was soon well behind its timetable. The troops finally left the valley and began to struggle up the steep ridges, under increasing fire from Turkish outposts. The enemy positions were rushed one after the other along the route, the 16th's riflemen fighting their way along the right flank of the advance. On the left, the 13th and 14th Battalions guarded that flank and drove the scattered Turkish defenders from ridge after ridge. The 15th formed the centre of the advance; at daybreak, with assistance from the 16th, they charged a Turkish post on a small hill, driving off the enemy group and establishing a strong position themselves.

The brigade reorganised itself on this high ground, overlooking a gully later named Australia Valley. The machine-gunners had not taken a direct part in this mobile fighting, but at some point Murray became involved in a bayonet charge on a Turkish position, probably the hill referred to above. A few Gurkhas from the supporting column on the 16th's right joined in also. Murray bayoneted a Turk, and was trying to extract the weapon from his victim's body when he was charged by another Turk. He was saved by one of the Gurkhas who brought down the attacker by throwing his *kukri* knife.[1]

By this time, early morning of 7 August, the northern assault columns had recovered somewhat from the disorganised start of their march, defeating all the forces opposing them and reaching a good position from which to complete the operation. The effort, however, had exhausted the troops. Virtually all of them were debilitated from illness, and the long march and sporadic fighting up and down the tangled terrain had used all their reserves of strength. They could go no further for the present, and the commanders decided that the force should dig in where it was, still well short of the objective, and try to recover some of its strength. The other columns of the northern force — the New Zealanders and the British and Indians — had also been forced to halt for the time being. On the same morning, at the main Anzac position to the south, the Light Horsemen of Victoria and Western Australia sacrificed themselves in the tragic charges at the Nek.

The next day, the 4th Brigade resumed its attempt to capture Hill 971. To add to the difficulties facing the troops, the tangled nature of the landscape had caused the brigade staff to mistake their location and they were in fact much further away from the final objective than was assumed, on a different ridge altogether. Advancing at dawn, the attacking columns found themselves running a gauntlet of Turkish fire from machine-guns and artillery emplaced on the heights ahead. Casualties mounted fast among the Australians, the 15th Battalion suffering particularly heavy losses as it pushed forward at the head of the assault. Finally the troops could do no more, and were forced to halt under the blazing sun and take cover well short of the objective. The brigade's organisation had broken down, and now a fresh danger arose, as a strong force of Turkish infantry began to move down from the north to counterattack, threatening to overrun not only the scattered riflemen but the headquarters elements as well.

The situation was saved by the arrival of the Australian machine-guns, which up to then had had no opportunity to influence the battle. As the *Official History* put it, 'At this moment there came up … the magnificent machine-gun sections of the 4th Brigade under Captain Rose, Lieutenants Black and Blainey [the 14th Battalion MG Officer] and Sergeant Murray, possibly the finest unit that ever existed in the AIF.'[2] There were four guns — two each from the 16th and 14th sections. Quickly positioned along the crest of the ridge, two on each side of a makeshift medical dressing station, they opened fire on the advancing enemy, breaking up the attack and driving the Turks to cover. Turkish artillery then tried to knock out the machine-guns with shrapnel shells, but their range was 100 metres too long. The Australians ceased fire to prevent the Turks from correcting their aim, then opened up again as soon as the bombardment stopped. With the enemy pinned down, the rest of the brigade gradually withdrew to the position it had occupied that morning, the machine-guns covering the retreat before eventually moving back themselves. 'We had been saved from certain disaster by the machine-gunners,' recalled Sergeant-Major Bain of the 14th Battalion after the war, 'who had worked their machine-guns red-hot in giving covering fire … otherwise it is doubtful if any one of us would have succeeded in getting back.'[3] Murray suffered a slight wound during the day, but remained on duty; perhaps this was the bullet that 'took some hair and skin off his head just above his ear,' as a colleague recalled many years later (Murray's service file recorded this as the second time he had been wounded, but it was actually the fourth or fifth).[4] Captain Rose, who seems to have been one of the unsung heroes of Gallipoli, commanded the rearguard with considerable skill.

The exhausted remnants of the brigade settled down into a strong defensive position on the heights around Australia Valley, which had been held by the 13th Battalion while the attack was taking place. A short distance to the north, a large British force had landed at Suvla Bay, but had failed to advance beyond its initial foothold, mainly due to inept leadership. The great effort of August had failed, and the Turks were still in control of the vital high ground. A despondent mood settled on the soldiers of the 4th Brigade, depressed by their losses (the brigade was now down to about a quarter of its full strength), the continued illness of many of the survivors and the sense of failure. Their chances of success in this operation had been minimal from the start, however. After the war, it was shown to be virtually impossible for even a fit, unencumbered man, making no errors in navigation, to cover that extremely difficult ground in anything like the time demanded by the plan. Again faulty planning had negated the dedication of the troops.

The Turks had followed up the retreating Australians, and they launched a determined attack on the 13th's lines early on 9 August. This was repulsed with heavy losses, as were further attacks over the next few days. On the same day Black's machine-gunners of the 16th, with 100 riflemen, moved to the right of the brigade's line, and set up a defensive position at the point called Number 1 Outpost. On 9 August also, Black was promoted to the temporary rank of captain. Earlier in the month he had been 'Mentioned in Dispatches' for the first time — that is, mentioned by name in the commanding general's regular reports as giving particularly good service without qualifying for a decoration; 'Mentions' were published in the *London Gazette* and the individual received a certificate.

Gradually, the situation in the north settled into some sort of equilibrium. Although the objectives of the advance had nowhere been achieved, the area occupied by the Allies had been greatly increased from the original cramped toehold around Anzac Cove, and the troops had a little more room to move. The longer distances added to the difficulties of keeping the front-line troops supplied with food, water and ammunition, but enough got through to maintain the position, and the myriad administrative details of the army continued.

At Cape Helles, at the tip of the peninsula, the British and French had been continuing a struggle which was at least as difficult and bloody as that at Anzac. The mainstay of the British forces was the 29th Division of the old regular army, one of the few British formations to earn the unreserved admiration of the Australians. The division had suffered shattering losses during the campaign and was particularly short of experienced junior officers. In a departure from precedent, nominations were called for from Australian NCOs to be considered for commissions in the 29th Division. Murray, always ready to try something new, sent his name in. It happened that the 29th was transferred north from Helles to Suvla at the beginning of August to take part in a renewed attempt to advance inland, and it seems that Murray was on the verge of being selected for a British commission. Word of this reached Colonel Tilney, former second-in-command of the 16th Battalion and now commanding the 13th, and he decided that Murray would not be lost by the AIF.

The 13th had suffered several casualties among its officers in the recent fighting, including its Machine Gun Officer Captain Legge, who was wounded on 12 August. As Tilney later told the story, 'I had seen [Murray] and Percy Black at Blackboy, and I immediately picked them out as thoroughly good soldiers. My machine-gun officer had just become a casualty, and I therefore asked that Sergeant Murray should be transferred to my command. Brigadier-General Monash agreed, the transfer was effected, and the sergeant was immediately recommended for and appointed to a commission.'[5] The next day, 13 August, Second-Lieutenant Murray reported to the 13th Battalion's lines to take command of the machine-gun section, accompanied by a note from Colonel Pope stating that he had no objection to Murray's transfer 'beyond the natural objection to losing a most excellent man.' On the same day, official confirmation of his sergeant's rank had come through, so on paper he went from lance-corporal to sergeant to second-lieutenant, all on the one day. For the next two and a half years, Murray would wear the 13th's two-blues colour patch with pride.

The 13th had just pulled back from the front line into reserve, relieved by a British unit, and Murray had a week to settle in to his new unit before it was called into action again. He would have had some knowledge of the men in his new section (and vice versa) owing to the close cooperation between the 4th Brigade's four machine-gun sections over the past four months.

Murray had absorbed a sense of British military traditions from his reading before the war, and he had no difficulty taking on the responsibilities of an officer. He quickly established himself in the 13th Battalion, incidentally adding another facet to his Australian connections: a Tasmanian resident in Western Australia, enlisted in a combined Western Australia/South Australia unit, and now serving in a New South Wales unit.

Not far from the lines held by the 4th Brigade was a low knoll known as Hill 60; this was in the hands of the Turks and formed part of their entrenched position facing the Anzac troops and the British in the Suvla area. The latter force was planning to launch another attempt to advance inland, and it was decided that Hill 60 would be assaulted by the Anzacs (with some British and Indian troops) at the same time. The 4th Brigade's part in this was to attack the right of the hill with a mixed force from the 13th and 14th Battalions, neither being strong enough to operate as a unit. The sick-list was growing daily as the Gallipoli diseases continued to spread, and most of those picked for the attack were weakened by illness. On the afternoon of 21 August, 500 men of the 4th Brigade charged across the Kaiajik Dere, through a murderous hail of fire to attack the network of Turkish trenches on Hill 60. The majority were killed or wounded in the charge, but the survivors managed to establish a foothold up the slope of the hill where they dug in, still short of the Turkish trenches.

The brigade machine-guns were distributed along the main position, and did their best to provide covering fire for the attacking riflemen. In the 16th Battalion's section of the line, one of Black's machine-guns (fired by Sergeant Sykes, a Blackboy Hill original) happened to be located so that it could shoot straight up part of the long Turkish communication trench leading to their front line. Firing at a range of 800 metres, the gun created havoc among the Turkish reserves moving to their front line. The trench was soon blocked by the bodies of the dead and wounded, and Sykes also cut down many of those who climbed into the open to get around the obstruction.[6] Murray, in his first action with his new unit, was in control of the 13th Battalion's machine-guns providing covering fire from their section of the line. Major Herring of the 13th commanded the attacking party, and he later credited Murray's guns with stopping any effective Turkish counterattacks on the captured position. The remnants of the attacking force were able to hang on to their foothold, although there was no chance of advancing any further against the Turks higher up the hill. Elements of the newly raised 2nd Australian Division had recently arrived at Gallipoli, and on 22 August the 18th Battalion of that division was ordered to attempt another attack. The inexperienced troops were driven back with heavy losses, and the fighting died down over the next few days as both sides consolidated their positions.

Among the 16th Battalion personnel in the area was Private Thomas Wilson, a well-known bush poet before the war (writing as 'Crosscut') who also contributed articles to the Perth *Sunday Times*. Wilson recorded an encounter with Percy Black during the Hill 60 operations:

> In a narrow, steep and dangerous sap [a type of trench] one day in the vicinity of Hill 60, and in the extreme heat of a Turkish summer it occurred to the officer in charge ... that it was a desirable thing ... to pass two battalions of men with all accoutrements in opposite directions at the same moment in time through a trench 20 inches wide. I was not well and had been deliberately depriving myself of the luxury of a drink to the limit of my endurance because water was then worth about a pound a drop. And then when I could stand it no longer and was about to put [my water bottle] to my lips, I found that a bullet had pierced it ... I was expressing my views eloquently upon things in general when Percy Black passed by in the smother of heat and crush. He took in the situation at a glance, saw the perforated bottle in my hand, and his own hand went to the carrier on his hip.
>
> 'Here, lad,' he said, 'take a sip of that,' and he handed me his bottle. And putting it to my lips I found that there was not an inch of water in the bottom of it! Was I the first to whom he had offered it that day? I do not think so.[7]

Another attempt on the summit of Hill 60 was made on 27 August, with the infantry attack to be supported by an artillery bombardment of the Turkish trenches. The right wing of the attack was allotted to the 4th Brigade, which managed to scrape together a mixed force of a few hundred semi-fit men. The operation began in the late afternoon when the bombardment commenced, but for some reason few shells fell on the trenches to be attacked by the 4th Brigade. From the main Australian position across the valley from Hill 60, the brigade's machine-guns sprayed the slopes of the hill in an attempt to disrupt Turkish movements, but without artillery support they were unable to fully suppress the enemy defences. The Australian charge was met by a torrent of fire which cut down most of the attackers, except for a small group that managed to capture a short length of trench.

As the few survivors fell back, the Turks in the double defensive line opposite the 14th Battalion's position stood up head and shoulders above the edge of their trenches to improve their aim as they fired at the retreating Australians. The 14th Battalion's medical officer, Captain Loughran, had found a good viewing point from which he had watched with anguish as the Australian attack had melted away. Realising that the over-eager Turks offered an inviting target, he had tried unsuccessfully to draw attention to it. To the right of the 14th's position, Black's guns of the 16th had been firing at the Turkish line directly to their front in accordance with their orders, when someone noticed the exposed enemy over to the left. Black immediately trained one of the 16th's Maxims on to this target (apparently taking over the triggers himself). From his vantage point Captain Loughran saw the Turkish trench 'traversed by a whirlwind — a dust storm apparently swept it from end to end and back again several times. We could hear a machine-gun firing furiously across our front and we realised that the 16th machine-guns … had spotted this lovely target.'[8] Across the valley he could see Turkish bodies sprawled all over their trench parapet, amid the clouds of dust raised by the bullets.

The 4th Brigade gained no real advantage from this blow however; concealed enemy machine-guns still covered no-man's-land and kept up a hail of bullets on the Australian lines, and there was no more to be done in this part of the battlefield. On the left, artillery support helped the New Zealanders and the Light Horse to capture part of the Turkish position, and Lieutenant Hugo Throssell won the Victoria Cross for his part in resisting counterattacks. The battle again subsided into a stalemate. The Anzac force had suffered further crippling losses for no worthwhile gain; another 200 casualties had reduced the 4th Brigade to less than a quarter of its full strength, with many of the 968 survivors weak from sickness. After the battle, Captain Loughran noted an odd reaction: 'I found the 4th Brigade remnant in nothing like as dejected a state as I expected. The fact was that every surviving digger, knowing the reception the attack would meet with, had expected that afternoon to be his last on earth, and was pleasantly surprised to find himself alive.'[9]

In the 13th Battalion, Murray had again made a fine impression with his handling of his machine-gun section during the action and in the following few days when the brigade held the line around Hill 60. He made use of his knack for choosing ground, setting up a gun in a concealed position from where he personally sniped at any Turkish movement he could detect. The battalion history noted that 'he worried the Turks tremendously and they retaliated, but they could never find his skilfully-hidden gun.'[10] He too was suffering from the effects of dysentery by this time, 'looking thin and ill.'

The brigade was pulled out of the front line on 31 August, and moved a short distance south to a somewhat quieter area along Cheshire Ridge, as part of the strong defensive line now established in the north of the battle area. The 13th called their new sector Durrant's Post — Major James Durrant was now acting commanding officer, Colonel Tilney having been hospitalised with illness. Murray set up his machine-guns as part of the strongpoint on the key height named the Apex. The unit remained in this position for two weeks, and at some time during this period Murray found himself in trouble with Durrant. As he later remembered the incident, 'the fault of mine was not very grave — leaving our trenches … one quiet afternoon for half an hour to see our Brigade MG officer without first having asked permission. Durrant strafed [reprimanded] me most thoroughly and then gave me kind and valuable advice, which I never forgot, and which later steered me through much troubled water.'[11]

In mid-September the depleted battalions of the 4th Brigade were relieved by the fresh units of the 2nd Division, and marched down to the beach. From here they were shipped off the mainland altogether, for several weeks rest on Lemnos Island. Some of the men and six machine-guns stayed behind however, to assist the new units to become accustomed to the conditions. The Apex position was the key point in the Anzac line in the north, and altogether thirty-one machine-guns from various units were concentrated there. The 16th's rear party included Black and twelve machine-gunners, and in the 13th Murray and Durrant stayed in the line as advisors. Durrant rejoined the battalion on Lemnos at the end of the month, but Murray's health had deteriorated further, and on 26 September he was evacuated by hospital ship to Egypt. Admitted to Ghezireh Hospital in Cairo, he was variously diagnosed with dysentery, colitis and enteritis. Murray hated Cairo, and he found the climate and atmosphere no improvement on Gallipoli, as he wrote to his sister Annie Cocker. 'More than anything I require a rest and change, both of climate and food ... how I would love a few days in dear old Tasmania.'[12]

It appears that he did in fact have the opportunity to return home, but in the event he turned it down in favour of remaining with his comrades. It is not clear exactly what happened, but Murray was certainly declared temporarily 'unfit for further service' on medical grounds during October. As well as the effects of dysentery, the continuing stiffness in his knee from the shrapnel wound may have been a factor also. Notice was sent to his mother on 9 October that he was being returned to Australia to recuperate, but when Murray embarked from Egypt, his destination was Gallipoli again. He reported back to the 13th Battalion and resumed his duties on 7 December. The story goes that on the day he was ordered to board a vessel for Australia, he managed to get himself instead on to a ship returning to Gallipoli, where his CO accepted him back without question. Another version, in a 1917 newspaper article, had it that 'he was offered three months' furlough but refused it'[13] — by that time Murray had attained considerable distinction, and the comment may have been a tactful version of what amounted to disobedience to orders, since technically, he had been ordered to embark for

Australia. Whatever the case, Murray was not one to leave a task unfinished; he had just begun to make his mark with the 13th and his men and his friends were still on the peninsula fighting. With little waiting for him in Australia, it is not surprising that he chose (with official approval or otherwise) to stay in the war zone.

On the peninsula, Percy Black had spent several weeks at the Apex position attached as an advisor to the 28th Battalion, together with the ubiquitous Captain Rose. The history of the 28th later recorded that 'to assist in the machine-gun work, and advise on local conditions, the battalion was fortunate in having attached to it for a time Captain Rose ... and that gallant soldier, Lieut Percy Black, DCM, 16th Battalion.'[14] Black rejoined the 16th on Lemnos on 8 October, and later in the month he was sent to Egypt on four weeks leave, the first time he had been away from the battle area since the landing. Back in Western Australia at about this time, some consternation had been caused by a false report of his death in the newspapers. An acquaintance from Black's Sandstone days, Frank Jensen,[15] had joined the AIF with the second contingent of recruits and went to Egypt with the 28th Battalion. There in late July he encountered some 16th Battalion officers, who told him of Black's exploits at Pope's Hill and the Bloody Angle. Jensen wrote back to Sandstone with the story, and his letter included the comment, 'the poor fellow paid the extreme toll.' He may have gained the impression that Black had been killed, or perhaps he was just referring to the wounds the latter had received (or had simply been misquoted). The letter was published in the local newspaper, the *Black Range Courier*, on 15 September, and picked up by the *Southern Cross Times* and the Perth *Daily News* shortly afterwards. The story appeared with suitable embellishments — 'The Hero Killed', 'recommended for the VC, only to be shot dead in the next engagement'. A distraught Miss Cassidy wrote through a friend to army headquarters seeking official confirmation. They replied that there had been no such report. There appears to have been no retraction of the *Daily News* article, although the *Southern Cross Times* realised that 'the report about Percy's death must have been false' after local friends received letters from him dated after his supposed death.

*16th Battalion on Lemnos, October 1915. Captain Percy Black is fourth from the left
in the front row. Lt-Col Pope is next to him, fifth from the left.*
(Courtesy Battye Library, Item 005035D)

Black, still very much alive, returned to Anzac from his leave on 21 November; he was temporarily assigned to Brigade Headquarters for the next two weeks before rejoining the 16th on 4 December. With Murray arriving back at Anzac a few days later, both men resumed command of their respective battalion's machine-guns in time for the final act at Gallipoli — the evacuation. The future of the expedition had been debated fiercely at the highest levels of the Allied command since the failure of the August offensives, among the first results being the removal of General Hamilton from command. His replacement, Sir Charles Munro, had the responsibility of recommending the next step, and he firmly advised that the entire force should be withdrawn as soon as possible. Munro had seen the difficulties of the terrain and the weakened physical condition of the men; winter was approaching, and the force was not equipped for the freezing temperatures that were expected. A storm in November had given an ominous warning of what could happen — numerous cases of frostbite (and some deaths from exposure at Suvla), flooded trenches and rough seas which disrupted the landing of supplies. As well, there was reason to believe that the enemy would soon be receiving many more heavy artillery pieces and increased supplies of high-explosive shells; their increased firepower might well blast the Allied army from its foothold.

General Munro came to the conclusion that the campaign could not be won without huge reinforcements of men and material, resources that were also being demanded on the Western Front. His recommendation was received with some dismay in London. Such an admission of failure after so much effort and cost in lives would have a shattering effect on British prestige in the Mediterranean. Prestige aside, a seaborne evacuation in the face of a well-armed and numerous enemy would be an extraordinarily risky operation; some estimates put the likely casualty rate as high as fifty per cent of the force. The government decided to send out the Secretary for War, Lord Kitchener, to assess the situation in person, and he arrived on the peninsula on 12 November. It did not take long for Kitchener to decide that Munro was right, and he ordered that the withdrawal should proceed. With careful planning, Kitchener felt, losses need not be unacceptably high;

some preliminary plans had already been drafted, and at Anzac the Australian staff now drew up a detailed scheme for full evacuation of the force.

The basis of the plan was to maintain an appearance of normality, continuing to hold the front line in apparent strength while gradually withdrawing troops from the rear areas. Ingenious ruses were employed to convince the Turks that nothing had changed and that the struggle would continue indefinitely. Indeed, until the last days few of the Anzac troops were aware that they were taking part in a complete evacuation; the first battalions withdrawn (initially to Lemnos) were under the impression that they were simply being given a short rest before returning to the front,[16] and they only realised in the last few days of the operation that they would not be going back. Through the first weeks of December, the force in the battle zone was gradually depleted, with the final abandonment of the position to take place on the night of the nineteenth.

As the truth dawned on the troops that the campaign was being abandoned, it sent a wave of conflicting emotions through the men. It had seemed to many of the men that the next big effort must surely bring success and vindicate the sacrifices of the last eight months. Bitterness at the admission of failure and at leaving behind the graves of their dead comrades was combined with relief that the long ordeal was coming to an end. The decision had been made however, and each man must now concentrate on carrying out his orders to complete the withdrawal successfully. For the machine-gunners of the Anzac force, controlling as they did its most powerful defensive fire-power, this meant forming part of the final rearguard to cover the retreat of their comrades against any interference from the Turks. During December, the numbers at the Anzac beachhead were steadily reduced, the troops being taken off quietly by night, until by 19 December only 10,000 remained. These progressively moved back to the beaches and embarked, until by 1.30 am on 20 December, the whole Anzac line was held by 2000 men. These last would pull out in three stages. In the 4th Brigade's sector in the north of the Anzac line, Brigadier-General Monash chose 'the pick of the 13th and 16th Battalions for our rearguard ... the last 170, the 'Die-hards', have been chosen from the most gallant and capable men in the brigade';[17] among these were the machine-gun officers of the two battalions, Second-Lieutenant Harry Murray and Captain Percy Black, each with a picked squad of gunners.

Choosing the final squads was a difficult task for the officers. The vast majority of the men volunteered for the honour of being among the last to leave, and there were anguished protests from those who were not selected. On the last night, the final stage of the withdrawal went ahead in accordance with the plan; at 2.05 am the last troops of the 16th, including Black and his gunners, moved quietly away from their trenches and began the walk down the track to the beach. At the same time, Murray's party of the 13th picked up their guns and moved off also, followed ten minutes later by the final five men of the 4th Brigade. Soon afterwards the 'Die-hards' were embarking for Lemnos; now only a few men of the 2nd Division remained, holding part of the original Anzac position. These were evacuated by 4 am, and the savage eight-month struggle was over, ironically finishing with the best-planned operation of the entire campaign — with only one or two men wounded where thousands of casualties had been expected.

The bulk of the 4th Brigade troops had disembarked at Lemnos and settled in to camp. The brigade turned out to welcome their rearguard, the band playing and the troops lining the route as the 'Die-hards' marched to the camp — 'a company of dirty ragamuffins who held themselves up like guardsmen.'[18] The men of the Anzac force were under no illusions: their great effort had failed but they knew also that the outcome was not the fault of the individual soldiers. Mixed with their disappointment and their sorrow at the loss of so many comrades, was an awareness for some that their young nations had established themselves in the eyes of the world, and indeed in their own eyes. A new consciousness of belonging to a nation distinct from their British origins had emerged during the fighting, and they now believed themselves to be at least the equal of any nation on earth. '1915. Australia's entry into the company of nations — no finer entry in all history ... to have leapt into Nationhood, Brotherhood and Sacrifice at one bound ... what a year — never can Australia see its like again,' wrote Captain F B Stanton of the 14th Battalion at the time.[19] For Harry Murray and Percy Black in particular, the two unknown bushmen had demonstrated their outstanding courage, determination and skill in action, and their qualities as leaders of men.

Chapter 5

WESTERN FRONT

The force spent only a short time on Lemnos; within a week, the first groups had embarked again for Egypt. The destination of the NZ & A Division was a camp at Moascar near the town of Ismailia, close to the Suez Canal, with the 1st and 2nd Australian Divisions camping at Tel el Kebir, fifty kilometres to the west. Egypt would be the setting for a series of major changes to the AIF's structure and organisation. All units increased their numbers when their sick and wounded rejoined them from the Cairo hospitals, and there were also many thousands of reinforcements waiting in the camps — recruiting in Australia had increased enormously in the previous months as the nation became aware that an extreme effort would be needed to win the war. Enough troops were available to double the size of the AIF, although weapons and artillery were still in short supply at this time.

For the 4th Brigade at Moascar, the first change was the breaking up of the NZ & A Division; there were now enough New Zealand troops available to form their own separate division, and this was duly done. As well as the 1st and 2nd Australian Divisions, the 3rd Division was beginning to form in Australia, and the Australian troops now concentrated in Egypt would be used to form the 4th and 5th Divisions. The method adopted was to split each of the existing sixteen battalions of the original four brigades in half, and use the new troops to build each half up to a full battalion. With the addition of the separately raised 8th Brigade, this produced an extra five brigades. Two of these (the 12th and 13th) were to combine with the old 4th Brigade to make up the new 4th Division. It was perhaps characteristic of the 4th Brigade that it thus made for an aberration in the AIF's otherwise logical numbering system — the circumstance whereby the 4th Brigade was part of the 4th Division would later puzzle German intelligence officers trying to determine their adversaries' order of battle on the Western Front. The battalions of the 4th Brigade were also allowed to retain the rectangular shape of their colour patches when the rest of the division later adopted circular patches.

The scheme to split the battalions was a sensible one, ensuring that the new 'daughter' or 'pup' units, as they were referred to, would have a solid core of experienced, battle-hardened officers and men, and also a strong link with the 'parent' units of the original force. The reorganisation was completed by early March 1916. But logical though it may have been, the split caused considerable distress to the troops. In the short period of their existence, the original battalions had created their own traditions in the heat of battle, and the men had formed strong emotional attachments to their units. Those selected for the new battalions were hit particularly hard, but the men remaining with the original units were almost equally devastated to see their old comrades departing. Each battalion's machine-gun section remained with its original unit at first, so Black and Murray stayed with the 16th and 13th Battalions respectively. Among the other officers who remained with the 13th was a Lieutenant Harold F Murray. This coincidence seems to have occasionally confused the 13th's orderly-room clerks; there is at least one entry in Harry Murray's service record that clearly relates to his near-namesake.

Within a few weeks, another change took place: each brigade's four machine-gun sections were detached from their battalions and combined to form a company attached directly to the brigade headquarters, regularising the informal arrangement that the 4th Brigade had introduced at Gallipoli. By this time the allocation of guns had been doubled to four per battalion, and the Maxims were in the process of being replaced by Vickers guns, basically an improved version of the Maxim. Each brigade's machine-gun company thus finished up with sixteen Vickers guns and their crews. To compensate for this loss of firepower, the infantry battalions would soon be equipped with the new Lewis guns, a much lighter, air-cooled automatic weapon characterised by its disc-shaped magazine over the barrel. Initially, each infantry company was allocated one Lewis, but the weapons proved so useful that the allocation increased to four per company by the next year.

Black and Murray remained with their respective battalions when the machine-gunners were detached, and took up duty in rifle companies (apparently by their own choice). Black, who had been a temporary captain since August 1915, was officially confirmed in that rank as of 20 January 1916, and on the same day Murray was promoted to full lieutenant. The reconstituted AIF now launched into a period of intensive training, both to bring the new recruits up to standard (many had arrived without rifles) and to refresh the old hands. Up to this time, Black's and Murray's service had been as specialist machine-gunners and machine-gun officers, but they now had the opportunity to show what they could do as leaders of 'footsloggers'. Black was appointed Officer Commanding 'B' Company of the 16th (one of his letters indicates that he was actually in that position as early as January, before the machine-gun section was detached), and on 1 March Murray was promoted to captain also; it appears that his posting at this time was second-in-command of the 13th's 'A' Company.

The 4th Brigade had relocated to the Tel el Kebir camp at the end of February, and here the 4th Division came into being. The new division's training continued through March and April, and it also commenced the difficult task of creating its artillery from scratch. By this time the 1st and 2nd Divisions had been sent to garrison the line of the Suez Canal, and these formations (the least disrupted by the reorganisation and with their artillery elements almost complete) were to embark for France to join the British Army on the Western Front. The 4th and 5th Divisions moved to the canal to take over the defence line and complete their training. It was during this move that the divisions' infamous desert march took place. The 4th Brigade (less the 16th Battalion, which was lucky enough to be sent ahead by train) was sent to march the seventy kilometres from Tel el Kebir to Serapaeum on the Suez, with full packs and limited water, through sand dunes in the furnace heat of the desert. Many of the men were still not fully recovered from their Gallipoli illnesses, and by the end of the three-day march, hundreds had dropped out and were lying exhausted along the last stage of the route. This nightmarish exercise caused considerable bitterness against the 'heads' (the higher commanders) for some time thereafter. The 14th Brigade of the 5th Division had an even more harrowing experience on this march, going by a more difficult route.

The divisions settled in and training recommenced, with each battalion taking turns to garrison the defences of the canal. There was elementary training for the large numbers of new recruits, together with advanced courses for specialists. Many of the officers and NCOs who had been promoted in the field at Gallipoli were sent to classes in military theory to back up their practical battle experience; Black and Murray would probably have attended such training. The units steadily improved in health and skills, and went through the process of filling vacancies at the different rank levels. At this time, an infantry battalion's full-strength 'establishment' included two officers of the rank of major; the 'senior major' was the unit's second-in-command, with another major as one of the four company commanders (the other three companies were commanded by captains, with each company having a less senior captain as its second-in-command). In the 16th, the senior major was E L Margolin; the officer selected to fill the battalion's other vacancy at this level was Percy Black, who was officially promoted to major on 27 April 1916.

It was just under twenty months since he had first enlisted as a private soldier, an astonishingly short time for such a rise, even allowing for the accelerated promotions that inevitably occur in wartime. 'They tell me it is about a record for the Australian army,' he wrote to his mother, and 'they' may well have been right. 'I have been given preference over a lot of officers that were senior to me but they don't seem to mind,' he added. When one considers that he had no more than a basic education, was near the upper age limit for enlistment when he joined, came from a blue-collar occupation and had no previous military experience at all (many 1914 recruits had some militia background), the achievement was all the more remarkable. His natural talent for leadership, his superb courage and effectiveness in combat, and his quick grasp of the skills of military life had brought him to the fore. Black was inclined to be flippant with colleagues about his success ('just luck') but his letters show that he took considerable pride in his achievements. He acknowledged to his mother that he had 'worked very hard'; it was in the same letter that he noted his feeling that he was the only one of the family who had been in a position to join up, and 'it was up to me to do my best for the sake of our name.'

By the end of May 1916, the 4th Division was considered ready for transfer to France, and the troops of the 4th Brigade embarked at Alexandria for Marseilles on 1 June. By this time, the 16th Battalion had a new commanding officer, E H Drake-Brockman, Colonel Pope having been sent to command the 14th Brigade. Marseilles was reached on 7 June, the troops marching from the docks to the railway station to entrain for the north and the fighting. Fears of potential rowdyism in Marseilles proved groundless, except for one incident in which Murray happened to be involved. The *Official History* relates that the reinforcement elements of the 4th and 5th Divisions were waiting at the docks on two ships when a group of 'bad characters' broke through the sentries, intending to enter the town and raise hell. Murray, as one of the officers supervising the landing of the troops, intercepted them at the dock gates. When they ignored his order to halt, he drew his revolver and faced the rioters 'with such obvious determination' that they gave up the attempt and returned to the ship.[1]

The early part of the journey through France was a source of intense pleasure for virtually all Australians who passed that way; most accounts speak of their fascination with the fairytale beauty of the countryside in the glorious June weather. The further north the trains carried them, the less attractive the scenery became, as they neared the devastated war zone. The

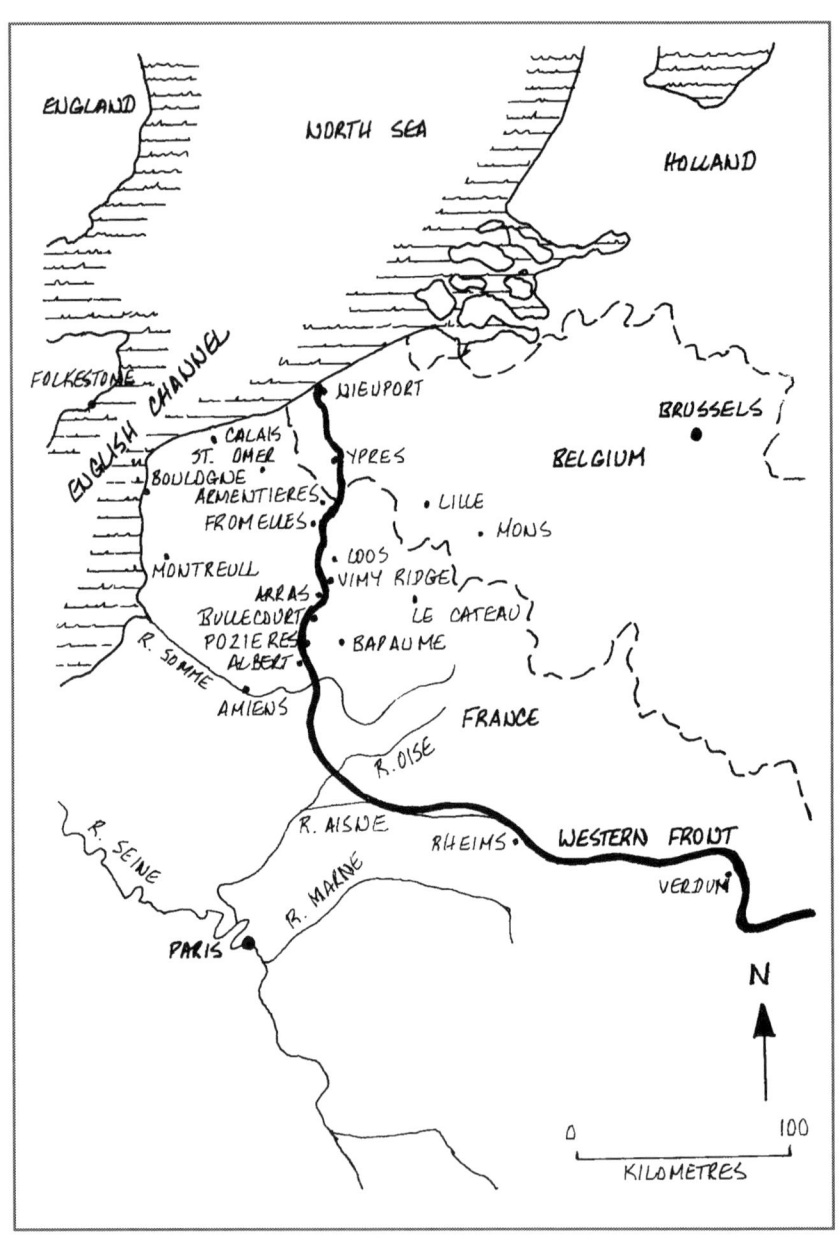

The Western Front in June 1916, before the Battle of the Somme.

Australians were about to plunge into a type of warfare that differed in many respects from that which they had experienced at Gallipoli. Following the comparatively mobile fighting early in the war, the German and Allied armies had settled into the long lines of earthworks which now stretched the whole 750 kilometre length of the fighting front; of this, the British sector in the north occupied roughly a quarter, the remainder being held by the French along with the small Belgian army. At Gallipoli, both sides had, of course, operated from trench systems, but the Australians had experienced nothing like the complexity and sophistication of the Western Front works. They also had much to learn about the battle tactics employed in the trenches. For the men of the 4th Brigade, the learning process commenced on 10 June 1916 when they detrained at Bailleul in French Flanders, within earshot of the rumbling artillery at the front line. They were in the northernmost part of the British sector, regarded as a comparatively quiet area and therefore suitable for introducing the troops to conditions in France. The divisions were grouped into two corps (I and II Anzac Corps) with the New Zealanders and one or two British divisions; the composition of the two corps was not rigidly fixed, and they were attached to different 'armies' of the British forces at different times.

A typical British trench system on the Western Front consisted of several parallel excavations, usually at least three lines: the front-line or 'fire' trench, the support trench several hundred metres to the rear, and the reserve trench still further back; some complex systems might include yet more lines in the rear. The lines were linked by a number of communication trenches that allowed troops to move below ground level between the various lines. The trenches were not simple straight ditches; had they been so, an enemy breaking into the trench would be able to fire right along its whole length. Instead the trenches were 'traversed' with straight sections ('bays') alternating with short right-angled sections ('traverses') to break up the straight line (see plan on page 102). Seen from above, the shape of the line resembled a battlemented wall. Communication trenches were dug in a simpler zigzag pattern, also to prevent enemy fire 'enfilading' the length of the trench. In front of the fire-trench was a wide entanglement of barbed wire, supported by stakes, and sometimes more wire between the front and support trenches. Beyond the front line was the

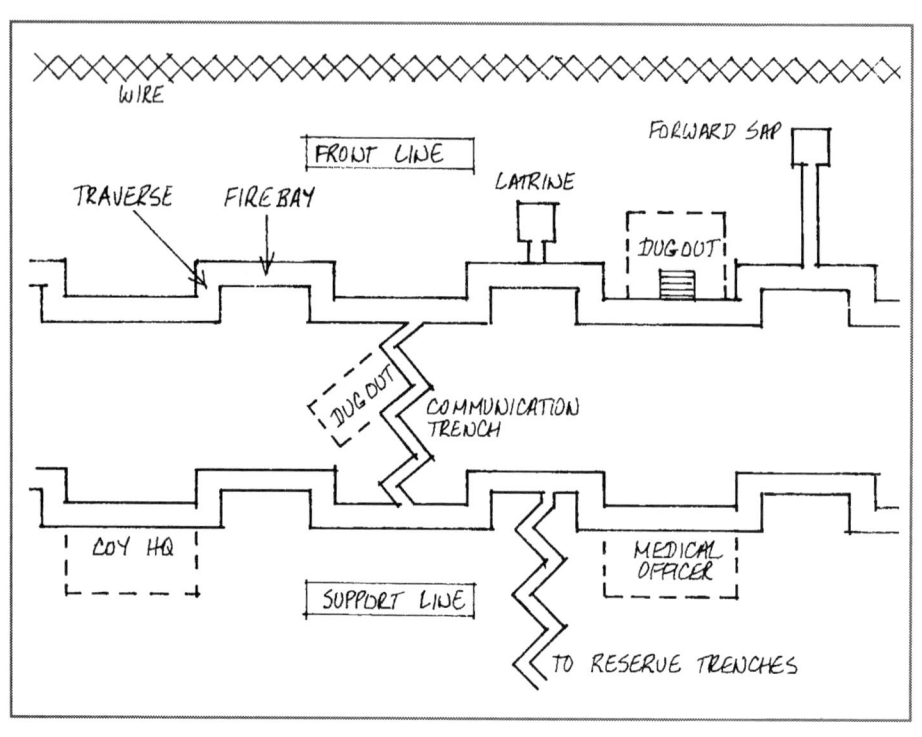

Plan of typical front line trench system.

desolation of no-man's-land, with the enemy's similar trench system on the other side.

A well-established trench was usually dug about ten feet (three metres) deep, the depth including a wall of sandbags (the parapet) up to a metre above ground level at the front of the trench, perforated with loopholes for observation and firing (see diagram on page 104). A similar low wall at the rear of the trench was called the parados. As the trench was deeper than a man's height, a 'fire-step' was dug along the inside of the front wall, so the troops could step up to fire through the loopholes or over the parapet. A timber bench-like structure was sometimes installed to form the fire-step. The trench would be interspersed with dugouts — underground chambers that provided some protection from shellfire. On the German side particularly, dugouts could be quite elaborately constructed and furnished. Machine-guns were mounted in strongpoints along the line, positioned to sweep the area in front of the trench with a deadly crossfire.

The Australians found themselves facing a number of differences in the weaponry and tactics used in Europe compared with the fighting at Gallipoli. In the first place, the artillery of both sides was vastly more powerful, both in the number of guns and the weight of shell. They would soon experience the devastating effect of a lengthy bombardment with heavy howitzers using high-explosive shells, which could smash an entire town to rubble, wreck a trench, bury men alive or blow them to pieces, and reduce the survivors to a state of mental breakdown. The other side of the coin was the availability of their own side's artillery to support them with similar pounding of the enemy. Ground loosened by shell-bursts turned into a quagmire in wet weather, which seemed to be most of the time, lice infestation was rife, and the trenches were home to countless rats. Over all hung the stench of death. Most of the soldiers smoked, as much to cover the smells of the battle area as for reasons of addiction — Harry Murray picked up the tobacco habit in the army, and also began to take the occasional drink, although it seems it took him a long time to develop a head for spirits.

The most effective weapon of defence for both sides remained the machine-gun, which the Germans were the more skilled in deploying and

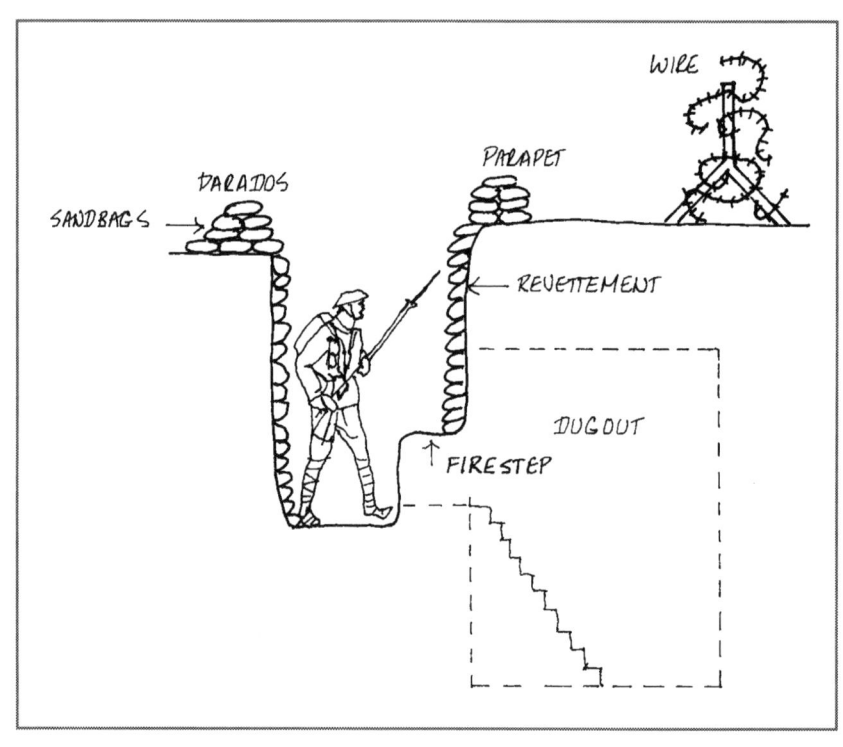

Section through trench.

which they used in great numbers at this stage of the war. The infantry of the British Army, however, was now using increasing numbers of Lewis guns; unlike the unwieldy Vickers and Maxim guns, these could keep up with the forefront of an attacking infantry group and give dominating firepower at the crucial points. The Australians soon learned to make particularly effective use of the Lewis gun in combat. For close-quarter trench fighting, probably the most important weapon was the hand grenade, which the British and Empire armies called a 'bomb'. At Gallipoli, the Australians had had no grenades at all to begin with, and found themselves at a great disadvantage, even against the crude bombs used by the Turks; only the makeshift 'jam-tin' grenades enabled them to hold their own. This aspect of warfare was more sophisticated on the Western Front. The Germans used stick grenades and smaller 'egg-bombs', both of which could be thrown further than the heavier British Mills grenade, but the latter was the more dangerous weapon. It had a larger explosive charge, and on bursting its segmented casing split evenly into flying pieces that could kill at a distance. All the troops carried grenades in action, and the battalions now formed 'bombing' platoons, specialising in grenade fighting.

A fight in the trenches would often see both sides flinging showers of grenades at each other until one gained an advantage and managed to drive back their opponents. Often the result depended on which side could maintain an adequate supply of grenades to the throwers in the front line. At Pozieres in July 1916, units of the 2nd Australian Division threw 15,000 grenades in the course of a desperate twelve-hour struggle, relays of 'bombers' throwing until their arms gave out. Both sides also used rifle grenades, which were projected from the muzzle of a rifle (using an adaptor and a blank cartridge) over a greater distance than could be achieved by hand, although with less accuracy.

Another weapon unknown at Gallipoli was poison gas, introduced by the Germans and then used by both sides. Several different types of gas, with varying degrees of frightfulness, were in use. Initially released in clouds from cylinders, by 1916 gas was usually delivered to enemy positions by means of special artillery shells. The 4th Brigade was fortunate in rarely experiencing a heavy gas attack, but gas masks had to be carried at all times when troops were in or near the front line. There was a lot to learn, and many officers and men were sent through the system of infantry 'schools' for detailed instruction in weapons and tactics. The troops were also issued with steel helmets for the first time in the war.

There were some advantages to the new theatre of war, not least of which was the opportunity to take leave in England or Paris, available with some regularity to the officers and less frequently for the rank and file. During quiet periods in the trenches, even in the front line, life remained uncomfortable and dangerous, but the level of tension was usually lower than that experienced in such positions as Quinn's Post at Gallipoli. In holding its allotted segment of the front, a brigade would often have two of its battalions in the firing line with the other two further back in reserve. A second brigade of the division would be alongside in the line, with the third brigade 'resting' in the rear. Units were rotated away from the front line with reasonable frequency — the actual time periods varied considerably, but a typical 'tour' in the firing line might be eight days, after which the unit was relieved by another coming from reserve. The process of relief could be a major trial in itself, with the new unit slogging through a long, narrow and often muddy communication trench, frequently under enemy artillery fire, to arrive at the front already exhausted. The troops going into reserve faced the same dangerous, tiring journey in reverse. Having got away from the forward zone, they would then be faced with a period of hard physical labour, carrying supplies and ammunition forward, road making, digging additional trenches, laying telephone cables and the like. When rotated further to the rear, however, they could look forward to at least a short period of safety among the French populace, and some limited recreation in the various *estaminets* (taverns) in the villages.

Combat was infrequent, particularly in certain areas of the front, but intermittent sniping and shelling went on most of the time. It was usually fatal to expose oneself outside the trenches during daylight, but after dark the battle area came alive, with carrying parties bringing supplies up to the line, and patrols from both sides creeping stealthily through no-man's-land. Most of these expeditions were intended to scout the enemy positions, but there were also occasional trench raids, when a strong force would enter the enemy trench following an artillery barrage, to capture prisoners and cause maximum damage. After-dark operations were not usually carried out in total blackness. Star-shells, flares and shell-bursts provided intermittent illumination, and with experience the soldiers' night vision improved to a remarkable degree. This phenomenon is mentioned in the writings of Captain George Mitchell of the 4th Division, who described in some detail how combat experience developed the senses, including the ability to distinguish between different weapons by their sound — the heavy rhythmic roar of the Vickers gun, the 'hurried stammer' of the Lewis gun, the differing explosions of British and German grenades.[2] A shattering, frightening noise from a machine-gun meant, by some trick of acoustics, that the gun was not pointed in one's direction, while the soft swish of bullets from a distant unheard gun was far more dangerous. Skills such as these helped the experienced soldier to survive the routine patrols and skirmishes, but made little difference in a saturating artillery bombardment or a massed attack into the crossfire of machine-guns and rifles, when death made no distinction between novices and veterans. Bitter experience showed that in major actions it was quite possible for a unit to be almost completely wiped out, and the practice arose of selecting a proportion of officers and men to remain in the rear as a nucleus for reforming the unit if necessary. These troops were designated as 'left out of battle'.

A full-scale assault on the enemy lines would begin with an artillery barrage, which could sometimes last for days. Some of the barrage would be directed at destroying the enemy barbed wire, a task which could also be attempted with mortar bombs. The trenches would be pounded with high explosives to wreck the defences and destroy machine-gun posts, unless the attack commander preferred to use shrapnel shells to keep the enemy's heads down and preserve the trench for occupation by the attackers. At the appropriate time, the artillery barrage would 'lift', lengthen its range beyond the objective and begin to pound the enemy reserve areas. The infantry attack would then go in, hoping to find little resistance. More often than not, the Germans would have been able to shelter themselves and their weapons in deep dugouts, to emerge once the barrage lifted and remount their machine-guns in time to open fire before the attackers reached the trench.

If the attackers managed to get into the enemy position, a bitter struggle would take place for its possession, each side tossing grenades into the next segment of trench ('bombing up the traverses') and following up with rifle and bayonet. In the meantime, support troops would be struggling across no-man's-land carrying extra ammunition and boxes of grenades to the fighting troops, a task that was at least as dangerous as the fight in the trench: both sides' artillery would be shelling the rear areas to cut off their opponents' source of supply. The constant traffic across no-man's-land included 'walking wounded', prisoners under escort, and the attack commander's runners carrying messages to headquarters, either verbal or scribbled on a message pad by whatever light was available, and returning with the replies. The commander could also communicate by flare signal, using a predetermined combination of colours to convey messages such as a call for artillery support. Compared to the weapons, signalling was still primitive, little different from the methods used at Waterloo. Had something like the Second World War 'walkie talkie' been available, the story of many 1914–18 battles might have been very different.

If the attackers succeeded in taking their objective, their next task would be to consolidate the position, setting it up to prepare for counterattacks which would probably be launched from the enemy's support line. The configuration of the captured trench would be the wrong way around for its new occupants, since it was originally built to defend against attacks from the opposite direction. A new fire-step would have to be dug in what had originally been the back wall of the trench, and makeshift emplacements made for machine-guns. At each end of the captured segment of trench, a barricade or 'bomb-stop' would be hastily thrown up from whatever materials were at hand. Working parties might now begin the task of digging a communication trench across no-man's-land from the original front line to the new position, to provide some sort of protection for troop movement. Heavy machine-guns would be brought up and emplaced, and signallers might start to lay wires for field telephones connecting with headquarters. Much digging and carrying would eventually see the position incorporated as part of a new front line (if it was held against counterattacks) — a few hundred metres of ground gained at a heavy price in lives.

For the most part, the Germans had remained on the defensive on the Western Front since 1914, while pursuing a more attacking approach against the Russians in the East. The British and French had launched numerous minor attacks, and several 'big pushes' on wide fronts in attempts to drive the Germans from French soil, but aside from a few minor gains of territory, all had failed in bloodbaths against the barbed wire and massed machine guns. At the time the first Australians began arriving in France, another series of major offensives was about to start. Departing from their established practice, in late February 1916 the Germans had forestalled the Allies' plans by launching their own offensive against the French at Verdun. The dreadful battle lasted for months and cost each side several hundred thousand casualties, the French barely hanging on under crushing artillery bombardments. The Allied offensive had originally been planned as a huge joint operation by the British and French, to be launched on both sides of the Somme River, which formed the boundary between the British and French sectors of the front. Verdun, however, meant that the operation would now be a mainly British affair, launched as much to take pressure off the French as to drive back the German line. The Battle of the Somme began on 1 July 1916, and the AIF would soon be taking part in this great blood-letting.

When the 4th Brigade arrived at the front line near Armentières in mid-June, it immediately began to relieve units of the 2nd Division, which had been gaining experience in this comparatively quiet 'nursery' sector since April. The 13th and 14th were the first of the brigade's units to occupy front-line positions, and were soon involved in patrolling and trench raids, as well as suffering casualties from enemy artillery. A couple of Murray's exploits during this period are recounted by Franki and Slatyer: on one occasion, while visiting his company's positions in the firing line after dark, he took a short cut across the open and surprised an enemy sniper. Although Murray had gone out unarmed, he bluffed the German into surrender and brought him in, the 13th's first prisoner in France. On another night, while patrolling with Captain Doug Marks (the young platoon commander who had impressed Murray at Gallipoli, now the battalion adjutant and a close friend), he crept into a German dugout and made off with a spiked helmet.

On 7 July, the 1st Division began to march south to be thrown into the Battle of the Somme, followed soon after by the 2nd Division. Within a few days the high command decided that more reinforcements were needed, and the 4th Division was sent south also. The line near Armentières was taken over by the 5th Division, and it was this formation which was the first of the Australians to be involved in a major action — thrown into an impossible situation at Fromelles and cut to pieces. On the Somme, the 'big push' had begun on 1 July. Preceded by a massive week-long artillery bombardment that was confidently expected to obliterate the German front line, the British infantry advanced across no-man's-land on a 25 kilometre front. All along the line, the German garrison emerged from the dugouts, set up their machine-guns and opened fire, mowing down the attacking lines like grass. By the end of the day the British had suffered nearly 60,000 casualties (19,000 killed outright) and the attack had been defeated almost everywhere. Some gains had been made, however, on the southern flank of the advance, where a few British and French units penetrated the German front line.

The British line was now bent forward to the south of the fortified town of Thiepval, which was still occupied by the Germans and formed a bastion preventing any decisive progress in this sector. The high command determined that Thiepval must be taken, and for the next two weeks the British Fourth Army hammered away at the enemy defences, with the intention of getting behind the Thiepval position and capturing it from the south-east. At great cost, the British managed to advance their line to a point where it swung across the German second-line trenches beyond Thiepval. The Germans quickly excavated a makeshift line roughly at right angles to their original front and parallel to the new British line. The new German position incorporated the small village of Pozieres and the high ground on which it stood, blocking the way to Thiepval.

From this point in the battle, the British tactics would consist of driving towards Pozieres and Thiepval in a succession of attacks on a narrow front — what C E W Bean described as 'giving a bang with the hammer every day or

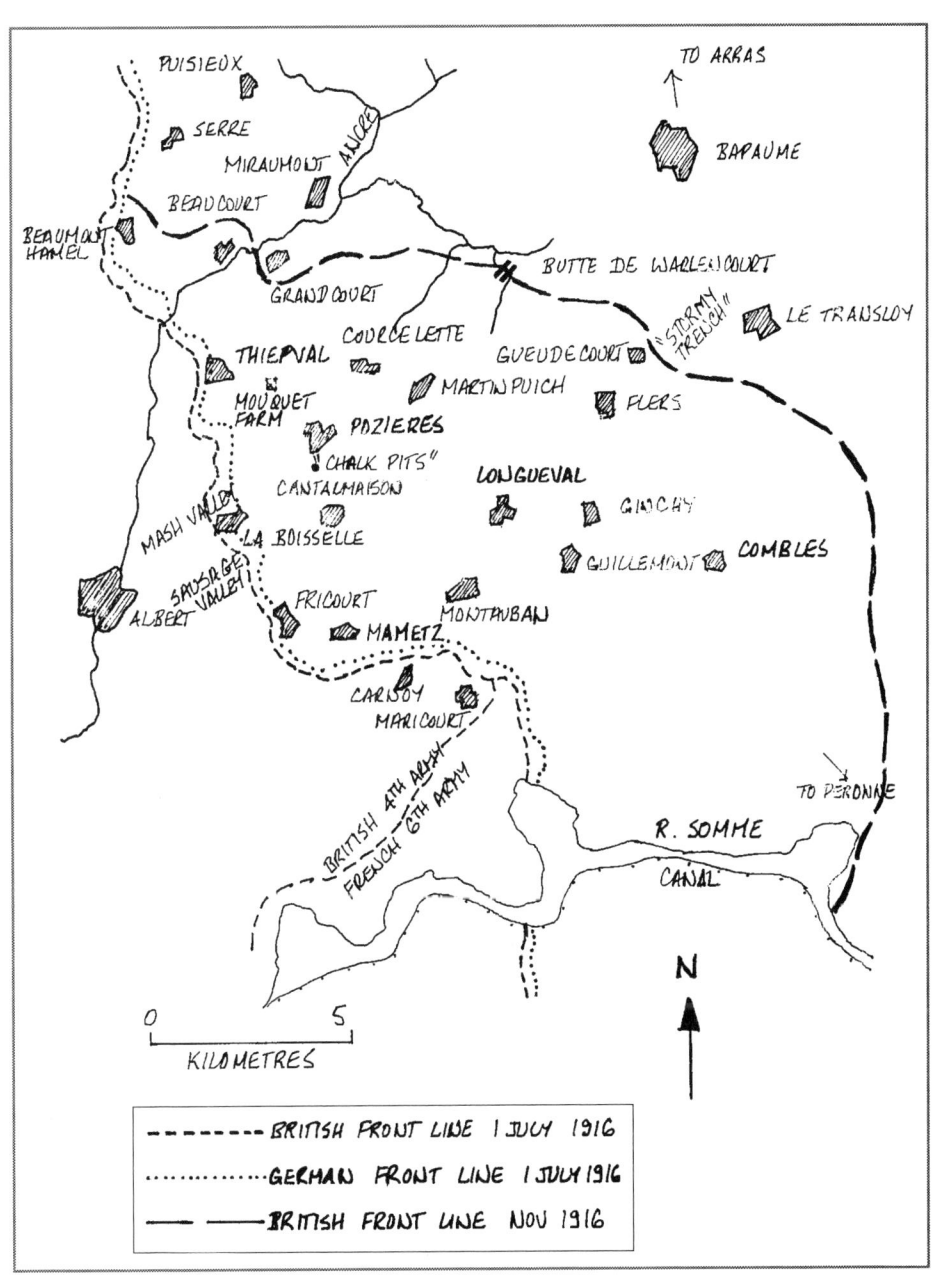

The British zone of operation on the Somme, 1916.

two to drive the wedge in another fraction of an inch.'³ The deeper they advanced, the more the Germans could concentrate artillery fire on them from different directions. A further difficulty was that the part of the old German second line (known as the OG lines) still occupied by the enemy was in such a position as to be able to fire into the flank of a force attacking Pozieres village; such attacks therefore had to be supported by more troops attempting to push further along the OG lines at the same time. The first British attack on Pozieres (17 July) was beaten off with heavy losses, and the exhausted units were relieved by the 1st Australian Division, just arriving from the north. The 2nd and 4th Divisions were following a few days behind. The Australian formations were now designated as part of the 'Reserve Army', and took over responsibility for operations against Pozieres.

The 1st Division attacked the Pozieres positions on 23 July, following a crushing artillery barrage which reduced the village itself to rubble and demolished sections of the OG lines. By early next morning, the village (or at least the place where it had been) was in the hands of the Australians, who now braced themselves for counterattacks. The German effort to retake this vital position took the form of a devastating artillery bombardment. For hour after hour the captured area was pounded with high-explosive shells, pulverising the remaining rubble of the village and reducing the surrounding earth to a powder. The troops of the 1st Division hung on grimly to their positions, suffering heavy losses in killed and wounded, with many more shattered mentally by the strain. The bombardment began to die away after three days, and the weary survivors of the 1st Division were withdrawn and replaced by the fresh troops of the 2nd Division.

The next objective for the Australians was part of the OG lines, still occupied by the Germans on the high ground overlooking the Pozieres position. After several nights of bitter, confused fighting over the churned-up wasteland that the battlefield had become, the 2nd Division secured its objectives. The Australians now held the Pozieres site and a considerable length of the OG Lines, but the cost in casualties had been enormous. The battered 2nd Division had to be relieved, and it was the turn of the 4th Division to go into the inferno of the Pozieres battlefield. The high command continued the tactic of inching forward on a narrow front deeper into the German lines. The way to Thiepval was still barred by a network of German trenches north-west of Pozieres, and beyond those was an important strongpoint in the ruined buildings of Mouquet Farm. It would be the 4th Division's task to capture that ground and keep the advance going. The 4th Brigade led the division into the battle area, moving up through the shallow depression called Sausage Valley, which would become familiar ground to all who served on that front. On the way they had passed the surviving troops of the 1st Division, just relieved from their nightmare experience. Edgar Rule of the 14th Battalion left a well-known description of this encounter: 'Those who watched them will never forget it as long as they live. They looked like men who had been in hell. Almost without exception each man looked drawn and haggard, and so dazed that they appeared to be walking in a dream, and their eyes looked glassy and starey … In all my experience I've never seen men so shaken up as these.'[4] The 4th Brigade had been given an indication of what was waiting for them as they marched toward the sound of the guns.

Chapter 6

MOUQUET FARM

As the 4th Division moved into the front line, the German artillery bombardment reached a peak of intensity. The 4th Brigade's foremost battalion, the 15th, attempting to relieve 6th Brigade units in the position called 'K' Trench on the night of 5 August, was stopped in its tracks by a furious hail of shells. The shelling eased off the next day, and they were able to complete the relief, but the brigade had received a sharp introduction to conditions around Pozieres. More was to follow; the 14th Battalion joined the 15th in the front line during the next night, and the German artillery again deluged the front lines with high explosives. Many of the Australians were able to take refuge in the old German dugouts in the trench system, but casualties were still heavy. At first light the Germans launched an infantry assault on the Australian position. They were thrown back with heavy losses, mainly through the efforts of Lieutenant Jacka, VC of the 14th Battalion, who led a handful of men in a counterattack against heavy odds. (Perhaps the most remarkable aspect of Jacka's action was that he was somehow not awarded a second Victoria Cross for his heroism in this fight.) It was obvious that the division's tour in the front line would be no picnic.

Over the next few days, the advance companies of the 16th and 13th Battalions moved forward to back up the 4th Brigade's other two battalions and prepare to continue the drive towards Thiepval. They found themselves in a scene of almost total desolation. By now the constant shelling had turned the area into a moonscape; the earth had been churned to powder by the shells, constantly turned over by fresh bombardments which uncovered, reburied and uncovered again the rotting corpses, German, British and Australian casualties from the battles of the preceding weeks. The trenches of both sides were constantly caved in by shells, painstakingly dug out again, then collapsed again, the troops often being buried alive; the lucky ones would be freed by their frantic mates, to emerge with their nerves strained to breaking point. Often the line of a trench could best be determined by noting where the dead and wounded were thickest. Edgar Rule of the 14th Battalion noted that the troops 'soon came to know what that spongy feeling underfoot meant' when walking along the trench floor — they were stepping on bodies only a few inches under the soil.

It was the division's task in this situation to advance the British line, thrusting northwards towards Thiepval through the maze of old German trenches, in a continuation of the 1st and 2nd Divisions' costly operations of the previous weeks. First to be thrown in was the 15th Battalion, advancing 200 metres on the night of 8 August to capture the part of the German front line known as 'Park Lane'. As often happened on this battlefield, the degraded condition of the partly demolished trench and the lack of landmarks made it difficult to identify the correct objective in the dark. Some of the troops advanced too far past the enemy position, but the 15th eventually secured its objective, only to experience another setback, one which would occur time and again over the next few weeks: the troops meant to be supporting their flanks (in this case the British 7th Suffolks on the left) were unable to advance in the face of heavy machine-gun fire from a German strongpoint. With its left flank 'in the air', the 15th eventually had to abandon the part of the position they had taken. Another attack was ordered for the following night; this time three companies of the 16th Battalion, led by Major Percy Black's 'B' Company, would advance on the left of the 15th.

Black had fought in desperate front-line combat throughout the eight months of Gallipoli, but always as a machine-gunner and machine-gun officer. Apart from training exercises, he had never led infantry riflemen in a pitched battle, so the coming action would be a test of his leadership in the field. The 16th's advance was carefully planned by the CO, Colonel Drake-Brockman. Part of their task was to capture the strongpoint designated as 'Point 78', which had held up the Suffolks the night before, and Drake-Brockman decided to approach it from an angle rather than frontally. This assignment was given to Black's 'B' Company; after taking the position, they would have to change direction in the dark and under fire, continue their advance to the final objective and link up with the rest of the 15th and 16th on their right. The brigade commander, General Brand, conferred with the battalions' commanding officers and company commanders to work out the final plans, and the 16th's officers and NCOs found vantage points in the Australian front trench from which they could study the ground over which they would be advancing.

At 11.55 pm on 9 August, the British and Australian artillery laid a devastating bombardment on the German lines, and five minutes later the 16th 'jumped the bags' and charged.[1] The attack was a brilliant success: under heavy fire, Black's men overwhelmed the German strongpoint, capturing three machine-guns, a flamethrower and fifty prisoners,[2] then wheeled to their right and rushed their next objective in the German position. The other companies of the 16th and 15th had also taken their objectives, and the Australians had advanced their line by 200 metres and occupied what had been the German front line. With the position secured, Black immediately moved along the front organising the important work of 'consolidation', setting up the captured trench to defend against counterattack.

In the event, there was no infantry counterattack, and it was not until the afternoon of the next day that the Germans were able to lay a heavy artillery bombardment on their former front line. At some point during this shelling, Black was buried up to the neck when a shell shovelled the trench wall in on top of him. He could do nothing but wait to be dug out, and a terrible pain in his right shin seemed to indicate a broken leg. He was soon freed, and

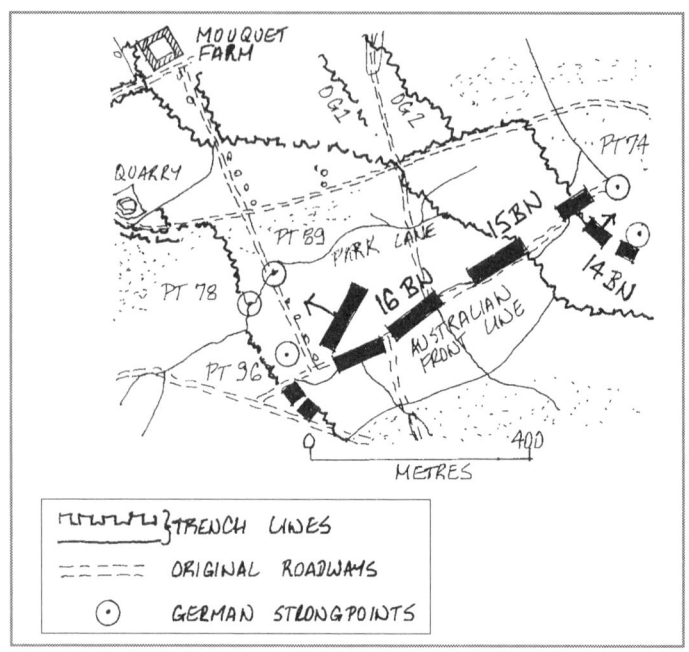

16th Battalion's advance towards Mouquet Farm, 9/10 August 1916.

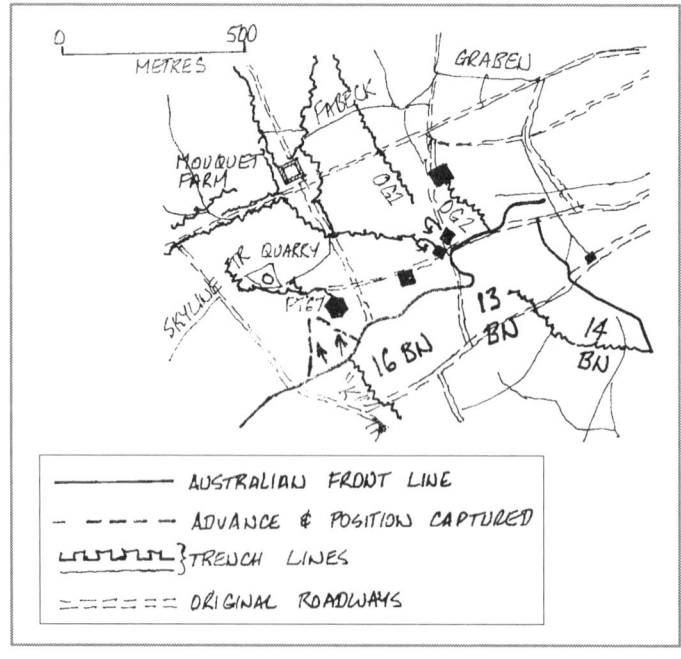

Second advance by 16th Battalion, 10/11 August 1916.

relieved to find that the pain was due to a burn from a hot piece of shell casing. A few minutes later, visitors turned up: Harry Murray and Captain Toby Barton, then commanding 'A' Company of the 13th. The 13th was in the process of relieving the 15th in the front line, and Murray and Barton had decided to call in on Black. Murray could see that his friend was somewhat shaken by his recent experience: 'I had a flask of whisky, which was strictly for wounded men. I considered he had qualified, and offered him a spot, and seldom have I seen a spot enjoyed so much. His eyes flashed, and he said "Harry, I've always said you were the right man at the right time, and you are living up to your reputation."'[3]

With the Germans believed to be off balance, another advance was ordered for the following night, 10 August. The 16th and 13th, the latter now in the front line, were to advance to another vaguely identified position about 200 metres further towards the piles of rubble which had once been the buildings of Mouquet Farm. In the desolate landscape, the confusion over locations was such that it was later realised that the 13th was probably already occupying the position it was supposed to take. In the event, the 13th simply followed their artillery barrage and dug in when the line of shell-bursts became stationary. Murray, second-in-command of 'A' Company at this time, had been 'left out of battle' for the attack. At some time during this night's battle the 'A' Company commander, Captain Barton, disappeared without a trace, and Murray took over the company. He had been keeping himself busy with more lone-wolf scouting excursions into no-man's-land in the few days the unit had been near the front: 'It was my happy hunting ground. I loved the freedom from the trenches,' he later wrote. It was presumably this type of activity, together with the daring in action that he soon began to display, that led to his being nicknamed 'Mad Harry' by the troops.

On the 13th's left, Percy Black again led the 16th forward across 200 metres of the wasteland, finding the trench they were supposed to capture to be almost non-existent due to the effects of artillery. The men went to work to dig a rough front line, on the edge of a shallow valley looking across to the German positions. The work was completed by first light, when the Germans began one of the heaviest artillery bombardments yet experienced by the

Australians. The new positions of the 16th and 13th were in direct view of the German observers, and as the narrow Australian front penetrated further into the German lines, it could increasingly be shelled from three sides. The hail of explosives went on hour after hour; casualties mounted rapidly, and the two battalions were forced to pull back a short distance from their front positions to avoid the worst of the shelling. In mid-afternoon, the Germans launched an infantry counterattack. The 13th and 16th, quickly moving back to their original posts, swept the attack away with fire from Lewis guns and rifles — the 16th troopers had kept their weapons under their tunics to protect them from dust and debris. The Germans fell back in disorder, hurried on their way by the British artillery.

After this repulse, the Germans turned again to their artillery, and the Australian line was once more pounded mercilessly through the night, the 16th suffering severely again.[4] Black later told Cyril Longmore how, during a barrage, he would 'walk along the line asking casual questions, such as "Got a match, lad?" He said this seemed to hearten the Diggers, on the assumption that things couldn't be so bad after all, if the Major was only concerned about little things like that.'[5] Some time during that night, Black sent word back for more Lewis guns to be brought up to the front line (either to replace unserviceable guns or for increased fire-power in case of another infantry attack), and the 15th Battalion, now in reserve, was ordered to send up six of its guns. One of the 15th's gunners carrying out this task left an account of his experiences that night,[6] which provides a valuable close-up of Percy Black. After struggling through the German barrage, the anonymous private managed to locate 16th Battalion headquarters by the light of flares and explosions, only to be told to keep going to the front line and deliver his gun to Major Black in person.

By this time the shells had almost obliterated the front-line trench, but about an hour before sunrise he finally came across a private of the 16th in a shell-hole, who informed him that this was in fact the front line. During a lull in the bombardment, he was directed further along to Black's company headquarters in a partly intact section of the old German trench. 'The place was a veritable graveyard, and gave forth a vile stench.' There was a dugout here, but Black was sitting on the trench parados in the half-light, calmly puffing on his pipe and looking, to the private, 'like a man who has just dismounted after a long ride and sought the shelter of a shady tree to rest … the only tranquil being I had met since I set forth from Chalk Pits that night.' Black accepted the gun from the private, handing it over to his company sergeant-major in the dugout.

'Where are the others?' he asked.

'They're at the back of me,' answered the 15th man.

'Will they be long? It won't do for you chaps to delay your return much longer. Want to be clear away from here before daylight,' Black said.

The private decided to make the most of the opportunity of speaking to Black, and recorded his impressions in detail.

> I had heard a lot about Black. His name had become synonymous with all that a soldier should be in the days of Gallipoli … Black was already an institution in the Fourth Brigade and one of the few men whose fame had spread throughout the whole Australian army … He had a magnetic personality … You instinctively say to yourself: 'I'd follow that man through hell!' and you mean it. There was an undercurrent of power about him, a purpose in the quiet, unassuming voice and the square chin. He seemed to me a typical bushman … I lit my pipe as I sat down beside him, and we talked about many things. As I finished my pipe, the first rays of the rising sun cast its early morning light over the wreckage around us.
>
> 'Better be tootling, lad!' he said simply.
>
> It was an order spoken very quietly, but for all that a command from a man born to command. I took it as such and rose to my feet … I looked back several times as I walked swiftly across the uneven ground on my way back to the unit. He had not moved. His reclining form was silhouetted against the rising sun. I felt a different man altogether on the

road home. A braver man. I had gained something — a trust
I have never lost. I had met one of the gods.

It was decided later that day to relieve the battered, exhausted 16th for the
next stage of the advance. The 50th Battalion (13th Brigade) moved up, and
after a difficult relief under yet another bombardment,[7] the 16th's weary
survivors made their way back to the support line. The battalion could be
pleased with its accomplishments in its first period of serious fighting in
France: although the cost had been terrible (over 400 killed and wounded)
they had made two highly successful advances, repulsed enemy counterattacks,
and stood up to furious shelling. The attacks that Black had led on two
successive nights were carried out so smoothly as to hardly rate more than a
few sentences in the *Official History*, or even the battalion's own history. The
CO, Colonel Drake-Brockman, however, was well aware of the difficulties that
had been overcome, and of how important Percy Black's faultless leadership
had been; on 13 August, he recommended Black for the Distinguished Service
Order (DSO).

The division pressed on with the short, narrow-fronted advances towards
the Mouquet Farm position. The 13th Battalion became heavily engaged over
the next few days, and Harry Murray would command a rifle company in
action for the first time (as with Black, all his previous battle experience was
with machine-guns). On the night of 12 August, the 13th advanced to a
position within 300 metres of the farm. The 50th on their left, however, was
held up and the 13th found itself occupying an isolated position ahead of the
rest of the Australian line. This turned out to be an unexpected advantage: in
attempting to counterattack the 50th, a German infantry force exposed its
flank to the 13th and was swept away by fire from Lewis guns and rifles. A
more ambitious attack was planned for two nights hence; the 13th Brigade
took over the line from the 4th Brigade, but the 13th Battalion remained in
the line, sandwiched between the 50th and 51st Battalions. The three
battalions were to assault the Mouquet Farm position on the night of 14
August: the 50th to capture the farm itself on the left, with the 13th and 51st
advancing up the old German lines (OG 1 and OG 2) to occupy the strong

enemy trench known as the Fabeck Graben, running to the east of the Farm. Murray was to be in overall command of the 13th's three companies ('B', 'C' and his own 'A') in the attacking force.

Zero hour was set for 10 pm; throughout the day of 14 August, the battalions huddled in their forward positions as the British and German artillery continued to pound each other's lines. The shells falling among the waiting infantrymen (including some inaccurate fire from their own side) caused numerous casualties, and those not hit were badly shaken. With so much damage done before the attack was even due to start, the commanders on the spot pressed for a postponement, but they were ordered to proceed. The troops set off as planned, but liaison between the battalions broke down almost at once. Both the 50th on the left and the 51st on the right were held up by machine-gun fire from concealed enemy positions, and lost touch with the 13th in the centre of the attacking line. The 13th, led by Murray in two waves, of 100 and 80 men, jumped out of their assembly trench straight into what he later described as 'the hottest fire I ever saw' — apparently one German unit was relieving another in the nearest trench, so it was crowded with twice the expected number of defenders. In spite of this, the 13th kept straight on, following the line of the old OG 1 trench; cheering and yelling, they swarmed through two minor German positions to reach the main enemy trench, the Fabeck Graben. A charge over the final thirty metres put the German garrison to flight, the Australians harrying them with rifles and grenades as they fled. Murray now moved to reorganise his men in the position they had captured.

The 13th had lost a number of men killed and wounded during their brilliant advance; Murray stationed his remaining men in several posts along the Fabeck Graben, occupying 200 metres of the trench running between the two OG lines. He placed another group further north along OG 1, about forty metres in advance of the main position. There had been no time during the charge to keep track of what was happening on the flanks, but Murray now made a quick reconnaissance westwards towards Mouquet Farm. He found no sign of the 50th, and shortly afterwards a German attack on the other flank showed that there was no support on the right either. At the same time, the advanced post had spotted the shadowy figures of numerous soldiers, almost certainly German, advancing towards the Australian position. Murray immediately sent a messenger to the rear seeking information, and set about rearranging his men to meet the threat. He brought two Lewis gun teams out of the main trench and positioned them in the open to back up the advanced post. There was a possibility that the troops to their front were a stray party of the 51st, but a challenge resulted in the strangers opening fire. Murray's Lewis guns opened up immediately and scattered the German force, but he was now convinced that the 13th were in a very dangerous position.

The 13th's own success had worked against them. With both flanks 'in the air', they were isolated in the enemy's lines, in danger of being surrounded and cut off. Other groups of Germans were beginning to close in, and the Australians were already down to their last twenty grenades, vital weapons in this type of fighting. Murray now withdrew the troops stationed in the Fabeck Graben and posted them back along the OG 1 line, at the same time organising parties to help the wounded back closer to the main Australian

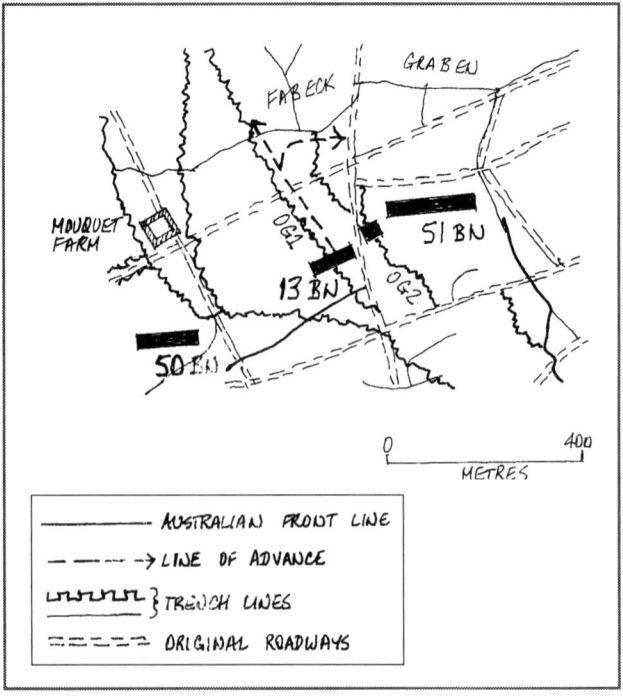

13th Battalion's attack at Mouquet Farm, 14/15 August 1916.

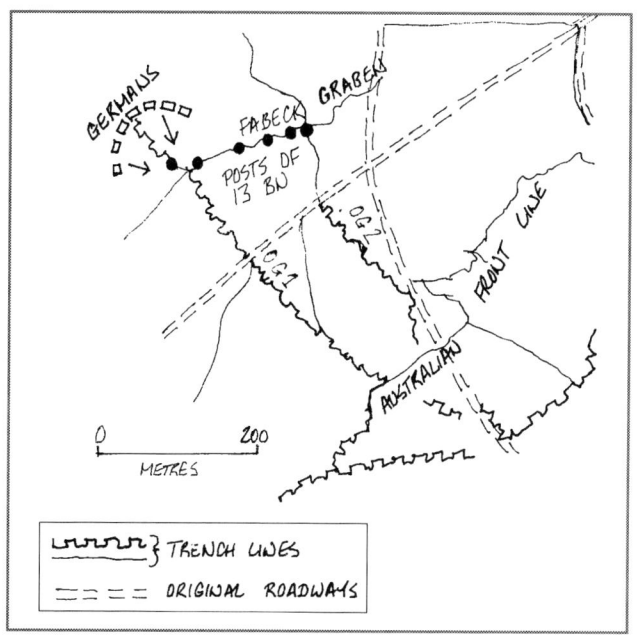

German counterattacks on the position captured by Murray.

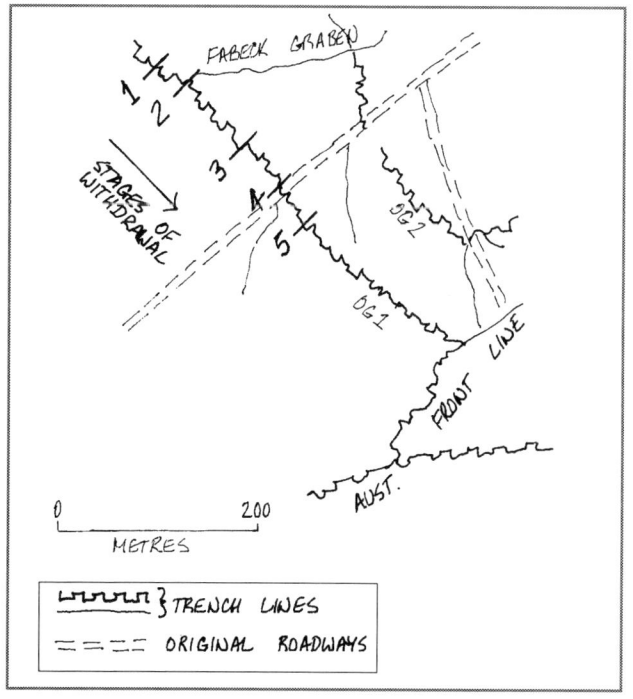

Murray's withdrawal.

line. Another German attack began, attempting to envelop the head of Murray's position from three sides. Point-blank fire from Lewis guns and rifles drove back the Germans advancing over the open ground, but those moving along the OG 1 trench were encouraged by the lack of grenades being thrown against them, and pressed forward eagerly. The Australians held their fire until the attackers crowded into the next bay of the trench, then mowed them down with a Lewis gun. The German attack was temporarily stopped in its tracks, but Murray had by now received a message confirming that there was no chance of any support on the flanks. His only course now was to get his men back to the main Australian position with the Germans at their heels.

Deciding to conduct a withdrawal by stages, Murray first gave orders for the wounded to be evacuated all the way back to the Australian lines. He then hastily formed a line of riflemen and Lewis gunners about fifty metres behind the men in the forward post, and withdrew the latter group through the new line, which kept back the pursuing Germans with steady fire. The withdrawn party then formed a line in their turn, and Murray sent most of the now front-line group back, staying a few more minutes with a few men to maintain fire on the pursuers before running back to the new position, which then covered the retreat. This leapfrogging tactic was repeated several times, Murray always the last to leave each successive post. With each of these progressive retirements, the Germans attempted to press the pursuit, but were continually stopped with heavy casualties by the fire of the covering posts. Murray long afterwards revealed his struggle with fear during the retreat: 'in those hectic moments I had experienced many a cold shiver, as I thought of the bayonets of the counter-attacking force, because it seemed to me, as I ran, that I was almost within reach of those lethal, shining blades.'[8]

As he ran back for the fifth time, with two of his men, a German grenade exploded in front of him, felling one of his companions. Assuming the man was dead, Murray made to hurdle the body, but suddenly realised that the soldier was still alive. At this point he fought what he later called, 'the hardest battle of my life,' his instincts demanding that he keep running but his sense of duty and comradeship telling him to stop and help a wounded mate. Duty and comradeship won out, and Murray hauled the man up onto his back and staggered on to the next post. Fortunately, the Germans, although following closely, had become more cautious after being checked so often by the Australians' covering fire, and the two made it safely.

Murray's problems were by no means over; they were still about 200 metres away from the main line, and had only six grenades left. Once these were gone, it would be only a matter of time before the Germans managed to close in and overwhelm them. A covering party on the left, under Lieutenant Meyer, was driven back, Meyer being wounded and captured. At this critical time, unexpected support arrived. The 13th's specialist 'bombing' platoon, led by Lieutenant Bob Henderson, had been operating in no-man's-land through the night, and Henderson had guessed that Murray was in trouble and brought his men up on the right of the retreating party. Murray heard Henderson's voice calling for him, and shouted back, 'Here I am, Bob — have you any bombs?'

'Any bloody amount!' Henderson replied, and then to his men, 'Throwers to the front!' The odds were suddenly reversed; Henderson's men carried thirty grenades each, and they launched an immediate counterattack which chased the Germans 100 metres back up the trench. With the pressure relieved, Murray's weary force safely made its way back to the Australian lines. Murray himself was not finished yet, however. A number of men were thought to be still lying wounded in no-man's-land, and before dawn Murray joined with Henderson again to scout the area and organise rescues. They nearly stayed too long, and 'themselves narrowly escaped being cut off,' according to the *Official History.*

Although it was finally unsuccessful, the operation on this night demonstrated Harry Murray's outstanding abilities as an infantry leader. He had led an overwhelming assault on a strongly defended position, and when forced to retreat, had shown remarkable control and ingenuity in a desperate situation. The official historian described the action as 'one of the most skilfully conducted fights in the history of the AIF,' while the 13th Battalion history noted that Murray's retreat was 'a masterpiece in defensive tactics.' A modern writer has commented that it was 'a perfectly executed example of arguably the most difficult military exercise, the opposed withdrawal, and showed outstanding leadership and skill by a man who had been

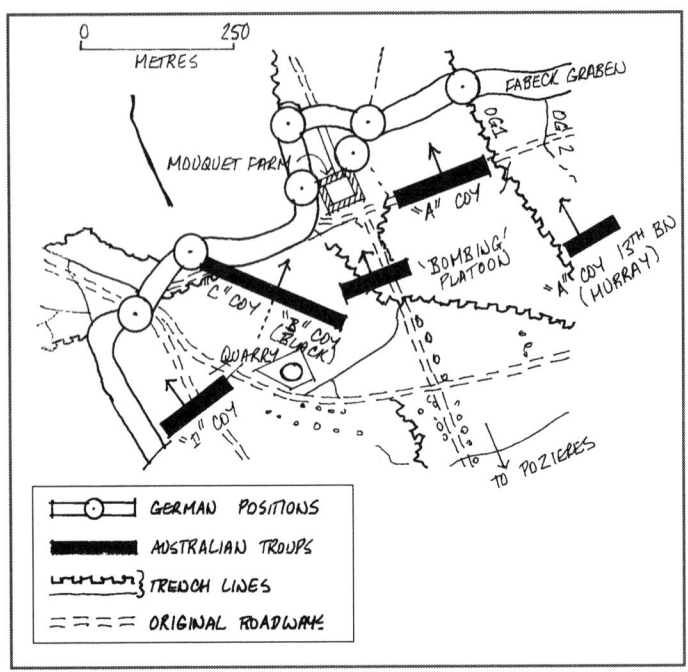

16th Battalion's attack on Mouquet Farm, 29/30 August 1916.

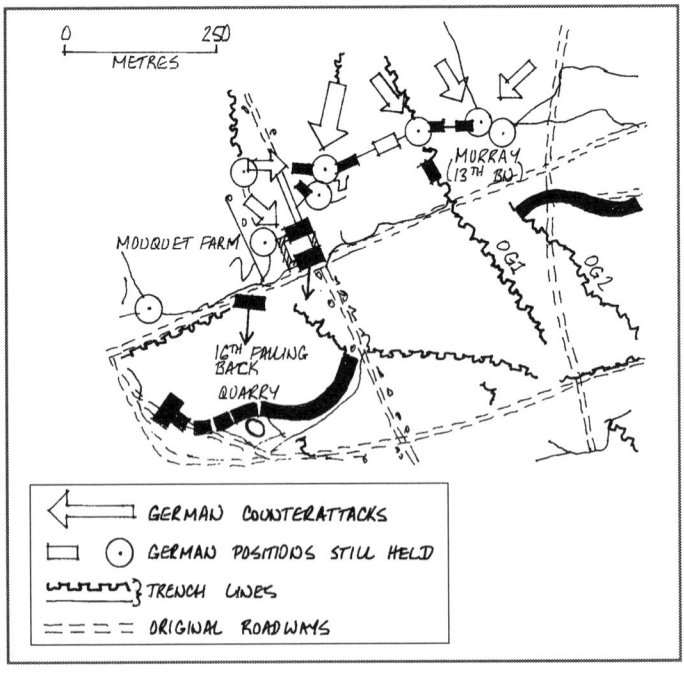

German counterattacks on 16th and 13th Battalions, 29/30 August 1916.

commissioned in the field without the benefit of any formal officer training.'[9] Strangely, though, Murray was awarded no decoration for his work on that night. It seems that several other outstanding efforts also went unrewarded during this period.[10] The battalion CO, Colonel Tilney, was very ill at this time, and this seems to have been the reason for the lack of recommendations. The unit history suggests some disappointment: 'Colonel Tilney's illness was rather unfortunate for several of the 13th's most splendid heroes, for fewer accounts of their deeds were written up, and consequently fewer decorations received for Pozieres by the 13th than by any other battalion of the brigade.'

Following this check to its previous steady advances, the 4th Division was relieved that evening by the 1st, and moved wearily back to the rear areas to recover its strength and replace losses. The division's casualties had amounted to over 4600 during the nine days of its tour on the Pozieres front. The 13th Battalion had lost 386 killed, wounded and missing, and Murray's 'A' Company had been reduced from 185 to 61 officers and men. The division spent a week in the rear, resting and taking in reinforcements. Colonel Tilney's illness showed no improvement, and he was ordered to hospital on 21 August. His replacement was James Durrant, who had been the 13th's adjutant at Gallipoli; he was to prove an extremely capable commander. Ahead in the front line, it was the 1st Division's turn to attempt the capture of the Mouquet Farm/Fabeck Graben position. A series of assaults achieved some initial success, but the Australians were eventually pushed back again almost to their starting point. The 2nd Division was then brought in, and went through much the same experience. It was becoming apparent that the Mouquet Farm position was more than just a series of rubble heaps and shell-holes: the cellars of the original farm were intact and had been extended by a system of dugouts to form an underground warren from which German reinforcements could emerge to fall on a disorganised attacking force and drive it back.

The high command was apparently unable to think of any better tactic than to continue the piecemeal head-on battering of the past few weeks, and now the 4th Division was brought back again for another try. On the night of 27 August, almost as soon as they got back to the line, the 14th Battalion was put straight in to try another assault. Their difficulties were compounded by the weather: heavy rain had begun to fall, turning the pulverised earth into knee-deep soupy mud. The rain caused trench walls to crumble, adding to the destruction caused by the inevitable shelling, and made any kind of progress slow and exhausting. The 14th made some gains, but was again unable to hold on to them, and the 13th and 16th were subsequently ordered to make yet another attempt.

Dawn on 29 August found the two battalions back in almost the same front-line positions they had vacated two weeks earlier, now choked with mud from the rain that continued to sheet down. The plan was for both battalions to attack in a single wave, each with its four companies more or less in line, with the 16th aiming for the Farm itself and the trenches on either side of it, and the 13th again assaulting the Fabeck Graben. All day the troops waited in the muddy trenches, while each side's artillery pounded away at the opposing lines. The Australians were also intermittently shelled by their own guns, the 13th in particular suffering from this due to its position being very close to the foremost German trench. Well before the time for the attack, the battalions had been seriously weakened by heavy casualties, and most of their rifles and Lewis guns had become clogged with mud and virtually useless. Nevertheless the attack went ahead at 11 pm. On the left of the line, the 16th struggled through the mud towards their objective; a sudden German barrage stopped one of the companies, and another lost direction, but Percy Black, leading from the front, took his 'B' Company straight at the Farm. They overran the rubble heaps and swept through to the far corner of the position, where Black spotted a German machine-gun; some of the Australians got the impression that the gun had been hoisted up from underground on a platform. As the gunner raised his head to fire, Black killed him with a single revolver shot, then fired two more into the gun mechanism to disable it. Moments later a German grenade exploded near him; Black was stunned by the blast, and wounded by fragments in the neck and left arm. But his men were now in possession of the Farm, and for the moment the attack seemed to have succeeded.

The 16th's ranks had been thinned by casualties however, and the German counterattacks now began. Like ants from a disturbed nest, their

Mouquet Farm.
(Australian War Memorial Neg Number E00005)

troops poured up from the dugout systems under Mouquet Farm. The Australians attempted to block the dugout exits with grenades, but the concealed openings were hard to detect in the dark, and the outnumbered Australians soon found themselves under attack from all sides. The Germans fought well and the 16th was eventually forced to fall back. It is not recorded exactly how Black got back to the Australian lines, except that Lawrence McCarthy later wrote that he was 'picked up on the top of Mouquet Farm dugout.' He regained consciousness and managed to give a report on the fighting to the battalion second-in-command (Major Margolin) but he was evidently concussed, as he could remember nothing of the conversation afterwards. His wounds were serious enough for him to be evacuated to the Casualty Clearing Station during the morning.[11]

Forming the right wing of the assaulting line, the 13th had 'jumped off' at 11 pm also. During the day they had lost 90 men as casualties to the combined shelling of the enemy and their own side. In Harry Murray's 'A' Company, on the left of the 13th's line, 38 men had been killed or wounded by the bombardment, leaving him with only 64 for the attack. Almost on zero hour, a single German shell had killed all nine men of a section. Murray's determination to carry out his orders was undiminished, but he was under no illusions as to what the end result might be. He took the risk of weakening his numbers still further by leaving a couple of Lewis gun crews in the jumping-off trench to provide cover in case he was forced to retreat. On the right of the 13th's line, losses forced the other companies to make last-minute changes to their dispositions; slogging through the mud, they were caught by heavy German machine-gun fire from beyond their right flank. A few unknown heroes on this side of the battlefield reached the enemy position, to be killed or captured. The effort was hopeless, and the survivors could do nothing but make their way back to their starting point.

'A' Company on the left of the battalion was not so exposed to the flanking machine-guns. Supported by the grenade throwers of Henderson's bombing platoon, they moved through the rain and mud up the line of the OG 1 trench in what was almost a carbon copy of their attack two weeks earlier. Again the company reached the Fabeck Graben to the east of Mouquet

Farm; with their rifles jammed with mud, grenades and bayonets were used to eject the Germans. After the experience of 14–15 August, Murray had made sure of a plentiful supply of grenades, and in the conditions of that night these were the main weapons against any counterattack. The company had captured about 150 metres of frontage, but casualties during the attack had reduced Murray's numbers still further to only about thirty men and officers. He quickly organised a thin garrison for the position: seven posts of three men each and the remainder as a mobile reserve to reinforce wherever the pressure was greatest. Two counterattacks came in from the right but were beaten off by the tiny Australian force. Contemporary writings recorded two incidents which may have occurred during this part of the battle: at one point Sergeant Marlin found himself isolated ahead of the trench and attacked by nine Germans, but Murray showed up to assist; the two Australians killed four of their opponents and scattered the rest. In the other incident, 'an enemy bullet started a man's equipment exploding'[12] (presumably the bullet set off the rounds in the man's ammunition pouch); ignoring the danger, Murray tore off the man's webbing equipment and hurled it away.

Murray was now in a situation almost identical to that of two weeks earlier. There were Germans on his right flank, from where the counterattacks had come, and although Henderson's remnant was supporting his immediate left, there seemed to be no sign of the 16th on that side. Murray decided to see for himself. Leaving Lieutenant Marper in charge in the Fabeck position, he took two men with him and moved off to the left. They had covered about eighty metres when two German grenades came flying out of the darkness and exploded amongst the patrol. One of Murray's men was wounded in the eye and the other's foot was blown off. Murray was hit by fragments in the back and thigh; reacting instantly, he 'sprang ahead' as he later described it, and found himself in the middle of five Germans lying on the ground. Two of them immediately jumped up and swung at him with 'knobkerries' (metal-tipped clubs used in trench fighting); one blow clanged off his steel helmet, while the second hit him in the chest. They then grappled with him, apparently with the intention of taking him prisoner. They had caught a Tartar. Murray, bleeding from his wounds and with his head ringing from the explosions and the club blow, had managed to keep a grip on his revolver. He immediately shot both his adversaries, whereupon the other three took to their heels, Murray throwing a grenade after them for good measure.

There was no sign of the 16th, and it was clear that the left flank was unsupported. Murray took his battered patrol back to the Fabeck Graben, he and the half-blinded man carrying the crippled man. Another counterattack was in progress as they arrived back at the position. This was repulsed, to be followed by yet another which was thrown back in its turn, despite 'A' Company now being down to only sixteen unhurt men. The battalion history recorded that 'Murray moved rapidly from man to man, fighting alongside one after another, or encouraging the lonely man. Not one but would gladly have died there for such a leader.'[13] A lull in the attacks followed, but the Germans then began to shell the trench and it was obviously pointless to remain any longer in the captured position. For the second time in two weeks, Murray sent his wounded back to the main line and then withdrew the remaining unhurt men. The retirement seems to have been accomplished with little interference this time, and by daybreak on 30 August the troops were back in their original front line, exhausted, disappointed and knee-deep in mud. The 13th and 16th Battalions had each lost about 230 officers and men killed, wounded and missing during the hellish night in trying to accomplish a task which was clearly too difficult for their limited strength.

Despite his wounds from the grenade, Murray insisted on remaining on duty, but the effort proved too much for him. He collapsed from loss of blood during the morning, and was evacuated from the front line and transported to the coast en route to hospital. His efforts in this battle would earn him the Distinguished Service Order, Colonel Durrant writing up one of his characteristically detailed recommendations a few days later. For the second time in as many weeks Harry Murray had proven himself a peerless infantry leader, as well as a lethally dangerous opponent in a hand-to-hand fight. The Farm was still unconquered however, and a few days later the 13th Brigade was sent in. At terrible cost in casualties (including Murray's cousin, Captain C H Littler, mortally wounded at the head of his company), they managed to cling to a corner of the enemy position until relieved by the Canadians. At the end of

September the high command finally abandoned the piecemeal attacks in this area and launched a major advance all along the line with four divisions, which eventually overran the Farm and advanced to Thiepval. The Australian effort at Pozieres and Mouquet Farm was later summed up by the official historian: 'On that crowded mile of summit the three Australian divisions engaged lost 23,000 officers and men in less than seven weeks … a ridge more densely sown with Australian sacrifice than any other place on earth.'

Among those casualties were Major Percy Black and Captain Harry Murray. On 1 September, Black embarked from Boulogne for England on the hospital ship *Jan Breydel*. Once across the Channel, he was admitted to one of London's military hospitals, at Denmark Hill. Murray seems to have been kept at the Casualty Clearing Station for several days (there is some confusion in the records here) but was eventually sent to England on the *Asturias* from Le Havre. He was also admitted to Denmark Hill hospital, on 7 September, where it was discovered that one of the grenade fragments had penetrated a lung. Details of the 'shop' that would have been talked once the two old mates were well enough to socialise must be left to the imagination, as no information has survived. Murray was the quickest to recover, and was discharged on 5 October; after spending some time on convalescent leave he had rejoined his unit by 19 October. A few days later came the good news that his DSO award had been confirmed. The 4th Division at this time was beginning a series of moves that would take it to the area around Flers and Gueudecourt, where the weather would prove to be at least as implacable an enemy as the Germans.

Black, whose DSO had also been notified early in October, remained in hospital or convalescing for another month. He was able to spend some time in the city, on one occasion renewing acquaintance with Cyril Longmore, former machine-gun instructor from the Blackboy Hill days. Longmore's frequent attempts to leave instructing for active service had finally been successful; he had been commissioned as a second-lieutenant in the 44th Battalion, part of Monash's new 3rd Australian Division. The division had been raised in Australia and sent straight to England, and was finishing its training on Salisbury Plain. The 3rd Division was a month or so away from moving to France, and Longmore found an opportunity to get up to London and meet Black for lunch.

In 1914 Black had been the raw recruit from the goldfields, who 'didn't know anything about this soldiering game'; now he was immensely the superior, in rank, honours and experience, of his former instructor. Longmore found him to be 'the same old Percy', however, and eagerly questioned him about conditions at the front.[14] Asked about his success, Black attributed it to luck! Later, crossing Piccadilly, he had to dodge a bus. 'I'll be glad to get back to the battalion. A man's not safe here!' he exclaimed as he reached the kerb.

Black would have a pleasant official duty to attend to while he was in London. He was summoned to attend an investiture ceremony at Buckingham Palace on 4 November, where he was presented with his DSO by King George V. Also during this month in London, he bumped into an old friend from Western Australia, Mrs A F King,[15] and they were able to spend a few hours catching up on old times. Mrs King was moved to write to Black's mother after this meeting, congratulating her on her son's success. 'All the honour and glory of his distinctions have not altered him one bit,' she wrote, 'he is still the same true, kind-hearted Percy Black I met in Western Australia.'[16]

Black was officially discharged from hospital on 13 November, and was back with the 16th three days later. By then the brigade was back in the area of the Somme battlefield, around the towns of Mametz and Ribemont (home of the legendary 'Incinerator Kate', an eccentric Frenchwoman who seems to have made an impression on every Australian who encountered her). One of Europe's worst winters in living memory was beginning at this time. Constant rain turned the roads into sloppy lanes of mud; the trenches took on the appearance of narrow canals, often two feet deep in liquid mud. Up to their knees in the morass, the troops were unable even to sit down during the day; many of them went out into the open at night, risking frost, snipers and artillery for the sake of a few hours sleep. In between periods of labouring duties in attempts to improve the trenches, the battalions took their turn in the front line near the wrecked villages of Flers and Gueudecourt. Driving rain and cold winds rarely ceased, but the atrocious weather fortunately tended to limit front-line fighting to skirmishing and artillery duels. The Germans regularly bombarded the ruins of Gueudecourt. During the 13th's spell in the front line, the restless Murray noted that the shells always arrived at fixed times, and took advantage of the lulls to explore the village and make sketches of its layout for headquarters.

The misery of the 4th Brigade troops was alleviated somewhat in early December when they were relieved by an unfortunate 1st Division unit. The brigade again made its way through the rain and mud to the back areas around Ribemont, which they found to be almost under water. Nevertheless some amusements were still available — the various *estaminets*, and observing the antics of 'Incinerator Kate' as she salvaged discarded equipment around the camp. The brigade was fortunate to be able to celebrate Christmas out of the front line, the 13th being in its billets at Coisy, and the 16th at Cardonette; Percy Black received an early Christmas present when it was announced on 16 December that the French government had awarded him the Croix de Guerre for his work in the August battles. As well as their decorations, both Murray and Black had been Mentioned in Dispatches during the year, the latter on two occasions.

Early in the new year of 1917 the 4th Brigade was back on the roundabout, moving again towards the front line and what would be a momentous period of combat.

Chapter 7

'SHEER VALOUR' AT STORMY TRENCH

The bitter winter dragged on. To support the French plans for a major offensive in April 1917, the British Army extended its front to release some of its ally's divisions. For I Anzac Corps, this meant placing all of its four divisions into the line, rather than rotating two in line with two resting and training. The 4th Division found itself back in its position around the ruined village of Gueudecourt, the site of Murray's explorations in November.

The British Army had its own offensive planned for the spring, and as part of the preparations for this, I Anzac was requested to keep the pressure on the Germans by aggressive actions against the enemy positions to its front. A series of small assaults was planned, including several against the complicated system of trenches in the salient (a bulge in the line) facing the 4th Division. To the 4th Brigade fell the task of capturing the section designated as 'Stormy Trench'. The operation was projected for mid-January, but the drenching winter rains had caused a delay — it had been decided to use trench-mortar bombs to cut the wire entanglements protecting the German position (it was so close to the Australian line that using high-explosive artillery shells was felt to be too dangerous) and the mortar emplacements had become waterlogged.

A change of weather at the right time solved the problem. The rains ceased and were succeeded by frosts, and a heavy snowfall on 17 January stayed frozen on the ground for a month. In spite of the cold, the frost was an improvement in many ways over the wet weather. The ground was dry and firm, and the now-frozen trench walls no longer collapsed; it became possible for the troops to move about more freely without creating a quagmire. The bright days and fresh air improved the men's morale, as did the easier transport of hot meals to the front line. From the military point of view, the frost and snow made it far easier for both sides to detect signs of traffic from aerial photographs; the positions of trenches, posts and pathways were easily checked and accurately mapped for the benefit of each side's artillery. Their shooting became much more accurate. For the Stormy Trench attack, the Australian trench-mortars could now be firmly emplaced for their wire-cutting task. They were in position by 30 January, and the 15th Battalion was selected to make the attack at 7 pm on 1 February.

Unfortunately, although the freeze enabled the mortars to be emplaced, it also caused an unexpected problem: the mortars began their bombardment on the 30th, but many of their bombs bounced off the frozen ground and exploded in the air away from the wire. The cold also seemed to affect the ammunition itself, many shells falling short. They managed to cut some of the wire, however, and on the following night, the 15th mounted its assault. Led by Major Mundell and Captain Dunworth and preceded by an accurate shrapnel barrage, the attackers followed the shell-bursts so closely that they were into the trench before the Germans had even managed to emerge from their dugouts. The right wing of the attack had been held up by uncut wire, but a party moved around it and 'bombed' along the trench to capture most of the objective on that flank. The 15th repulsed two strong counterattacks and consolidated the position. So far their operation had been brilliantly successful, but things began to go wrong from this point. The supply of grenades faltered under a furious German artillery barrage, and the countering fire from the Australian artillery for some reason fell away, allowing a strong counterattack by the German infantry to get to close quarters. Under a shower of grenades to which they were unable to reply, the

15th was forced back to its own lines with a loss of 144 officers and men. Stormy Trench remained in German hands.

The brigade was determined to make another attempt, and selected the 13th Battalion for the task, to be carried out at 10 pm on 4 February. The 13th took over the forward positions from the 15th, Murray taking the earliest opportunity for another nocturnal crawl into no-man's-land with some of his officers and scouts, familiarising themselves with the geography of the area. Colonel Durrant had only received definite orders for the operation at 8 pm on 3 February, but he made maximum use of the short time for preparation. Two hours later, he was conferring with his company commanders to explain the plan, and later that night, following Murray's lead, they all made an exploration of no-man's-land. Durrant and his officers had consulted with the surviving officers from the 15th's attack, and were aware of their difficulties with grenade supply and artillery support. A reserve of 20,000 grenades was organised: 12,000 at the jumping-off positions ('Grease' and 'Shine' trenches) and 8000 at Battalion Headquarters in the small quarry known as the Chalk Pit. One thousand rifle-grenades were provided; each rifleman was to carry six grenades in his pockets (the troops would wear greatcoats in the freezing weather). The specialist 'bombers' of each company carried at least twenty extra, and the companies all had carrying parties of twenty men carrying another 24 grenades each. Murray's 'A' Company would have an immediate supply of over 2000 grenades with them when they started the attack, the other three companies having similar quantities. Conscious of the 15th's problems with artillery support, Durrant improved coordination by arranging for the senior artillery officer to work from the infantry headquarters, one of the first times this had been done in the AIF.

A mood of enthusiasm was sweeping through the battalion. Eight men due to depart on leave insisted on staying for the 'stunt'; Lieutenant R H Kell of Murray's company left a sickbed to take part. Murray himself had caught a severe dose of influenza. Captain Winn, the 14th Battalion's Medical Officer,[1] came to Murray's dugout to look him over. Winn found him obviously ill with a temperature of 103, and started arrangements to evacuate him.

'You can cut that out,' said Murray, 'I'm not going away.'
Winn was amazed.

'Not going? You'll get pneumonia if you don't. In fact, I'm not too certain you haven't got it already.'

'Pneumonia or not, I'm not going to hospital. I'm going to take Stormy Trench tomorrow.'

'Don't be silly. You're not fit. All you're going to take is a pill.'

'I tell you I'm going to take Stormy Trench; and what's more, let me tell you, I'm going to keep it.'[2]

Colonel Durrant held a final briefing for his company commanders at 4 pm next day, six hours before zero. 'A' Company was to take the right of the attack, with 'C', 'B' and 'D' in succession to the left. Durrant expected the heaviest weight of the inevitable counterattacks to fall on 'A' Company, and stressed this to Murray.

'If the enemy ever get my trenches back,' he replied, 'they will only find a cemetery.'[3]

This grim attitude seemed to be all through the battalion during the desperate events of the next twenty-four hours. After the frustrations and losses at Pozieres and Mouquet Farm, the 13th Battalion, and Captain Harry Murray in particular, were not to be thwarted this time.

After the conference, the company commanders briefed their junior officers and made sure that the plan was explained in detail to the troops. The front line was held during the day by two platoons each from 'A' and 'B' companies; to avoid observation by the Germans, the other two companies stayed in the second line until after dark before moving forward to their jumping-off positions. The remaining two platoons each of 'A' and 'B' had moved up in twos and threes late in the day. The men all wore sandbags over their feet to muffle the noise of their boots on the frozen ground during the assembly; they had been fortified by a rum issue, unusual in the AIF before action (it was normally issued afterwards) but approved on this occasion because of the cold. The battalion contained a high proportion of new recruits, replacements for the heavy losses in the Pozieres and Mouquet Farm battles. The coming battle would be the first major action for these men, but in the event they would behave like veterans.[4]

'A' Company settled quietly into its positions in the shallow front trench, Murray shivering violently with the effects of his flu. Lying on the frozen snow in the light of a full moon, there was nothing for the men to do but wait for zero. With twenty minutes to go, a whisper reached Murray for permission to smoke; after a quick glance to make sure the men were keeping low, he gave it, provided one cigarette was lit from another to avoid too many flaring matches. Behind them, their guns began to fire a few shells to warm their barrels in preparation for the full bombardment. With three minutes to go, Murray ordered 'Smokes out'; the men made a few final checks of their weapons and braced themselves for the onslaught.

The drama that was about to begin would be described by a number of people at the time and in later years: the following narrative of the night's events is drawn from several of these sources.[5]

Zero. Watching behind for the artillery to commence, Murray jumps a little as the horizon suddenly lights up with myriad gunflashes; the roar of the guns reaches the men as shells begin to swish overhead. They are out of the trench and moving steadily forward, in perfect alignment in the moonlight. The shrapnel shells are bursting in the air about 200 metres ahead, spraying the enemy trench with their deadly pellets. Murray can see that the red flashes of the bursts are almost in a straight line over the objective — close to a perfect barrage. As he gets nearer to the trench, he sees that the wire in front of it is still mostly intact. But he has expected this — the artillery's forward observers had reported earlier in the day that it might not have been cut completely, and he has already planned to work around it to the left and then attack down the trench. The barrage will 'lift' in two minutes — they need to be right behind it then to catch the Germans before they have time to recover. They move almost too quickly; with twenty seconds to go, Murray calls to the troops to get down and crawl to avoid being hit by their own shrapnel. The shells are now exploding in the air behind 'A' Company, the shrapnel whistling over their heads and the expended nose-caps and casings of the shells whining through the air and bouncing off the frozen parapet of the German trench.

The barrage lifts! The company springs to its feet and Murray leads his men around the broken end of the entanglement; they pour down into the deep, wide trench, the 'bombing' sections now taking the lead. The wire has prevented the attackers from hitting all sections of the trench at once, and although many of the Germans have been caught in their dugouts by the swiftness of the Australian advance, resistance stiffens further along the position. On their own initiative, some of the attackers run in the open outside the trench to save time. Those Germans who manage to emerge from the dugouts fight back with grenades, but they are quickly overcome by the Australians, and those who are not killed or captured flee along the trench to the right. So far the trench has sloped downhill. The company reaches the lowest point, crosses a flat portion and starts to move uphill towards the point of its final objective, another 100 metres further along.

Corporal Roy Withers calls into a dugout entrance for the occupants to surrender. A shot from within cuts his ear. Enraged, he hurls two grenades down the shaft. Seven of the eight men in the dugout are killed; the eighth, a terribly injured officer, manages to stagger up the steps. With no hope of survival, he is given what attention is possible, and dies during the night. The fighting in the trench has now died down, and Murray has a moment to think. If they continue along the trench to the top of the rising ground, they will have gone well past their planned objective and will almost certainly be bombarded by their own artillery. Their original objective, however, has turned out to be partway up the slope, and holding at that point will give the Germans the advantage of throwing their grenades downhill with the Australians having to throw uphill. Murray knows a grenade fight is inevitable when the counterattack comes, and he quickly decides to pull back to the bottom of the slope, leaving sixty metres of flat ground in front, and hold on there, 100 metres short of the planned objective.

He orders the building of a 'bomb-stop' at this point. The Australians quickly scavenge the captured trench for materials, and improvise a barricade from duckboards, planks, sandbags and clods of frozen earth. Sergeant 'Scotty' Thompson sites his three Lewis guns and their crews along the position, and twenty minutes after taking the trench Murray is satisfied the Australians are ready to defend it. He sends one of his runners back with a one-word message for the CO: 'Set'.[6] The runners, Rollings and Stewart, will make many round trips that night, taking Murray's messages and returning with the replies, often bringing ammunition and grenades as well. On the left, the other three companies have quickly taken their objectives, again following the barrage so closely that they are on top of the Germans before an effective defence can be organised. They have captured an advanced machine-gun in no-man's-land on the way across, and sent back many prisoners. The 13th has won a quick victory, but they are all aware that the real test is still to come.

The German counter-stroke begins with a hurricane of artillery and mortar fire all along the captured trench. More shells crash into the communication trenches and the Australian lines, disrupting the carrying parties and support troops. On the right, 'A' Company stays alert under the storm for the infantry assault which must follow. The bombardment ceases abruptly at 10.40 pm; the dark figures of men are seen moving ahead of and around 'A's right flank. Those towards the right rear may be a party of Australians from the 58th Battalion, who are meant to be digging across to link up with the 13th, but those to the front are certainly Germans. Murray moves across to one of the Lewis guns and directs its gunner to fire at this group. Suddenly a shower of German grenades explodes among the Australians at the barricade; seven of the nine men are killed, and those alongside them recoil twenty metres back along the trench. Murray immediately orders the SOS signal fired to bring in artillery support, and calls up the reserve bombing section from further down the trench. They race to the right flank and start flinging their grenades at the attackers in what Murray later describes as 'a bomb fight of the first magnitude', while Corporal Robertson calmly and methodically lobs his rifle-grenades into the German section of the trench.

The Australian artillery barrage has responded instantly to the SOS, and is falling between the attacking Germans and their support lines, cutting them off from reinforcements and extra supplies. By now the German grenadiers have gone to ground in shell-holes and old trenches, and from their concealment are beginning to get the upper hand over the Australian bomb-throwers. Murray decides they will have to drive the Germans away hand-to-hand. Revolver in hand, and still shaking with fever, he leads a bayonet charge over the top against one of the German posts; jumping into a group of six opponents, he shoots three in seconds, and the others throw up their hands in surrender and are sent to the rear. His party puts the remaining Germans to flight. Murray carries three wounded Diggers back to the trench one by one. Although his uniform has been torn by bullets in several places, he is unhurt. On the other sides of the position, more bayonet charges — and Roy Withers running along the parapet hurling grenades despite an injured knee — have driven off the remaining groups of Germans. There is a short lull; taking Robertson with him, Murray leaves the trench to explore the surrounding area, identifying likely concealment positions that the next German attack might make use of.

The Australian artillery is still bombarding the enemy's positions, and now the German barrage descends again on 'A' Company. The storm of shells shatters the sides of the trench into great boulders of frozen earth. The company's casualties mount up; some men are blown to pieces, others killed or wounded by splinters, some buried under the frozen blocks. Through it all the survivors stick grimly to their positions. Parched with thirst, they find that the water in their bottles has frozen, and try to dig out pieces of ice with their pocket-knives.

The next counterattack comes at 11.50 pm. Again the SOS flares bring down the Australian artillery to isolate the attackers from their supports; again the Germans fling showers of grenades into 'A' Company's position. The Australians mount more bayonet charges and drive their opponents back again, but the Germans return again and again, five separate attacks in all, at intervals of only a few minutes. To his men, Murray seems to be everywhere at once, advising and inspiring, fighting in person with pistol and grenade, at one point carrying another two wounded men back to the trench. At last the Germans have had enough and pull back to regroup. 'A' Company's strength has dwindled further, but there is no thought of abandoning the fight. After another pause, which the remaining Australians use to rebuild their barricades and clear some of the rubble from the trench, the German artillery starts up again.

Throughout the ferocious fighting around the trench, the 13th's carrying parties have moved back and forth across the shell-swept ground between Stormy Trench and the Australian support line, bringing up the vital supplies of grenades and ammunition and helping wounded men back whenever they can. A specially selected company of the 14th Battalion, occupying the original jumping-off trench in support of the 13th, is pounded with particular severity by the German artillery, but keeps up a constant stream of ammunition and grenades to the 13th, particularly to 'A' Company on the right. (Murray later wrote: '[I saw] nothing to equal the work of the 14th carrying parties; often without officer or NCO; with men staggering under impossible loads, and continually scourged by heavy shell fire … continuing until supplies in the trench were greater than our needs.'[7]) Their commander, Captain Hansen, is mortally wounded that night.

Another lull follows, and those of the Australians who are still on their feet return to the weary work of rebuilding the barricades on their right flank and shoring up the sides of the trench. At 2.30 am, another storm of German artillery and mortar shells bursts over the battered trench. This continues for twenty-five minutes, when Murray sees the German infantry approaching yet again in another desperate effort to regain the position. As before, he moves up and down the trench exchanging a few words with each man and moving on quickly to the next. The bombardment ceases, to be followed by the inevitable shower of grenades from the German assault troops. As they begin advancing towards the Australians, Murray leads his men over the top to charge them again with bayonets. Their first wave gives way; Corporal Brown leads another charge against a second wave, and Murray joins in this one also. Roy Withers, who had been sent back to the rear to have his injured knee treated and insisted on returning to the front line, repeats his earlier heroics, flinging grenade after grenade into the German positions. Finally this German attack is repulsed like the previous ones. It will be their last attempt.

Murray now has 60 men left on their feet out of 149 who began the operation.[8] He himself has suffered a laceration to one hand at some point *during the battle, but is otherwise unhurt. The German artillery recommences after a pause, but there will be no more infantry attacks. Stretcher-bearers move constantly back and forth from the front line to the Australian rear area, carrying back the most seriously wounded. Murray goes out of the trench again to look for wounded men, finding two more and carrying them back. The Australian guns keep up a precautionary shelling of the German lines, while the survivors of 'A' Company wait for the dawn, resuming their attempts to chip ice from water-bottles to slake their raging thirsts. Daylight comes at last. 'Gone was the admirable trench we had captured, and in its place there remained a boulder-strewn depression — boulders of frozen earth.'⁹ The mantle of snow has disappeared for a hundred metres to the front and rear of Stormy Trench, blasted away by the artillery shells. Murray counts sixty-one dead Germans and twenty Australians over a distance of seventy metres. The company stays alert for another counterattack — Murray believes he can still deal with one more — but none comes. The other companies have held their positions through the night also, and the 13th Battalion has secured its victory.*

Daylight showed the captured section of trench securely held by the battalion. The other three companies had also been shelled and assaulted by infantry during the night, but the Germans had put the main weight of their effort into trying to turn the right flank of the position, where 'A' Company had held on at great cost. They were in obvious need of relief, and the 16th Battalion was requested to provide a company to take over from them. The whole battalion volunteered, and Captain Ahearn's company was picked.[10] The 16th's CO sent a message: 'Heartiest congratulations. Tell Murray we are all delighted he got through safely.'[11] The relief could not be carried out until darkness fell again, and 'A' Company waited in its position, still under intermittent shellfire, until 8 pm that night before the 16th took over and they could at last make their way back to the support line. Here they came under the wing of the 16th, as they had virtually swapped with one of the 16th's companies. As the close support battalion, the 16th were doing much heavy carrying and digging work; as Murray later wrote: 'we were supposed to

German prisoners captured at Stormy Trench, under interrogation by a British officer.
(Australian War Memorial Neg Number E00180)

take our share, but Colonel Drake-Brockman gave us two hours work only on any night, and we had a big, safe dugout to sleep in.' Their main worry seemed to be a shortage of cigarettes and money to buy them with! Pooling of financial resources in a 'tarpaulin muster' and a trip to the brigade canteen solved that problem.

Assessing the results of the operation, Colonel Durrant reported that they had captured 600 metres of the enemy trench, which included sixteen dugouts accommodating about 150 men. Prisoners totalled 77; under questioning, some of these said they had been attacked by picked storm-troops, and marvelled at the speed and efficiency of the Australians. The 13th had suffered a total of 61 killed and 172 wounded,[12] the greatest proportion from 'A' Company; Hansen's gallant company of the 14th had suffered the worst, with 95 casualties out of 120 men, testimony to the hazards of the support role. Seeking details of the fighting, Durrant was given much information about the deeds of the troops by Murray and the other companies' officers, but he was unable to extract any details from Murray about his own efforts. The CO eventually pieced together much of the story from others' accounts, and on 7 February he recommended Murray for the Victoria Cross. As well as describing his actions in the battle, the recommendation noted his 'sheer valour' and included the comment: 'His Company would follow him anywhere and die for him to a man.'[13] Many years later, Durrant was to say, 'Harry Murray was not recommended for his VC because of one action. He was recommended because he gave more than brawn; he gave brains over a sustained period of 24 hours.' Withers and Robertson were also recommended for the VC, but in the event only Murray's was approved and Withers and Robertson each received the Distinguished Conduct Medal. Apart from Murray's VC, the 13th Battalion's decorations for Stormy Trench included three DCMs, three Military Crosses, and no less than fourteen Military Medals.

The battle was not quite over for the 13th. 'B', 'C' and 'D' companies stayed in the trench for another four days, suffering from the regular German shelling and the continuing freezing weather, while a start was made on converting the position into a part of the Australian front line. Two defensive machine-gun posts had already been set up by the 4th Machine Gun

Company, and work was started on digging new communication and support trenches. On the night of 9 February, the 46th Battalion moved in to relieve the 13th. It was a relief in every sense as the weary men marched for the back areas, fortified by a hot meal on the way, and a rum issue when they arrived at the huts at Mametz.

The Australians continued to extend their newly captured position over the next few weeks; the 46th gained another 150 metres of trench on 11 February and a further 25 metres three nights later. The 57th Battalion made a 75-metre gain the next night, and the position was also extended to the left, the 45th Battalion capturing several hundred metres of trench in an outstanding effort on 21–22 February. Although the Stormy Trench operations would be classed as minor, the Australians had captured a useful position overlooking part of the enemy's back area, and shown the best of their fighting qualities. The victory owed much to thorough planning and preparation at short notice, and as much to the skill and determination of the Diggers in the front line. 'A' Company had the lion's share of the honours, but above all the battle was a personal triumph for Harry Murray. Bean wrote of Murray, 'He was a leader whose presence always raised other men to heights of valour and energy.'[14] At Stormy Trench, his inspiring leadership had tipped the balance between victory and defeat.

Chapter 8

DEATH IN THE WIRE

The clear frosty weather ended shortly after the Stormy Trench action, and the rain started again. The terrain quickly reverted to its former muddy quagmire. This did not stop preparations proceeding for the planned British offensive further north, including the transfer of a large proportion of the Fourth and Fifth Armies' artillery to the Arras front. This left I Anzac Corps' sector of the Fifth Army's front particularly weak in artillery. The corps still had all its divisions in the line and was still carrying out local attacks on its front. General Birdwood considered it vital to arrange some sort of rest period for the troops before they were required to attack again in accordance with the operations planned for April. As a compromise, he ordered the 4th Division withdrawn from the line, and the other three to thin out to cover the whole corps frontage. The 4th was relieved on 24 February 1917; this coincided with the startling discovery that the Germans were in the process of abandoning their front trenches in the southern part of their line and withdrawing from the Arras salient. Since September 1916 they had been constructing an immensely strong line of trenches and barbed wire behind their original position; the German code-name for this system was the

Siegfried Line, but it has become known to history by the Allies' name for it: the Hindenburg Line. Now the German Army was falling back to this fortification, with the object of disrupting at least the southern part of the anticipated offensive by the Allies, and also saving troops by reducing the area they were required to hold. It was also part of their strategy to hold off the Allied armies while their U-boat campaign slowly strangled Britain.

The British Army set off in pursuit of the retreating Germans. In the Australian sector the 1st, 2nd and 5th Divisions took up the running, with the 4th following up in reserve. The long marches through rain and wind were brightened for the 4th Brigade and for the 13th Battalion in particular on 12 March when word came through that the award of the VC to Murray had been confirmed. It was the 13th's first VC, and the third for the brigade since the beginning of the war. There was time for a celebratory banquet, and the news was quickly reported home to hearten the public, particularly in Western Australia. On 17 March a story on Murray's Victoria Cross appeared in the *West Australian*, which noted that he was 'well known at Comet Vale, on the goldfields, and at Holyoake and Dwellingup,' and gave a short summary of his military career.

The story was picked up by the labour newspaper *Westralian Worker* and run under the heading 'Another Timber Worker VC', proudly pointing out that he was 'a good member of the Timber Workers Union.' The paper also noted (inaccurately in Murray's case) that two of the three VCs awarded to West Australian enlistees had been to sleeper hewers, the first being Martin O'Meara of the 16th Battalion. Murray's name was inscribed on the Honour Board in the Perth Trades Hall. There was more publicity in the following month, the *Sunday Times* publishing a longer article which gave some further details of his family background and quoted from the citations of his previous awards, but the information offered on Murray's VC action was quite inaccurate, dating it to December 1916 and saying that it was fought 'waist deep in mud and water.' An account of Stormy Trench by the official war correspondent, C E W Bean, appeared in the *Western Mail* on 27 April, but in accordance with the 'no names' convention, Murray was identified only as 'the company commander, a Tasmanian,' and there was no mention of a VC recommendation. It would have taken an extremely perceptive reader to make the connection.

By this time, events in France had moved on. The pursuit of the enemy's retreat continued through March and into the first week of April, through continuing cold weather including the occasional snowstorm. Finally on 9 April the 1st Division pushed the German rearguards out of Hermies and Demicourt, the last of the string of fortified villages screening the Hindenburg Line. The Line itself, with its belts of rusty barbed wire in front of a double line of trenches, was visible only a few kilometers from the Australian front. Further north, the British spring offensive was due to begin, with a planned starting date of 8 April. General Sir Hubert Gough, commanding the Fifth Army, was anxious to assist by attacking the Hindenburg Line as early as possible. The original plans for the Fifth Army's part in the offensive had been disrupted by the German withdrawal, but the vigorous pursuit of the Germans had brought the Fifth Army's spearheads within reach of the line with relatively little loss of time. An immediate attack, however, would require new plans made in haste. The task set for the Fifth Army was to capture the sector of the line on either side of the village of Bullecourt, which was incorporated into the German defences as a bastion. The double German trench system bore a strong resemblance to the OG system encountered at Pozieres in the previous year, and the 4th Division used the terms OG 1 for the front-line trench and OG 2 for the support trench. Success here would put further pressure on the northern part of the German forces under attack around Arras, as it would seriously interfere with any retreat by those troops to their final reserve line — a 'switch' trench running northwards from the Hindenburg Line near the village of Queant.

The capture of Bullecourt itself and the line to the left of the village was to be undertaken by a British division, and the sector between Bullecourt and Queant was to be attacked by the 4th Australian Division, which had come back into the front line. The normal difficulties of a Western Front attack across no-man's-land were compounded for the Australians by the German front line forming a 're-entrant' in the section they were required to attack;[1] as they neared their objective, they would have enemies on both sides (in

Bullecourt on the left and Queant on the right) as well as in front. It was intended to solve this problem by suppressing the two village bastions with artillery fire. As well as taking the designated sector of the Hindenburg Line, a further objective for the Australians was added by the Fifth Army commander: to also capture the village of Riencourt, about 900 metres beyond the Line, and then to advance further to the village of Hendecourt, link with the British on their left, then wheel to the right to face the Germans in their 'switch' trench running northwards from the Line.[2] It was altogether a formidable task, depending for success in the first instance on the barbed-wire entanglements being destroyed by the fire of artillery which was already depleted by the transfer of batteries to the north.

The bombardment had started on 4 April with the few batteries that were in position, even before the villages in front of the Hindenburg Line had been cleared. The fire increased as more batteries came up: the guns were attempting to demolish a formidable obstacle, broad double and triple belts of wire, starting fifty metres in front of the first German trench, laid out in an angled design to split up an attack and enable machine-guns to fire along the edges. Another single belt of wire was positioned between the first and second trenches of the Line. The main attack in the north was to start on 9 April, and Gough's orders to the Fifth Army were to mount their operation at dawn the next day. On 8 April, however, the General was informed that not enough progress had been made in cutting the wire: reports from air patrols and infantry scouting had indicated that although some damage had been caused, the wire was still largely intact. It was reluctantly agreed that the attack would have to be postponed. The next day, the Third Army launched its attack at Arras, with immediate success: the Canadians captured Vimy Ridge, and part of the German front was overrun around Arras itself. Frustrated at being unable to do anything to assist, General Gough was ready to accept the radical proposal that was now presented to him.

Attached to the Fifth Army was a company of twelve tanks; these machines were still experimental and mechanically unreliable to some extent, with the best tactics for their employment not yet settled. Nevertheless, their senior officers came to Gough on the afternoon of 9 April with the suggestion that the tanks be grouped together and sent in ahead of the infantry, without an artillery barrage, to break through the wire into the trench system, with the infantry following behind to occupy the position. The General seized on the idea immediately and ordered the attack to be carried out at dawn the next day. The tank officers were somewhat taken aback by such haste, but hurried off to work out the details with the Australian staff. In spite of their considerable doubts,[3] the Anzac leaders agreed to proceed with the scheme and arranged for the 4th Division's two front-line brigades (the 4th and 12th) to form the infantry component of the attack. It was planned that all twelve tanks would precede the infantry, four in front of each brigade and the remaining four attacking up a shallow valley in between the brigades. Hasty verbal orders were passed to the division and brigade commanders late in the afternoon, passing down to the battalions during the evening. Hurried conferences were arranged at brigade and battalion level to pass on the arrangements to junior commanders; it was probably on this night (Murray later recalled it as 'one or two days before Bullecourt') that Black and Murray found a few minutes to talk. During the conversation Black said calmly, 'Harry, this will be my last fight, but I'll have that bloody German trench before they get me.'[4]

The division began to form up. Although there had been no time as yet to dig a proper front line, advantage had been taken of several features of the landscape. The Australians had occupied a railway cutting running parallel to and about 900 metres away from the Hindenburg Line; a kilometre and a half further back, many of the troops were billeted around Noreuil village and various sunken roads near it. Forward of the railway, another sunken lane made a useful forming-up position, and some assembly trenches had also been dug. The battalions began moving up into position around 10 pm, and all were in position by 4.15 am, waiting on ground covered by a thin dusting of snow. The plan called for the tanks to come up from the rear during the night and then move off ahead of the infantry at 4.30, with artillery opening up on Bullecourt and Queant villages at the same time to protect the flanks. The infantry would begin its advance at 4.45 am. The imagination of the troops had been caught by the novelty of the scheme, and there was an air of excited confidence. This began to dissipate as the start time grew nearer and there was no sign or sound of the tanks. As dawn approached, the Australian commanders and staffs were growing increasingly anxious: if the infantry was still waiting when the sun came up, virtually in the open and clearly visible against the snow, they would be slaughtered by the German artillery. Their worst fears were confirmed just before 5 am, when a report came in from one of the tank officers that the machines had been hopelessly delayed by loss of direction in a snowstorm and could not arrive in time.

With disaster looming, the decision was made to get the troops to the rear immediately. The message from Brigadier-General Brand to the 4th Brigade was: 'The stunt is off. Dispositions as yesterday. Move.' There was no time for an orderly march-off; the men simply got to their feet and walked back like 'the departure of a crowd from a Test match.'[5] With the light improving, there was every chance that they would still be seen and bombarded by the enemy, but discovery was delayed by a fortunate snow-squall which screened them for long enough to get clear. A German barrage did come down to cause a few casualties at the end, and the Germans had certainly seen enough to realise an attack had been planned.[6] The troops' confidence had all but evaporated. The 13th Battalion historian described the men as 'dog-tired, disappointed and more pessimistic than at any other period in their history concerning the higher authorities.'[7] The 13th's experience was typical: hard physical work during the preceding week (road making, carrying supplies and so on), an all-night march into position with the tension of impending action, only to have to slog back to Noreuil again and then another five kilometres to their billeting area near Favreuil. It was late afternoon before the tail of the column arrived, many of the exhausted men flinging themselves down to sleep immediately.

Any hopes for a night's rest were soon dashed. While the troops had been on the march, Gough was informing his corps commanders that another attempt was to be made before dawn the next day. The Australian leaders protested that the fiasco of the morning had shown that the tanks could not be relied upon; Gough appeared to be wavering, but a telephone call to the commander-in-chief resulted in a firm order that the attack must be carried

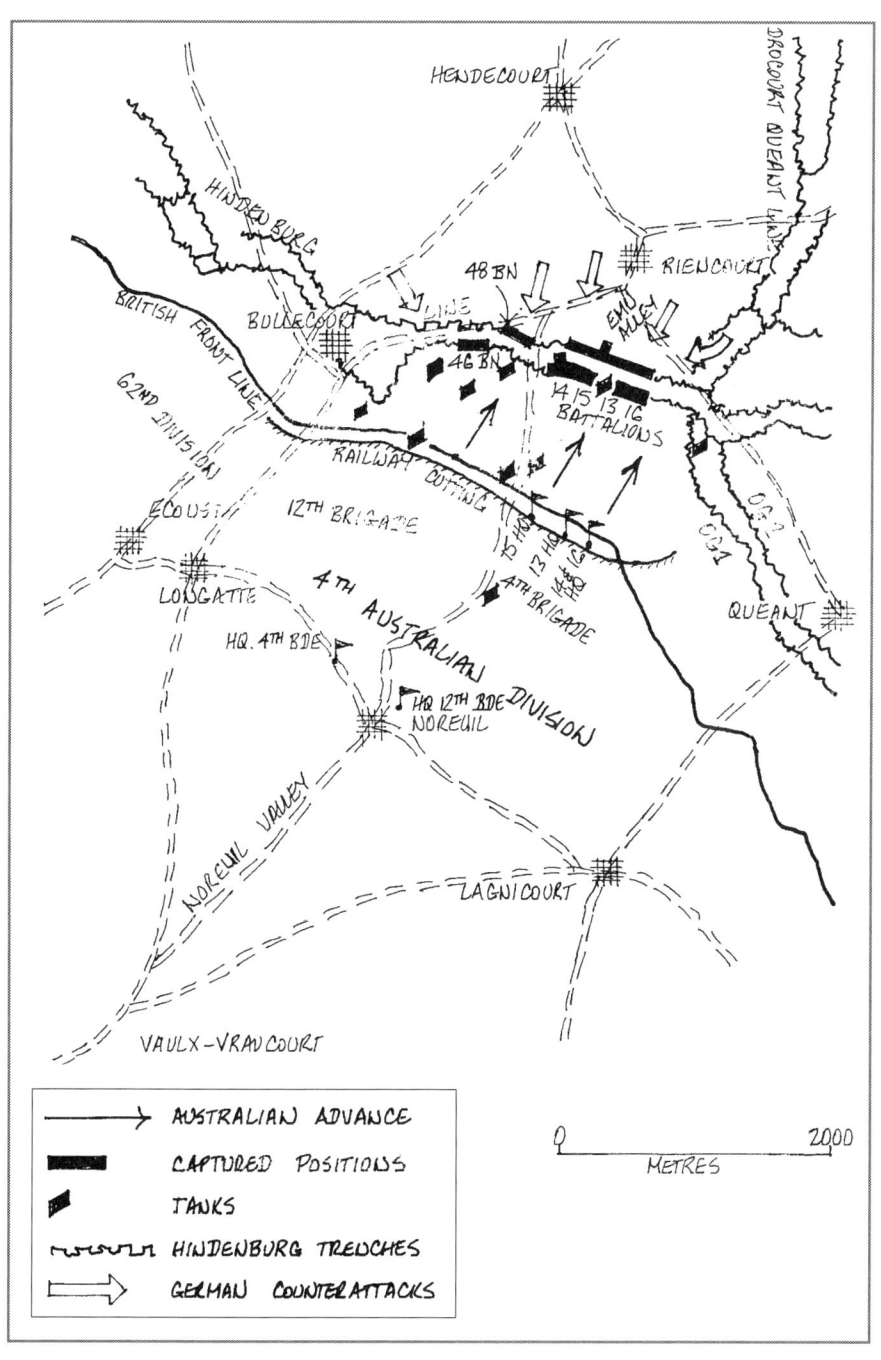

The battlefield of Bullecourt showing the situation at about 9.30am on 11 April 1917.

out. Orders came out again to the units, and at around 9 pm the troops began to retrace their steps back to the assembly areas. Midnight conferences at brigade and battalion level discussed final details. In the 16th Battalion, Colonel Drake-Brockman conferred with his company commanders from 12.15 to 2 am, sorting out the final dispositions of the companies. As the conference broke up, Black, with the premonition still upon him, said quietly to Drake-Brockman, 'Well, good-bye colonel — I mayn't come back, but we'll get the Hindenburg Line.'[8]

By about 3.30 am, the 4th Division was in position for the attack, 4th Brigade on the right, 12th on the left. The front line of the 4th Brigade, 700 metres away from the Hindenburg wire, comprised the 14th and 16th Battalions, each of their companies in four lines. Both battalions' COs and their staffs had set up a joint headquarters in the railway cutting. In the 16th, Black took his place with the rear platoon of his 'B' Company on the far right of the line. He was the senior officer in the battalion, indeed in the whole of the 4th Brigade's attacking force, and would be de facto commander in action. Several hundred metres behind, the support line had formed up, the 15th on the left to back up the 14th, and the 13th on the right following the 16th. These troops were in 'artillery formation' — single file by platoons. Murray, commanding his 'A' Company on the right, positioned himself a few metres in front of his men. He was not confident about the outcome; while waiting for the final orders, he had found himself hoping that the attack would be called off, but as always, now that the die was cast, he put aside his doubts to focus on the task before him.

The tanks, on which everything depended, did not have as far to travel this time, but they were again behind schedule. A single tank got into position ahead of the 4th Brigade infantry at 3.20 am, and another two clanked up during the next hour. Others had broken down in the back area. Captain Jacka of the 14th, doing his best to guide the tanks into position, had seen another ignore his instructions and strand itself in a sunken road. (The furious Jacka had to be restrained from shooting the tank crew.) Jacka had found out from the tank officers that they had no hope of reaching the Hindenburg Line in the fifteen minutes allowed for in the plan; this meant that the infantry would

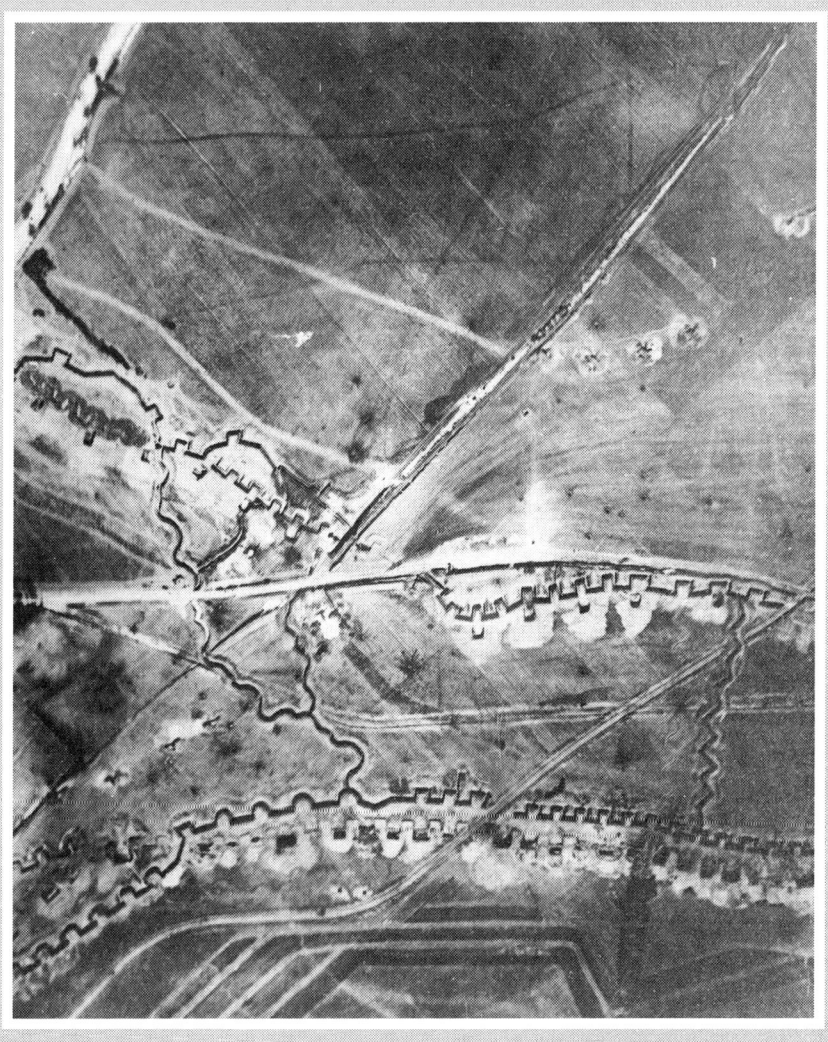

Bullecourt: aerial photograph showing a section of the Hindenburg Line.
The pattern of the trenches, with bays and traverses, can be clearly seen.
The grey bands at the bottom of the photograph are belts of barbed wire.
(Australian War Memorial Neg Number A01121)

reach the wire before the tanks. Jacka swiftly reported this to the battalion headquarters in the railway cutting; Colonels Peck and Drake-Brockman made a last-minute attempt to have the timings changed. 'Stick to the program' was the answer from above. By the planned starting time of 4.30 am, only three tanks were in position in front of the 4th Brigade, and none with the 12th Brigade on the left. A disaster was in the making.

At 4.30 the tanks in front of 4th Brigade moved off. A few German shells began to land in the infantry area, and one wiped out the 4th Brigade's mortar battery. Flares began to rise from the village of Bullecourt on the right of the German line; the tanks had been detected, and some of the enemy machine-guns opened fire. The infantry moved off, 'punctual to the second,' at 4.45 am. It was still dark, with visibility about fifty metres, but in the light of flares and explosions watchers could see the battalions perfectly aligned as they moved steadily across the open ground. In the 13th, Lance-Corporal Bert Knowles, leading a section of 'A' Company, watched Murray in front of the company, 'strolling along as if death was something which only came with old age.'⁹ Halfway to the objective, the leading lines of the 16th and 14th crossed a gentle crest and found that they had caught up to two of the tanks. The infantry had to keep moving, and they swept past the tardy monsters and continued towards the wire. It was now 4.50, and flares began to rise from the Hindenburg Line directly in front of the advancing infantry; the leading battalions had been seen, and a storm of fire broke out from myriad rifles and machine-guns. The Germans were firing through their wire, and the leading Australians could see showers of sparks flying from the entanglement as bullets glanced off it. They had left the tanks behind, they were facing uncut wire with no means of clearing a passage, and men were rapidly going down under the fusillade.

They were at the point of no return. Percy Black strode from his position in the rear wave to the front of the 16th Battalion, calling out, 'Come on, boys, bugger the tanks!' He led them into the entanglement, looking for a passage. There were ways to get through; a few gaps made by shells were located, and there were areas where shell-bursts had loosened the strands. One or two passages left for access by German patrols were found. Somehow the 16th, and the 14th on their left, struggled through the obstacle — two successive bands of barbed wire, each waist high and eight metres wide at this point. Scores of dead and wounded were left in the wire, but Black led the survivors across the open ground beyond the wire and into the foremost trench (OG 1). With bayonets and grenades, they drove out the German garrison.

The 13th had followed behind the 16th in support. Shortly after starting, the right flank started to lose direction and come in towards the centre, tending to follow a roadway slanting across their front. Murray saw this, and Corporal Knowles watched him deal with it. He 'strode across and simply said "Right incline, 13th," and it was done without any fuss.'[10] Another few metres and a whining torrent of machine-gun fire suddenly lashed the battalion. About thirty men went down immediately; Bert Knowles' section was reduced to himself and two others in moments. Murray could tell from the shifting arc of the fire that the Germans had not actually seen them in the gloom, but were searching all too successfully for targets. 'Get down, 13th, till it passes,' he called. ('Setting the example myself,' he later wrote.)[11] The hail of death swept past. The light had improved by now, and Murray looked up to see the 16th ahead struggling through the wire, the machine-guns mowing them down. Bert Knowles heard again 'the same wonderful voice in front': 'Come on, 13th! The 16th are getting hell!' The 13th covered the remaining 200 metres to the wire at a jog-trot, as more machine-guns and rifles were turned on to them. Ahead, a single tank following behind the 16th had flattened a path through the first wire belt but had been stopped in the second belt, its shape clearly outlined in sparks struck from it by the bullets rattling on its sides. The 13th charged up the narrow gap in the wire; reaching the stranded tank, Murray at first tried to move through on its left, but found the intact wire on that side too much of an obstacle. Dashing around to the other side, he suddenly saw, only ten metres away in a short trench projecting into the wire belt, the machine-gun that had caused many of the 13th's casualties in the approach. With suicidal courage, the German crew was still firing even though they were now surrounded. They were quickly shot, but they had done great damage in the Australian ranks.

The 13th now tried to find a way through the remaining wire, some even stepping across the top from one strand to another. All the time the flanking machine-guns were sweeping the area and cutting down the advancing troops, many collapsing into the wire to be hung up on the barbs. A bullet grazed the back of Murray's neck; he dropped for a moment with the shock before realising he was unhurt. Finally the survivors were through and into the OG 1 trench; most of the Germans had fled under the 16th's assault, but a number were routed out of the dugouts by grenades, and the 13th sent sixty prisoners back to the Australian lines. There were many of the 16th's dead and wounded in the trench, but Black had already led his remaining fit men on to assault the second part of their objective, the German support trench, OG 2.

This was about 150 metres behind the front line, protected by another wire entanglement halfway across the intervening space: only a single narrower belt, but it was completely undamaged. As the Australians hesitated at the barrier, the Germans opened fire on them again. Black walked calmly along the entanglement searching for an opening, and soon found one of the narrow gaps left for patrol access. He called his men to the spot and sent them scrambling through the opening. As the last few passed, he turned to his runner, Private Ellis, and ordered him to take a message to the battalion commanding officers at the railway cutting: 'Tell them the first objective is gained and I am pushing on to the second.' They were his last words. As he finished speaking, a German bullet struck him in the head and he fell, killed instantly.

There was 'no time to weep.' Ellis set off on his perilous journey to deliver the message, and the 16th troops, led by such men as Captain Dan Aarons, rushed OG 2 and again used their rifles, bayonets and grenades to kill or drive out the Germans. Behind them, Murray was leading the survivors of his 'A' Company of the 13th forward to assist. In the improving light, others of the 13th located a few of the communication trenches leading between OG 1 and OG 2, and used these to advance into the second line. The two battalions completed the capture of the position on their flank of the attack, while on their left the 14th and 15th had also taken their objectives despite also suffering cruel losses from the German fire, including three of the 14th's four brilliant company commanders. By 5.30 am, the 4th Brigade, depleted by losses of probably sixty per cent in killed and wounded, held about 800 metres of the German first and second trenches. On the left of the

Death of Major Black, by Charles Wheeler (detail).
(Australian War Memorial ART03558)

attack, the 12th Brigade, let down to an even greater extent by the tanks, had managed to get into the trenches on that side also. The Australians had done what was thought impossible: broken into the Hindenburg line, against uncut wire and without an artillery barrage. But they now faced an even greater challenge: to hold on to their gains.

In the 4th Brigade's area, the battalions were mixed together all through the position. Murray was by now aware of Black's death; he had refused to believe it at first, searching desperately until he saw his friend's body.[12] The situation of the battle demanded his attention and he fought down his grief. Murray now made sure the right flank was secure, ordering a barricade built to defend against counterattack on that side. A few men of the 16th were still trying to get further along the trench on this side, throwing grenades ahead of them as they went. Murray ordered them to stop, only to receive the reply, 'Oh, we're going a long way yet!' He had to repeat the order; an officer of the 16th arrived at this point, and Murray handed over control of the flank to him and set off back down OG 2 to the left. He was carrying out the practice he had developed in previous battles, hurrying from one end of the position to the other, assessing the situation all along the 800-metre length of the line. As he went, he organised the defences, positioning Lewis guns and posting sections of men into key positions. With Black gone, the officers of all battalions tended to look to Murray for overall leadership, and before long it was accepted that he was in charge of the brigade in the trenches.

As soon as OG 2 had been taken, Murray had sent back a brief message advising headquarters. It was 7.15 am, and having completed his survey of the position, Murray sent a more detailed message, which would become famous and be quoted almost in full in the *Official History*:

> We hold first objective and part of second. Have established block on the right of both objectives. In touch with 14th on the left. Expect heavy bomb fighting in evening. There are six tanks at a standstill, apparently damaged — just behind the first objective there are four, and two near second. Quite impossible to attack village. 'A' Company 13th badly cut

about by machine-gun fire in wire, some of all other 13th companies here all O.K. We will require as many rifle and hand grenades as you can possibly send, also SAA [small arms ammunition]. Most of Lewis machine-guns are O.K. Have four Vickers guns. Fear Major Black killed. Several officers killed and wounded … Have plenty men. Have about 30 prisoners of 124 Regt. Will send them over at dusk. Look out for S.O.S. signals. Send white flares (as many as possible). With artillery support we can keep the position till the cows come home.[13]

This situation — the trenches captured but no further advance possible — had been allowed for in the plan, with an arrangement for the artillery to lay down a barrage beyond the trench line to disrupt infantry counterattacks and to suppress the flanking villages and also Riencourt village beyond the lines. Five minutes after sending his message, Murray noticed a German counterattack forming up around Riencourt and fired off the SOS flare signal to bring down the barrage. There was no response. Altogether the signal would be made eighteen times — *eighteen times* — during the morning, but the artillery stayed silent. The problem was that the higher echelons had received reports from spotter aircraft and artillery observers stating that the Australians had already captured Bullecourt and Riencourt and even that they were advancing further into German territory. Whatever the reason for this fatal optimism (the official historian Bean believed the errors to be caused by the deceptive visibility that morning), the result was a refusal to allow the guns to open fire. For the rest of the battle, the Germans could move up reinforcements and ammunition with impunity, and their own machine-guns and artillery were allowed to cut off the Australians from their supports without interference.

Small parties of the 16th and 13th had made their way into a communication trench ('Emu Alley') leading almost directly into Riencourt. They pushed up the trench close to the village, and could clearly see Germans in the upper floors of the village buildings sweeping the captured position with rifle and machine-gun fire. A few artillery shells would easily shatter these strongpoints, but the bombardment did not come. Machine-guns in the flanking villages were now sweeping the tops of the trenches and raking the area behind the Australians, cutting them off from reinforcements and supplies. The Germans' own artillery had begun to shell the Australian back area. One shell landed in the 13th Battalion Headquarters, killing six of the staff and wounding five others including Murray's close friend Doug Marks, who was badly injured. Colonel Durrant escaped untouched.

Now the Germans began to launch infantry counterattacks against the captured positions. At six different points along the 4th Brigade front, groups of Germans attacked behind showers of grenades; the Australians replied with deadly effect using their heavier Mills grenades, supported by Lewis guns placed in shell-holes in advance of the trenches and by the Vickers guns of the 4th Machine Gun Company, which had followed the infantry in the attack. The German attacks were repulsed without much difficulty, but supplies of grenades were running short. The troops had carried minimal numbers of grenades with them — according to the plan, they were supposed to be fighting in the open beyond the Hindenburg Line rather than engaging in 'bomb fights' in the trenches. Murray had ordered the collection of grenades from the dead and wounded, and the trenches were searched for German grenades; these were nowhere near adequate, but no supplies from the rear could get through the storm of machine-gun fire that had isolated the Australian front line. Having repulsed the first round of counterattacks, the 4th Brigade seemed reasonably secure for the moment, occupying the deep, well-constructed trench system, with barricades in place and their Lewis and Vickers guns well placed by Murray and other officers keeping the Germans' heads down. But without support from the artillery, it could only be a matter of time before they were forced out. Murray's message had arrived at Battalion Headquarters at 8.45 am (the runners taking ninety minutes to make their way back through the fusillade) and the Australian commanders at battalion and brigade level needed no further convincing. In his dispatch on the battle, Bean later referred to 'a message … from one officer whom everyone could trust.' But their demands for the artillery to open fire were rebuffed. The 4th

Brigade Headquarters diarist noted, with what must have been extreme understatement, 'a most aggravating telephonic communication took place.'[14] The infantry would be left to fend for themselves.

Ammunition was running low in the trenches. The troops had already been ordered to refrain from shooting at long range, saving their ammunition until they could be sure of hitting a target. At about 10 am, the Germans launched another series of heavy counterattacks all along the line. Numbers of them thrust into the gap between the 4th and 12th Brigades, which was supposed to have been occupied by the tanks, and began to attack along both trench lines. Others attempted a frontal attack, but were kept down by the Australians' fire. Another attack up the trenches from the 4th Brigade's right flank began to make headway as the Australians rapidly used up their remaining grenades. The 13th's Captain Gardiner, commanding on this flank, hurriedly conferred with Murray and several other officers to decide on the best course to follow. Gardiner wanted to move the brigade out of the trenches, find nearby shell holes to occupy, and hold out there until evening. Although this was Gardiner's first fight in France, he was on paper senior to Murray, who deferred to his seniority at first, and agreed to try the move.

Dan Aarons of the 16th volunteered to run the gauntlet back to HQ with a further plea for artillery support. He somehow managed to get back unscathed, but by then the situation in the trenches had deteriorated further. Gardiner's group on the right had used their last grenade, and the Germans were able to creep closer; some of the Lewis guns on this flank had been knocked out by enemy grenades, others had run out of ammunition. Murray organised a line of riflemen along a bank spanning the gap between the two trenches; these kept the Germans' heads down for a while, but the end was now looking inevitable. The observers in the railway cutting at the rear watched with increasing dismay as the white smoke-puffs from German grenades steadily advanced along the line of the Australian position, with fewer and fewer answering bursts from Australian grenades.

As the flanks of the Australian position in OG 1 were driven inwards, those occupying OG 2 were in danger of being completely cut off. Murray shepherded the survivors back to OG 1 and they pushed the Germans back for a short distance on each flank, but he knew there was now nothing left to do but retreat as best they could. On the left of the captured position, part of the shattered 12th Brigade had already been forced to retreat.[15] Murray moved rapidly along the trench, passing the word to pull back, positioning the few remaining Lewis guns to cover the retreating riflemen for a few minutes. Sergeant Blackburn, in charge of a Lewis gun section of the 14th Battalion, later recalled Murray coming up to their section of trench: 'Hopping on to the parados, he addressed us something like this: "Well, men, we are just about out of ammunition, and it doesn't look as if anything more can be done. We either stay here and get skittled or be taken prisoners, or we can get out while our luck is in. What do you say?" [Lance-Corporal Bamford] sings out: "We're with you, Harry, whatever you do." "Well boys," says Murray, "out we go. Hand over all your ammunition, except ten rounds, to the Lewis gunners; but listen you chaps" (turning to us), "don't be too long after we go."' The gunners stayed to give covering fire for a further five minutes, then made the attempt themselves.[16] Murray continued to move along the trench, passing the word to as many of the troops as he could reach, to many groups calling out, 'There's two things now — either capture, or go into that!' ('that' being the hail of death from crossfiring machine-guns and rifles sweeping the open ground back to the Australian lines). It was every man for himself.

Many had already been cut off and forced to surrender. Most of those surviving made the attempt to get back, but scores were cut down by the storm of fire (Murray later described it as 'like expecting to run for hundreds of yards through a violent thunderstorm without being struck by any of the raindrops'); the wire entanglements which blocked them in the advance that morning now formed a barrier hampering the retreat as well. Murray stayed almost to the last with a group of ten men attempting to give some cover to the withdrawal. With the Germans closing to within ten metres, Murray ordered any copies of code signal lists torn up and trodden into the mud, then led his little band out of the trench to attempt their retreat. The eager Germans followed them into the open; Murray's group jumped into a shell-hole and turned to face their pursuers for a final stand. At that moment the distant German machine-guns, confused by the clouds of dust and smoke, opened up on their own men. Those who were not cut down scrambled for cover, and Murray's group was free to continue their escape.

Murray never remembered how they managed to negotiate the wire for the second time. At some point a bullet grazed his back, just breaking the skin. Once through the wire, there was nothing more Murray could do except save himself, and the mental, physical and emotional strain of the past seven hours suddenly caught up and almost overwhelmed him. He found himself exhausted, hardly able to move more than a few metres without rest. Finding some shelter in one of the few shell-holes (the area had not been heavily bombarded), the party could see no more cover ahead. Just as they had decided to take their chances in the open, a shell whined overhead and blew a convenient crater twenty metres in front; they stumbled forward and into the hole, pursued by a burst of machine-gun fire. Murray's hand touched a piece of hot metal from the shell-casing; the pain had the effect of restoring some of his energy, and he set off again for the Australian lines with his now diminished group. Through an increasing bombardment from the German artillery, Murray and three others managed to reach the Australian front line at last. The horror was not quite over; within moments of reaching the line, Lieutenant Tom Morgan was killed by a shell-burst. Somehow, Murray had come through the whole battle, the advance, the fight in the trenches and the retreat with no more than grazes from two bullets, one of which did not break the skin (presumably he would also have collected cuts and abrasions getting through the wire). The remnants of the 4th and 12th Brigades were relieved by the reserve 13th Brigade, and at dusk the weary troops moved off towards the back areas.

Murray's lethargy returned, and he found himself again unable to walk more than a few metres at a time, wanting only to lie down and sleep. German shells continued to fall in the area, and Colonel Durrant personally saw to it that Murray kept moving in spite of his protests. A few nips of whisky from Durrant's flask had no effect, but he was at last able to get Murray out of the front line and on the way back to Noreuil. The 13th's quartermaster met them halfway, bringing their horses up, and Murray was able to mount and leave it to the animal to carry him the rest of the way. Durrant took Murray with him to a meeting of the battalion COs with General Brand at Brigade Headquarters, and in the grim atmosphere of the gathering Murray began to regain some of his strength and energy. By then he would no doubt have been aware that as well as losing one great friend in the battle, another in Douglas Marks had been desperately wounded and might not survive. But these were only two of the appalling losses suffered by the division, and by the 4th Brigade in particular. Total casualties of the brigade were 2339 killed, wounded and captured out of 3000 men who entered the fight; the 12th Brigade lost 950 out of 2250. Of the total casualties for the division, over 1000 had been taken prisoner by the Germans, by far the largest number of Australians captured in one battle throughout the war. Many of the prisoners had been wounded in the fight and were cut off by the Germans in the trenches, or were collected by the Germans as they swept through the battlefield during the afternoon.

The disaster that had befallen the 4th Division was not of its own making; the troops had been sacrificed for the sake of an experiment and, when in spite of all the difficulties, including slipshod planning, it had achieved some degree of success, a tragic communication breakdown between infantry and artillery ensured that there would be no reprieve from disaster. In Bean's words, 'everyone was aware that the 4th Australian Division had been employed in an experiment of extreme rashness, persisted in by the army commander after repeated warnings, and that the experiment had failed with shocking loss … a magnificent instrument recklessly shattered in the performance of an impracticable task.'[17] But in spite of their anger and despair, the survivors were at the same time proud of their achievement in breaking the Hindenburg Line without artillery. Many years later, Brigadier-General Brand summed up the feeling:

> … the most disastrous, the most bloody and yet the most glorious day in the history of the 4th Brigade. With its sister Brigade, the 12th, it advanced 1000 yards over open country under terrific frontal and enfilade fire, hacked a way through

a maze of wire entanglements, seized the famous Hindenburg Line, and, cut off from reinforcements or assistance of any kind, held on without artillery support for six hours, repelling several counter-attacks backed up by powerful artillery. As a feat of arms surely there was nothing finer in the whole war.[18]

One loss in particular reverberated throughout the AIF. As well as being regarded with enormous affection and respect by the 16th Battalion and the 4th Brigade, Percy Black was known at least by reputation across the whole AIF. The 15th Battalion's history described the death of 'the pride of the 4th Brigade.' 'The greatest individual loss in the brigade that day was that of Major Percy Black ... None fell that day with more glory, yet many fell and there was much glory,' wrote the historian of the 14th Battalion.[19] On hearing the news, Major-General Cox, the former 4th Division commander, wrote, 'The bravest and best soldier in the AIF has this day made the supreme sacrifice.'[20] Cyril Longmore, now serving with the new 3rd Division, wrote of the 'pang of regret' through the rank and file: 'a real Australian had gone West, one who typified all those qualities of manhood the Digger admired.'[21] Murray refrained from making his feelings public, except to note in his letter to Longmore two weeks after the battle that he was 'frightfully grieved'.

The loss of his seemingly indestructible old companion and the enormous casualties in his company and in the battalion, coming as the culmination of almost continuous combat since the previous August, seem to have temporarily shaken Murray's iron composure. The battle had, however, demonstrated another level of his military capacity. Nominally commanding one company out of sixteen in the assault, and not the most senior officer involved, he had taken charge of four battalions in a crisis and led them with unfailing determination and cheerfulness through a desperate struggle against odds that became overwhelming. In taking on the responsibility for the conduct of the battle and the eventual decision to withdraw, he had shown a moral courage equal to his undoubted physical bravery. He had done all that was humanly possible in the situation. A few days after the battle, Colonel Durrant recommended Murray for another decoration, a bar to his DSO, noting in the document, 'He is not only brave and daring but a skilful soldier possessing tactical instinct of the highest order.'

After the battle, the depleted, exhausted battalions of the 4th Brigade moved away to the back areas to rest and rebuild for the ordeals still to come. The AIF referred to this battle as the First Battle of Bullecourt, although it was generally regarded in British records as a part of the Battle of Arras. The Second Battle of Bullecourt began on 3 May, when the 2nd Australian Division was flung at the same sector of the Hindenburg Line. This time a more conventional plan was used, the infantry attacking behind an artillery barrage. Again the Australians broke into the German trenches, and hung on against ferocious counterattacks and bombardments. With the artillery support that had been withheld at First Bullecourt, the Australians managed to keep open a narrow supply route to the captured position. In succeeding days, the 1st and 5th Australian Divisions were drawn into the fighting. Eventually the Germans gave up their efforts to retake the trenches and reconstructed their line around this section, while the Bullecourt trenches were incorporated into the British front line. The victory of Second Bullecourt was a remarkable achievement, but the fighting cost Australia a further 7000 casualties, a high price for a position of doubtful value.

Percy Black's body was never recovered. It may have been destroyed by some later bombardment, or perhaps buried in a mass grave by the Germans. After the war, his name was one of those listed as 'missing' on the Australian memorial at Villers-Bretonneux. The preliminary casualty reports published after the Bullecourt fighting listed Percy Black as 'wounded', and it was several days before this was corrected to 'killed in action', around Anzac Day of 1917. Anne Black was informed of her son's death promptly;[22] she would survive him by only four months, dying on 9 August 1917.

The news of Percy's death gradually became public in Australian newspapers during April, and on 26 April, flags were flown at half-mast in Southern Cross and Bullfinch: 'the last tribute of respect to our Yilgarn hero' as the *Southern Cross Times* reported (calling him 'Colonel' Black). 'Percy's death ... has cast a gloom in WA,'[23] wrote Miss Cassidy to Black's sister Jessie Adamson. When the news reached Victoria, the flag on the little schoolhouse at Beremboke was lowered to half-mast also.

There were many former 16th Battalion members back in Perth at this time, repatriated through wounds or illness, and Black's death affected them deeply. A group of them arranged a public meeting at the Perth Town Hall to discuss a suitable memorial. The meeting was held on 17 May, and was chaired by Lieutenant-Colonel L E Tilney, former second-in-command of the 16th Battalion and more recently commanding officer of the 13th. After a number of what the press called 'expressions of appreciation of the character and worth of the late soldier,' the meeting decided initially on two measures. Firstly, a commemorative plaque of brass and marble, paid for by the 16th veterans, would be placed in St George's Cathedral. A telegram was immediately sent to Mrs Black in Melbourne, offering sympathy and seeking her approval,[24] to which she soon replied in the affirmative. The second proposal was to obtain an enlarged photographic portrait for hanging in the Soldiers' Institute building in the city, the headquarters for the state's returned servicemen. A committee of nine was appointed to make all the arrangements; they were also charged with looking into the possibility of erecting a public memorial, but nothing seems to have come of this.

Ten days later, the *Sunday Times* printed a moving tribute to Percy Black written by 'Crosscut' (Thomas Wilson), the poet and former 16th Battalion man. Black, he wrote, was 'loved for his modesty, his unassuming splendidness of character, in a word his beautiful personality ...'

> Starting as a private, and with no greater backing than his own good personality; with no more education than was necessary to carry him through the tattle of life; with no more prospect of military advancement than the career of any ordinary, everyday ... common or garden sort of bloke would indicate, he did deeds that it will be hard to find a parallel for in all the archives of gallantry. Within the small space of a

couple of years of active service he attained successive ranks through every grade from private to major …

He won those splendid honours without incurring the animosity of any of his fellow-soldiers from private to general. Every step of his upon his upward path was applauded with heartfelt pride by those who had the honour of being his comrades … Advancement in all avenues of life rarely fails to incur heartburnings, jealousy, discontent and bitterness on the part of some who have perhaps been distanced in the race. In the case of Percy Black it is not too much to say that his successes only made him dearer to the hearts of his friends. Enemies he had none.[25]

The memorial plaque was ready within a month of the meeting. Mounted in the south transept of St George's Cathedral, it was unveiled by the Governor of Western Australia, Sir William Ellison-Macartney on Sunday 17 June 1917, during an evening service conducted by Archbishop Riley, who was both Chaplain-General of the Australian forces and Anglican Archbishop of Perth. The Governor spoke briefly, beginning by saying that the memorial was erected in honour of a gallant soldier and a distinguished man. 'When the call of the Empire came, Major Black and his comrades saw clearly before them the path of duty. He trod that path with certain, sure and shining steps. He pursued his duty with great gallantry, and, in the course of so doing, he jeopardised his life until death. Amid a band of brave men his great personal qualifications and characteristics attracted respect, admiration and affection.'[26]

A bugler sounded the last post. Archbishop Riley prefaced his sermon with another tribute, outlining Black's military career and concluding: 'His comrades described Major Black as having been a quiet, retiring man, but a man who, when occasion demanded, had been full of energy and resource.' At the end of the service, the congregation stood while the 'Dead March from Saul' was played.

The following Sunday, the portrait photograph was unveiled at the Returned Soldiers' Institute in Perth in front of about 300 guests, mostly returned soldiers. The Soldiers Welcome Committee had decorated the building to present 'a pleasing spectacle with a great many huge palms placed on the spacious verandah, while the interior was decorated with a profusion of wattle blossoms, violets and other blooms,' as the press reported.[27] Again the Governor presided, speaking another eulogy of Percy Black.

> In a short military career lasting barely two and a half years, Major Black received a series of distinctions which were very remarkable. But probably the one upon which he would himself have laid the greatest stress was the fact that he had obtained and retained in the most remarkable manner the respect, affection and esteem of all his comrades. He was one of those men whom on first acquaintance, the superficial observer would take to be a man of extraordinary modesty, but his natural capacity and his gift for always doing the right thing at the right moment soon brought him to the front … Major Black was a brave man among brave men.[28]

The portrait, covered by a Union Jack, was then unveiled by Colonel Tilney.[29] Messages from Black's family were read out, together with a cable from the 16th's original commander, Colonel Pope, and several patriotic musical items were performed. In the genteel manner of the time, the function concluded with afternoon tea served by the ladies of the Welcome Committee. Western Australia had said its farewells.

Chapter 9

THE PATH OF DUTY

On the other side of the world, the wreckage of the 4th Brigade struggled wearily back to Favreuil on the night of the battle, and to Bapaume the next day, the brigadier and the battalion commanders in tears as the sadly depleted units marched past. The battalions entrained for transport to Albert, and from there marched the final few miles to their old hutted camp at Mametz. On 14 April, General Birdwood inspected the brigade and made a speech acknowledging 'this disaster that has befallen your brigade' and disassociating himself and his staff from the faulty planning of the battle. Cold comfort for the survivors, but most of the troops seem to have accepted Birdwood's sincerity. It would be some time before the brigade, and indeed the division, recovered in numbers and morale.

From the day of the battle, 11 April, Murray had been temporarily promoted to major to replace the wounded Marks, and was now acting second-in-command of the battalion. Later in the month, the division withdrew further to the familiar rest area around Ribemont. Training programs commenced, inducting the many replacements coming into the units,[1] and providing refreshers for the diminishing number of old hands.

Colonel Durrant, concerned about the effect of Bullecourt on Murray's state of mind, added the job of Battalion Musketry Officer to his duties to ensure he was kept fully occupied. When Murray wrote to Cyril Longmore on 26 April, informing him of Percy Black's death ('the very best of us, the bravest and coolest of all the brave men I know'), he also mentioned that he was expecting to go on leave to England on 8 or 10 May.

He was still in France on 12 May however, when General Birdwood attended a full divisional parade, held in a field near Ribemont, on the Albert–Amiens road. The division formed a large hollow square, and Birdwood presented decorations and medal ribbons to a number of recipients. The award of a bar to Murray's DSO had been approved a few days before, and he was the first to be called up, to receive 'the ribbon of the DSO' (presumably with the rosette representing the bar) from the General. The troops were seated casually on the ground during this part of the parade, and Lieutenant George Mitchell recorded that 'the unusual sound of unchecked applause was heard as different recipients stepped forward.'[2] Birdwood's main purpose was to farewell the division, which was now under orders to move to the Flanders theatre, where it would join the new 3rd Division in II Anzac Corps around Messines. Murray, however, would first be proceeding on leave to England. Having been delayed by the divisional parade, he would now be attending an investiture ceremony to receive his decorations from King George V. At the beginning of June, Murray was in London preparing for what was to be an unusually elaborate event.

For the first time in the war, an investiture ceremony would be held in public, and in Hyde Park rather than at Buckingham Palace. The event was scheduled for the afternoon of Saturday 2 June, announced in advance to ensure a good turn-out. An enclosure was prepared in an area of the park between the Serpentine and Knightsbridge Barracks, and a canopied pavilion set up for the King to make the presentations. Areas were set aside with seating for various dignitaries, and for several hundred wounded servicemen from the hospitals in the London area, and there was 'ample space for thousands of the general public,' as *The Times* reported.[3] No less than 351 presentations were scheduled, including fifty posthumous awards to be

4th Division parade at Ribemont, 12 May 1917. Murray (uncharacteristically wearing a peaked cap) being presented with his DSO ribbon by General Birdwood.
(Australian War Memorial Neg Number E00450)

received by next-of-kin. Murray, who was to receive his VC and his DSO and bar, would be in good company, with ten other VCs to be presented also.

Saturday 2 June 1917 was a beautiful summer day in London. Spectators and guests began to assemble in the early afternoon, and at 2 pm the massed bands of the Brigade of Guards, leading a guard of honour from the Scots Guards, began to march up Constitution Hill to Hyde Park Corner, and along The Row, which was lined with spectators, to the enclosure in Hyde Park. The men and women[4] receiving decorations filled several rows of seats in front of the pavilion. Observers noted the wide variety of uniforms, and the row of people wearing black, who were receiving the awards of their dead relatives. The reporter from *The Times* was moved to note that the gathering included 'men of every class and from many walks in life … who, before the war had no thought beyond peaceful employment … gathered here to receive from their King … decorations for acts of war which three years ago would have seemed impossible to them.' The King left Buckingham Palace at 2.35 in the royal carriage, accompanied by the Queen and Princess Mary, and followed by further carriages conveying various aides and equerries (including Sir Ian Hamilton, erstwhile commander-in-chief at Gallipoli). The royal party was cheered enthusiastically by the large crowd during the ten-minute drive to the pavilion; alighting from his landau, the King saluted as the Royal Standard was broken out, inspected the guard, and mounted the pavilion to begin the investiture.

The recipients were allocated numbers designating their place in the order of appearance; these had been published in the press with the corresponding names, and were displayed on large cards around the area as each came up to the King. Number one on the list, first of the distinguished company to march up the ramp, was Major Henry William Murray of the 13th Australian Infantry Battalion.[5] It was most unusual to present a VC and a double DSO to one man at the same time, and it was reported that the King spoke to Murray at considerable length; one account said for fifteen minutes, but this was probably an exaggeration since the whole investiture was scheduled for only an hour and three-quarters.

The Times, taking note of the wording of Murray's VC citation, commented that 'he seems to have accomplished nearly every task it was possible to set himself in an attack,' a statement with which it would be hard to disagree. One can only imagine Murray's feelings at this point; given his natural reticence and dislike of public attention, he would surely have felt uncomfortable at being, however briefly, the centre of attention in front of thousands of people. On the other hand, a man of his fervent patriotism would have been delighted at receiving high honours at the hand of his sovereign. In any case, he was probably relieved to have gone up first, getting the ordeal of public scrutiny over early before marching off the dais to receive the congratulations of a group of well-wishers.

Shortly after the investiture, Murray travelled to Scotland to complete his period of leave, a trip that proved to be significant in his personal life. In Scotland, he and several other officers of the 13th enjoyed the hospitality provided by a landed family of Kinross-shire. Maud Purvis-Russell, born in Kinross-shire, had spent most of her early life in New Zealand before returning to Scotland to marry Sir Henry Montgomery, a baronet of the shire. In 1917 they were at Hattonburn House on their estate near Loch Leven and the village of Milnathort with their seventeen-year-old daughter, Clementine (Clem).[6] Two of their sons were serving in the forces, and it was no doubt Lady Purvis-Russell Montgomery's New Zealand connections that led to her making her home available to Anzac soldiers on leave or convalescing.

Writing to the family of Lieutenant George McDowell, another visiting 13th Battalion officer, Lady Purvis-Russell Montgomery described her youngest daughter as very good at games, and 'a shy girl … the boys don't make much headway with her.'[7] Her particular sport was golf and she was Scottish Ladies' Champion twice during the 1920s. Harry Murray and Clementine hit it off together immediately, and the two formed a close attachment, though how deep will probably remain a matter for speculation. If Clementine had indeed caught the eye of the dashing Major Murray, VC, he nevertheless only spent a few days at Hattonburn on this trip. He would return, however.

After a 'glorious time' (according to Lieutenant McDowell) in Scotland,

Murray returned to the Continent later in June and rejoined his battalion in Flanders, where he resumed command of 'A' Company and found that he had reverted to the rank of captain. The 4th Division was by then attached to II Anzac Corps, and backed up the 3rd Division in the latter's successful baptism of fire at Messines. The 4th Brigade found itself operating as the reserve for the division, and the 13th Battalion commenced a period of frequent rotation between support and front-line duties, the latter mostly patrolling and 'mopping-up' in the wake of the great British assault at Messines. To quote the battalion history, 'In 25 hours we marched in, relieved a front-line battalion, advanced 400 yards, dug in, handed over, and were again on our way out.' From 13 to 17 June, the 13th was occupied in 'digging and carrying' in support of the front line, then moved to the rear for further fatigue duties, road-making and burying cables for field telephones. Details of Murray's activities during this period are restricted to a few glimpses; young Sergeant Eric Evans, rejoining the battalion about this time after a long convalescence in Australia, recorded in his diary that he was warmly welcomed by both Colonel Durrant and Murray,[8] although Evans was not in Murray's Company. On 27 June at Bailleul, the Duke of Connaught (the King's uncle) held an inspection of elements of the 3rd and 4th Divisions. Murray was among those representing his brigade, as was the great Albert Jacka of the 14th Battalion. This parade was notable for an unseemly clash between the two divisional commanders, General Holmes of the 4th Division and General Monash of the 3rd, over who should have the honour of presenting Murray and Jacka to the Duke.[9] Monash may have felt this was within his rights, having been the original commander of the 4th Brigade, but the bad blood between the two generals over this incident had not been resolved when Holmes was mortally wounded by an artillery shell several days later.

The 13th continued its labouring work until 8 July, then moved for another short period in the front line: five days in a system of outposts and trenches near the River Lys. The trenches were among the worst the 13th had encountered, swarming with lice and rats, and vile-smelling pools of contaminated water all around. The battalion carried out a series of

The scene at Hyde Park, London, on 2 June 1917,
for the presentation of decorations by King George V.

[Inset] Murray leaving the dais after receiving his decorations.

(The Times History of the War, Vol XII)

aggressive patrols into no-man's-land during this period, reconnoitring the enemy positions and attacking their patrols. On the night of 9 July, Murray led a party of ten men to raid a German strongpoint, but suffered a sharp repulse with the loss of half of the patrol. In spite of this setback, Murray made a number of daring nocturnal sorties to reconnoitre no-man's-land and the German positions, making his way between their posts as far as the river bank. A story went around the troops that 'Mad Harry' even swam across the river to examine the far bank. Sergeant Evans, for one, thought this likely: 'Nothing surprises me about the man. He is the most complete soldier I have ever encountered.'[10]

Colonel Durrant himself was wounded on 11 July, and the next day Murray was promoted again to major, this time as permanent rank, and took on the acting command of the battalion. On 14 July, the 13th again returned to reserve duties, with considerable sickness in the ranks from the unsanitary conditions. A short time away from the front line improved the men's health and outlook, but three weeks later the battalion was again rotated towards the forward areas, spending another period of labouring works, under intermittent shellfire, in support of the 16th. The rapid rotations continued, the 13th returning on 20 August to the front line around the village of Gapaard, a waterlogged quagmire where the trenches were often waist-deep in mud. Although there were no major actions during this period, the battalion suffered a steady stream of casualties from artillery fire and the ever-present machine-guns. Major Doug Marks, by now recovered from his Bullecourt wounds, returned to the battalion on 23 August; as the senior major, he took over as acting CO, with Murray reverting to second-in-command.

There are indications that the strain of more than three years of front-line combat was beginning to tell on Murray; at about this time, he confided to another 4th Division officer, Arthur Maxwell, 'You know, with me it has come to this. I have to go up the line by myself now, so that they do not see me duck at the shells.'[11] The notes of the official correspondent, Charles Bean, indicate that Murray was to be given a short rest away from the front ('everyone knows they ought to have pulled Murray out long before'),[12] but it is not clear if this actually occurred. Possibly he was offered a break or even the option of going home, but declined; 'strongly object to the "done enough" idea,' he wrote in a letter a few months later. In any case, the 13th Battalion as a whole came out of the line at the end of August.

Two months earlier, Murray and his young friend and admirer, Lieutenant George McDowell, had discussed the factors which kept them going in the trenches. They agreed that the main ones were: 'righteousness of the cause; love of country and loved ones at home' and 'love of Battalion'. For them — and this point is made by other AIF soldiers — the battalion was not just the present living members, but also those who had died under its colours — 'their spirits live and are a motive power.' Both officers also agreed that their reasons for joining up in the first place were 'altogether another batch and more superficial.'[13]

Murray's reputation as one of the AIF's outstanding fighters was, of course, well established by now, particularly in the 4th Division, and it is no exaggeration to say that he was the 13th Battalion's unquestioned hero. It was said that when men of other battalions encountered those of the 13th, one of the first questions asked was 'Murray killed yet?' to be answered with 'No, still going strong,' followed by a story of some new exploit, real or imagined.[14] Among the troops, there would often be comparisons made between Murray and Jacka, much as the cricket followers among them might have debated the relative merits of, say, Victor Trumper and Clem Hill as batsmen.

On 1 September, the 13th was rotated back to the rear to camp around Lisbourg, supposedly for a long rest. In the event, the rest only lasted two weeks, time enough for some sporting events, and for a 'strenuous but splendid musketry and Lewis gun course arranged by Murray,' in his capacity as Battalion Musketry Officer. The battalion historian later said that Murray 'trained the Battalion to as perfect a state of efficiency with the rifle as any battalion ever was trained … No prize marksmanship about their training, no special sight or gauges, but every contest under active service conditions … Any platoon could charge across a hundred yards of rough country, take cover, fix sights and open out on any target that might suddenly appear for a few seconds on any part of their front.'[15] Seven months later, at a place called

Hebuterne, the 13th would see the practical results of this training.

Unexpected orders to move forward again put a sudden end to the 13th's brief rest. After a passage through 'filthy billets [and] filthier farms,' the battalion struggled through mud and heavy enemy shelling to reach their front-line position near Zonnebeke in the vicinity of Ypres on 23 September. The 4th Brigade played its part in the Battle of Polygon Wood on 26 September. The 13th Battalion again found itself in support to the brigade's other battalions, following closely behind them in their attack in the northern part of the battle area, digging communication trenches through to captured positions and mopping up German posts bypassed by the assaulting units. Support duties were no easy task; in a few hours, the 13th suffered 66 casualties out of 400 men in action, mostly from the German artillery. The battalion was relieved that night, and marched back by stages to the Ypres Canal, south of the city. Arriving around midnight, the weary men found that a hot meal had been organised by Murray. With his usual care for the troops' welfare, he also made several journeys to find and guide a number of stragglers, lost in the maze of winding tracks leading to the camp area.

In early October came another rotation back to the forward area. Here the battalion suffered its first serious gas attack on 15 October, in which most of the men were affected by the poison gas to some degree. Then followed another spell in the front-line trenches. The 4th Division was to play a supporting role on the right flank of the series of desperate attacks in appalling conditions in front of the village of Passchendaele. The British offensive petered out in the Flanders mud, leaving both sides too exhausted to do much more than hold their positions as the winter approached. However, it seemed that the 4th Division would at last get its often-promised long rest in the rear.

From the Passchendaele battlefield, the 13th made its way to its allocated rest area at Woincourt, near Dieppe: an initial march of sixteen kilometres, then sixty kilometres by train, another fifty in buses, and a further week's marching. Here they found uncomfortable billets, and Murray went around the district, accompanied by Lieutenant T A White as interpreter,[16] in an attempt to obtain supplies of straw for the men's bedding and places for baths and stables. The mayor of the district at first assumed that Murray was a sergeant, and refused to believe that he was a major and second-in-command of the unit. 'When enlightened he was astonished,' White later wrote,[17] 'saying that an English sergeant-major once billeted there had far more shiny buttons, stripes and badges than Murray, who was dressed like a Digger, except for the dark crown on each shoulder, a Sam Browne [the distinctive belt worn by officers, with a strap over one shoulder], and his VC, DSO (bar) and DCM ribbons. The *maire*'s idea of rank was the amount of shine, colour and gold braid.'

During November, Murray had another short stint as acting CO of the battalion. Yet another change of orders followed within eight days of the 'rest' period commencing; the 4th Division was suddenly sent up to Peronne, where a German counterattack after the Battle of Cambrai had broken through the British front. Here the division formed the reserve for the armies on that front, but the danger passed without the need to throw it into battle again. It remained in the area however, and as winter advanced the troops were occupied with training and working on improvements to the defences. It was at this time that the 13th's highly respected CO, Lieutenant-Colonel Durrant, was posted away from the battalion to a staff job in the 2nd Division. Douglas Marks was promoted to lieutenant-colonel and took permanent command of the battalion. This brilliant young officer was still only 22 years and 7 months of age at this time, and he led the 13th with great distinction for the rest of the war.

An important organisational change took place for the AIF at the end of 1917. Hitherto the five Australian divisions had been grouped with the New Zealand Division and several British divisions to form I and II Anzac Corps. The British high command now agreed to the Australian government's request for the five divisions to be combined into a single Australian Corps. It had originally been proposed to disband the veteran 4th Division, which was the most weakened by casualties, and use its personnel to reinforce the others. This expedient was avoided by a scheme to retain the 4th as a 'depot' division in reserve, rotating with other divisions depending on which suffered the most casualties in action. The 4th Division thus avoided disbandment, to the relief of those of its members who were aware of the proposal, and in the event all five divisions were thrown into the climactic fighting of 1918. The Australian Corps came into being in the new year, under the command of General William Birdwood.

Early in January 1918, a memorandum from Birdwood was circulated through the AIF seeking volunteers for an exotic and mysterious adventure. In the chaotic military situation in the East that followed the Russian Revolution, most of the Russian forces keeping the Turks out of Persia were withdrawn. A plan was devised to send a cadre of officers and NCOs from the British forces to provide leadership to the local population and some Russian remnants resisting any Turkish advance in the area, and volunteers were sought particularly from the Dominion armies in France. Birdwood's circular to the Australians mentioned Murray specifically as an example of the type of officer being sought, and hinted that Murray himself might volunteer. Although he had undoubtedly needed a break from the strain of battle earlier in the year, Murray, bored and restless with the comparative inactivity of the previous months ('Have been very sick of things lately, done nothing since August and not much then,' he wrote to Cyril Longmore about this time), immediately nominated for the new force. Despite his original encouragement however, Birdwood now reversed himself and vetoed the release of Murray and three other officers who had volunteered — Albert Jacka, and the two Maxwell brothers, the brilliant Tasmanian giants from the 13th Brigade. Murray may have felt that he had 'done nothing since August', but it had been enough to earn him his second Mention in Dispatches, published in January 1918.

Murray's disappointment at missing the Persian expedition was assuaged to some extent when he was granted five weeks 'Blighty' leave on 12 January. He took the opportunity to again visit Scotland and Hattonburn House, a Scottish winter no deterrent to the prospect of spending more time with the Montgomery family and enjoying the close companionship of Clementine. Relaxing on the estate — 'this is a lovely place, right on the banks of Loch Leven ... and our hostess is one of the very best women that the Empire has produced' — he would return refreshed to the front in mid-February 1918.

There he would soon face not only a dramatically altering military situation, but a significant turn in his career. As he wrote to Longmore (incidentally hinting at a possible reason for Birdwood's veto on his Persian ambitions): 'There's some talk of a command.'

Chapter 10

COMMANDING OFFICER

At the end of his leave, Murray returned to the Continent and rejoined his unit. During January, the 13th had been moved back up north to Flanders, initially to Bailleul again and then into the front line. The sector remained quiet, and Colonel Marks took the opportunity to go on leave himself early in March, Murray taking over as acting battalion commander. The usual rotations between front line and reserve continued, and the battalion moved back to billets around the village of Neuve Eglise on 2 March. Here the 4th Brigade occupied the time with a sports competition, although the area was still within range of German artillery, and the intermittent shelling caused a number of casualties. The troops were all aware that the lack of action would not continue for much longer — none doubted that the Germans would soon be launching a massive assault on the Allied armies.

With the collapse of Russia at the end of 1917, Germany was able to transfer large numbers of troops and guns from the Eastern Front to reinforce its armies in France. In early 1918, the Germans held a numerical superiority on the Western Front, but they were well aware that this would not last for

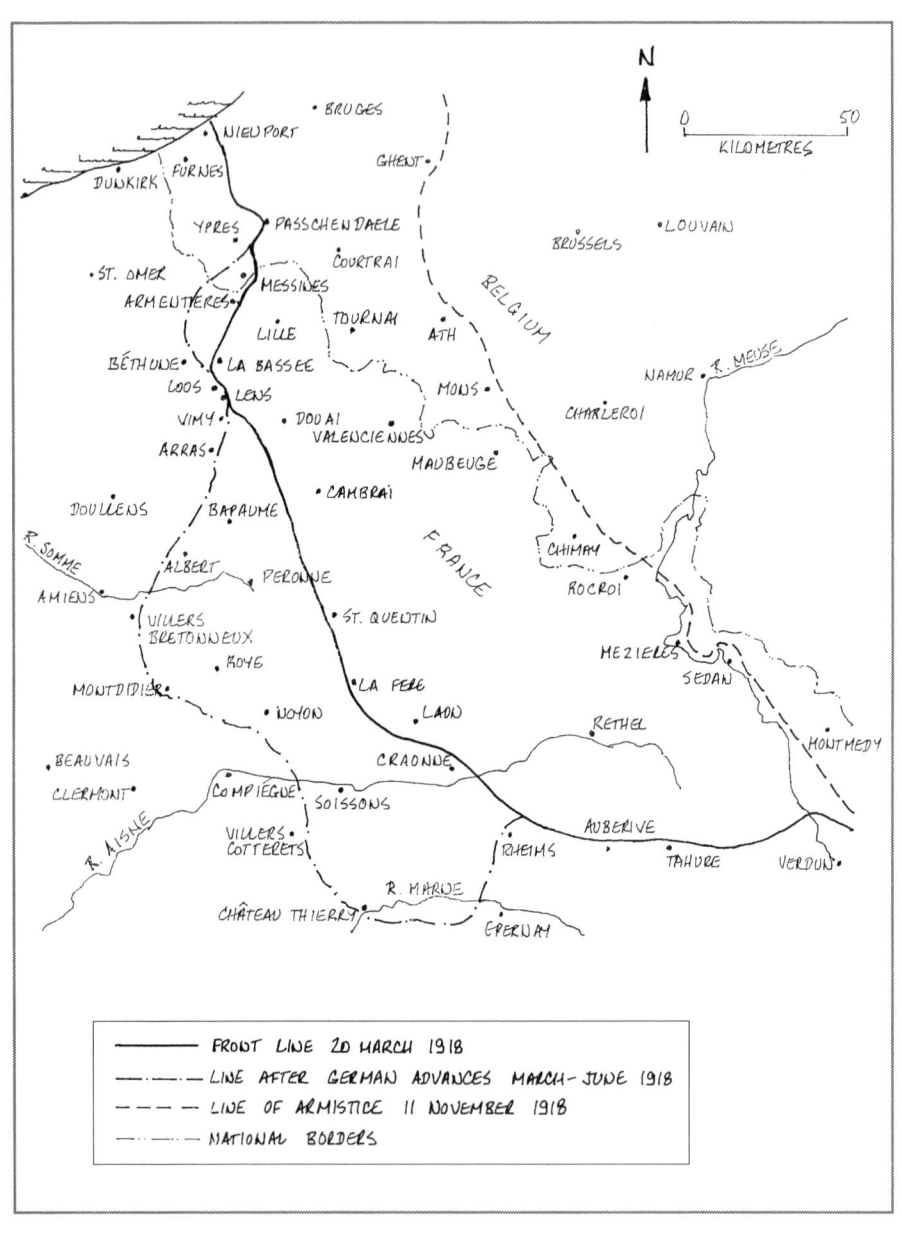

N

0 _____ 50
KILOMETRES

- BRUGES
NIEUPORT
FURNES
DUNKIRK
GHENT •
YPRES • PASSCHENDAELE
• LOUVAIN
BRUSSELS
• ST. OMER   COURTRAI
ARMENTIERES • MESSINES
LILLE   TOURNAI   ATH
BÉTHUNE • • LA BASSEE
LOOS   LENS   MONS •
VIMY •   • DOUAI   CHARLEROI
ARRAS •   VALENCIENNES
          MAUBEUGE •
DOULLENS   BAPAUME   • CAMBRAI
R. SOMME   ALBERT •
AMIENS •   PERONNE   CHIMAY
• VILLERS   ROCROI
  BRETONNEUX   • ST. QUENTIN
  • ROYE   MEZIERES
MONTDIDIER •   SEDAN
      • NOYON   • LAON
BEAUVAIS •   CRAONNE   RETHEL   MONTMEDY
CLERMONT •   COMPIEGNE
R. AISNE   SOISSONS
VILLERS •   AUBERIVE
COTTERETS •   RHEIMS   TAHURE   VERDUN •
        R. MARNE
CHÂTEAU THIERRY •   EPERNAY

BELGIUM

FRANCE

NAMUR • R. MEUSE

FRONT LINE 20 MARCH 1918
LINE AFTER GERMAN ADVANCES MARCH–JUNE 1918
LINE OF ARMISTICE 11 NOVEMBER 1918
NATIONAL BORDERS

The Western Front in 1918. German offensives and Allied counteroffensives.

long. The United States had been steadily building up and modernising its forces since entering the war in 1917, and the first American troops were now beginning to appear in France. It was only a matter of time before the American trickle became a flood and the defeat of Germany would be a certainty. A decisive attack in the early months of 1918 was Germany's best chance to force a victory in the war before the odds turned finally against them. It was clear to all that the supreme crisis of the war was approaching — the only question was where and when it would occur.

In the meantime, steady developments in machine-gun tactics led to a key reorganisation in the British and Empire armies — the final separation of the heavy machine-guns from the infantry units. With the lighter Lewis guns now providing fire-power for the infantry companies in close combat, the Vickers guns were being used increasingly for long-range support of attacks. Batteries of these guns were now positioned to lay down curtains of fire on the enemy's lines as an adjunct to artillery, as well as their traditional task of providing concentrated firepower in defensive positions. In 1916, a machine-gun company equipped with sixteen guns had been attached to each of the three infantry brigades in each division; shortly afterwards, each division had formed a fourth company, directly under control of the divisional headquarters. This made a total of 64 guns and their crews per division. In early 1918, the final step was taken of combining each division's four companies into a machine-gun ('MG') battalion, commanded by a lieutenant-colonel; this officer would thus control all the division's machine-guns and report directly to the general commanding the division. The new machine-gun battalions were numbered according to their division number, and the officer appointed to command the 4th Australian Machine Gun Battalion was Harry Murray, who was promoted to temporary lieutenant-colonel on 15 March 1918.

Murray's achievement in rising to this rank from private was very rare in the British Empire forces during the war. There were a few other AIF soldiers who also accomplished this — Norman Marshall and Maurice Wilder-Neligan are two examples. The former was a well-known sporting champion before the war, and the latter a well-educated Englishman of some wealth: backgrounds that gave both these brilliant soldiers something of a head start in reaching command rank.[1] Murray had been an unknown rural working man when he had enlisted three years and six months before ('the sleeper-cutter colonel', a post-war newspaper called him) and it was nothing more than the revelation of his extraordinary abilities that had brought about his advancement.

Murray now began the task of setting up the organisation of his new unit, prior to its officially coming into being. He did not immediately break away from the 13th Battalion however, continuing to administer command of that unit as well, pending Marks' return from leave. Other events suddenly took priority: on 21 March, General Ludendorff launched the long-expected German offensive on the Western Front. The British Army should not have been surprised, but it was; differences between British Prime Minister Lloyd George and his commander-in-chief, Sir Douglas Haig, over strategy for 1918, had delayed the dispatch of reinforcements to the front, leaving the British spread too thinly. At the same time, the French and British commands had only recently been able to reach some sort of agreement on joint plans. Some preparations had been made to meet the German attack, but these proved to be inadequate against new German tactics which included the use of specially trained storm troops to carry out deep penetrations into the opposing defences.

The enemy assault hit the British line where it was particularly weak, in the sector occupied by the British Third and Fifth Armies. After a short, crushing bombardment, the Germans stormed through the British positions and forced a gap between the two opposing armies, through which the main German force began to roll. Two hundred and fifty square kilometres of ground had been lost by the end of the first day, an enormous area by comparison with earlier battles. For the first time in the war, the British front was broken and the Allies were facing disaster. A hundred kilometres to the north, the news began to reach the Australian Corps over the next few days. They heard of the rapid German advance with amazement and disbelief — within days, the enemy had recaptured ground that had previously been taken from them only after many months of dreadful fighting, in which the Australian sacrifice was at least as great as that of any other part of the Allied forces. Hearing the names of familiar villages back in the hands of the enemy again, the Australians were swept with a burning enthusiasm to get back to the south and get into the fight. All sensed

Officers of the 13th Battalion in March 1918.
Major Harry Murray, acting CO, is in the centre of the front row.
(Australian War Memorial Neg Number E01728)

that this was a decisive time in the war, and they wanted to play their part in it.

There was not long to wait. Urgent orders arrived for the Australian Corps to begin moving south to close the gap in the line, with the 4th and 3rd Divisions first to leave. Murray issued a detailed movement order for the 13th Battalion on 24 March, and with the rest of the 4th Brigade as the spearhead of their division, the troops set off in a convoy of trucks early the next day. After several changes of orders during the day, the 4th Brigade troops found themselves heading towards the village of Hebuterne, on the edge of the old Somme battlefield, where another German breakthrough was rumoured. It was during this movement that the famous scenes occurred when French villagers, hastily preparing to flee from the advancing Germans, went back to their homes when they realised that the Australians had arrived. Leaving their vehicles a few miles short of Hebuterne, the brigade spent the night billeted in various small villages, setting out on foot for the battle zone the next day, 26 March.

Lieutenant-Colonel Marks, hastening back from leave, caught up with the 13th Battalion at Laherliere village about midday and resumed command from Murray, who remained with the battalion for the time being. By now, rumours spoke of German armoured cars or tanks advancing unchecked beyond Hebuterne. The Australians found themselves the only troops heading towards the front, while the roads were crowded with demoralised British troops in full retreat (some accounts say rout) in the opposite direction. These included a speeding carload of staff officers, greeted with a shower of disparaging comments from the Diggers as the vehicle roared past. Soon the forward troops of the 13th saw in the distance ahead some sort of vehicles coming along the road, apparently the dreaded tanks.

Murray decided to deal with this threat himself; he took charge of one of the 13th's platoons and led it on ahead, stationing the men on either side of the road to fire on the vehicles' crews. Murray himself moved a hundred metres further up the road to get a close look and give warning. At the last moment he realised that the supposed tanks were actually French farming machinery, and called to the men not to fire. With the tension temporarily relieved, the 4th Brigade continued its march to Hebuterne in high spirits, ready to meet the real German thrust, which would be upon them over the next few days.

This incident marked Murray's final departure from the 13th Battalion, and he now turned his full attention to his new command and its 800 men. The original machine-gun companies — the 4th, 12th and 13th companies, linked with the brigades of the same numbers, and the 24th Company controlled by 4th Division Headquarters — were, of course, fully operational in the combat zone already. The 4th Company in particular was working with the 4th Brigade infantry, and became heavily involved in the fighting on 27 and 28 March in front of Hebuterne. Here the brigade had dug in to meet the renewed enemy advance, with the formidable New Zealand Division holding the ridge on their right. Several massed attacks by the German infantry were swept away, mainly by the long-range rifle fire of the 13th and 15th Battalions — the 13th Battalion history credited their success largely to the musketry training Murray had conducted in the previous year. 'It is safe to say that fewer bullets were wasted at Hebuterne than at any other time in our history.' Machine-guns of the 4th Company broke up a marching German column at a range of 1500 metres during 27 March, and the next day the guns shattered an enemy party trying to attack the 15th Battalion's position.

By this time, the 4th Division had been temporarily split up. It had been intended that the 12th and 13th Brigades would move in behind the 4th Brigade in support, but an urgent order now arrived sending the 12th and 13th (with the divisional headquarters and artillery) marching thirty kilometres further south to meet another enemy advance in the country around the town of Albert. The 4th Brigade remained holding the line at Hebuterne, with the 4th Machine Gun Company in support. Murray's other three companies went south with the main body of the division, and although his own movements are not documented at this time, it seems likely that he accompanied them, given that his post was with the divisional headquarters. The weary troops of the two brigades reached their destination during the night of 27 March and dug in, their front-line posts occupying the line of a railway embankment between Albert and the village of Dernancourt, north of the River Ancre. From the railway, the ground sloped up to the Albert–Amiens road, with the supporting troops located on the face of the slope. The 12th Company's sixteen machine-guns were positioned amongst the infantrymen in the firing line.

The German assault began at dawn on 28 March, under a heavy artillery barrage. The Australian defences were briefly penetrated in several places, but the attackers were eventually beaten off. At one stage a strong German force advanced under cover almost up to the position of a 12th Company machine-gun, at the point where the right of the Australian line linked with a British brigade. The gun could not get at the enemy troops, so some of the gunners drew their revolvers and joined with the British to charge the German party, while others dragged the gun into a better position and opened up at point-blank range. The surviving Germans retreated in disorder to Dernancourt village, seeking cover in the houses, and the machine-gunners pursued them with fire that ripped through the flimsy walls. The German attack had failed all along the line, and the enemy force fell back for several hundred metres. For the rest of the day, the 12th Company gunners kept up harassing fire on any Germans who left cover. A party of enemy engineers trying to build a pontoon bridge over the River Ancre was cut to pieces by two of the 12th's guns. The fighting died down in the evening, with both sides exhausted.

Things were comparatively quiet around Dernancourt for the next few days, but the Germans kept up the pressure at many other points along the British zone, including another unsuccessful attack on the 4th Brigade at Hebuterne. The 13th Brigade moved into the line at Dernancourt alongside the 12th, and again the machine-gun companies were positioned to provide defensive fire-power. The Australian position at Dernancourt was a particularly difficult one to defend, with its broad exposed slope behind the front outposts; this was open to view from the German side, and the enemy could observe, and fire at, any movement of reserves in this area. Halfway up the slope, behind the 12th Brigade sector, were positioned two machine-gun batteries from the 24th Company, each with four guns, one in a quarry and the other in a trench. Open to enemy view as they were, the crews had been ordered to keep their heads down and the guns dismounted during daylight hours unless the Germans launched an attack. On the right, some of the 13th Company's guns had also been posted on the slope, with others at intervals along the infantry firing line.

During the lull, the Germans had built up their strength in front of Dernancourt to more than two divisions, and on the morning of 5 April this

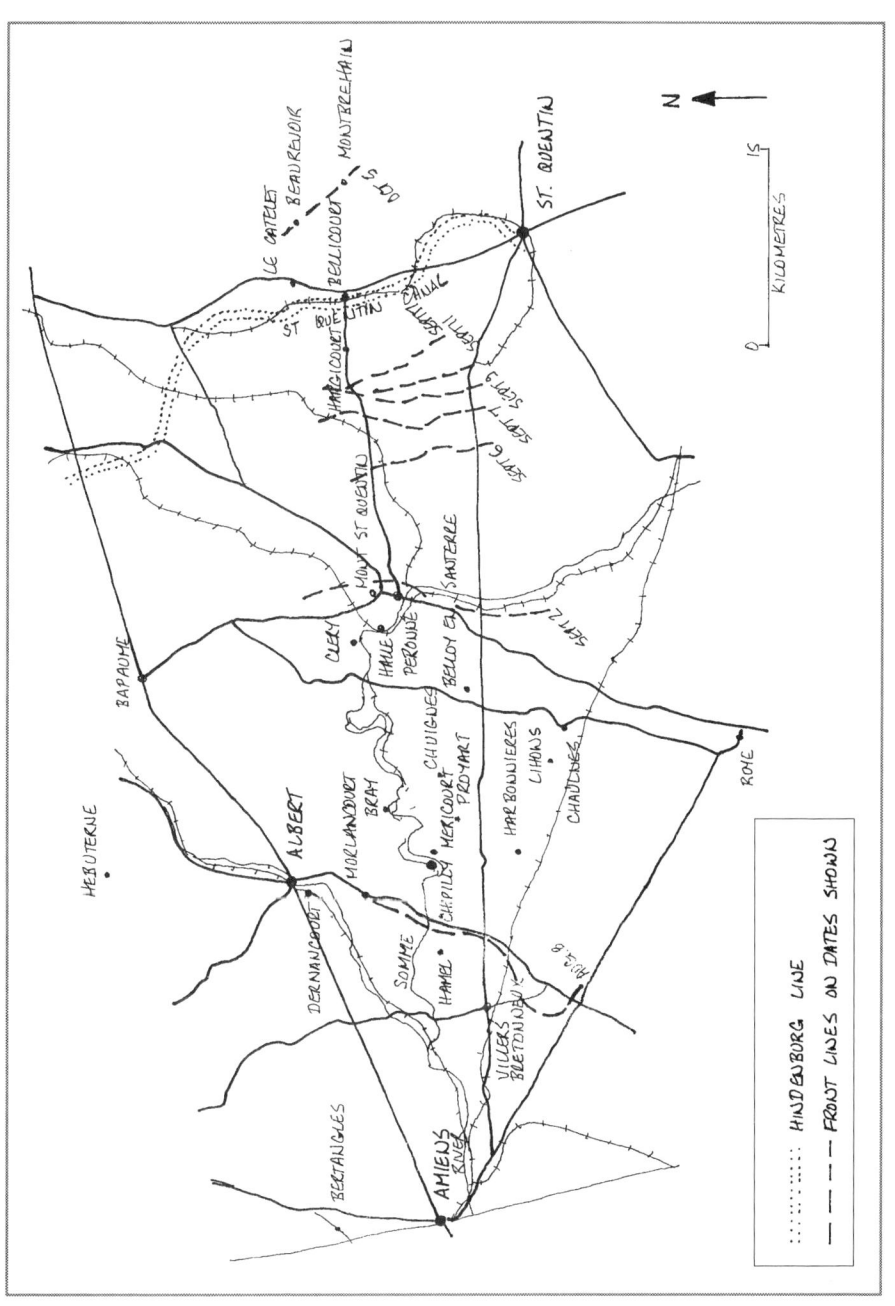

Area of operations of the Australian Corps, 1918.

force was hurled against the two Australian brigades in their precarious positions. The attack had been expected, but it was so powerful that the thin line of defenders was pushed far back up the hill, and the Germans came close to a complete breakthrough. A desperate counterattack by the Australian reserves stopped the enemy thrust after savage fighting, and the defenders managed to establish a new line near the top of the slope. The front was now stabilised, and the Germans made no further attempts in this sector.

The 4th Division machine-gunners experienced mixed fortunes in this battle. On the right, the 13th Company guns poured fire into the swarms of Germans in the first stage of the attack at the railway embankment, preventing them from making any progress on this flank of the battlefield. Two of its guns nearer the centre of the line were encircled and captured by the Germans later in the battle, after putting up considerable resistance. In contrast, both of the 24th Company's four-gun batteries on the slope were overrun by the enemy without firing a shot. The German artillery barrage and heavy covering fire from their machine-guns had kept the guns' crews under cover, and the morning fog hampered observation. The gunners had only realised at the last minute that enemy infantry were attacking, and before they could get their weapons set up for action, they had been surrounded and forced to surrender, the survivors of the crews being hustled off as prisoners. These machine-guns had been expected to block any attack in the centre of the position, and with their loss the way was open for the Germans to penetrate deep into the Australian line.

In the confusion of the battle, no-one on the Australian side was aware of exactly what had happened, and a story quickly spread that the battery of four guns in the quarry had been heard firing after being surrounded, and had fought to the death. Murray was at the battlefield during the morning and had apparently observed the surrender of the second battery in the trench on the slope, supposedly also after a gallant defence.[2] Hearing these reports, he somewhat unwisely passed the story on to the war correspondents without seeking confirmation, and it reached the newspapers in Australia. The *Sydney Morning Herald*'s version was typical: 'One group of four machine guns was seen fighting to the last, when the Germans actually swamped them, the men dying at their guns after inflicting terrible losses.'[3] The truth emerged nine days later when two of the captured gunners made a daring escape from the Germans and got back to the Australian lines where they made a full report on the circumstances of their capture.

No doubt the two captured batteries had faced considerable difficulties during the action, but the general feeling was that they had put up a rather feeble effort. The incident must have been something of a jolt for Murray; on the credit side, however, the rest of the 24th Company had fought well, and the other three machine-gun companies had performed with great effectiveness in the heavy fighting of the past week. All this had occurred before the new battalion had even been officially established, but by 7 April the unit's headquarters staff had been selected, and the 4th Australian Machine Gun Battalion came into existence a week later. It is of interest that the battalion's Regimental Sergeant-Major, John Dwyer, was also a Victoria Cross winner (and another Tasmanian). Few if any other units can have had VCs as both commanding officer and RSM.

The forming of the AIF's machine-gun battalions did not happen without some degree of resentment from the original companies, who did not welcome the loss of their independent status and the breaking of their links with the infantry brigades. The history of the 6th Machine Gun Company (2nd Division)[4] frankly acknowledges this attitude, and Murray later wrote that 'as new battalions, the MG companies were not easy to weld together.' Murray did have several advantages coming into the command, however. In the first place, he was one of the personalities of the 4th Division, known at least by reputation to all personnel, and as an infantry leader he had worked closely with the 4th Company for the last two years. He was of course a former machine-gunner and machine-gun officer himself, a veteran of the 4th Brigade gunners' desperate fighting at Gallipoli, and some of his comrades from those days were still serving in the companies. These included a few of the original 16th section from the Blackboy Hill days (which must have seemed a lifetime away): Bert Sykes, Peter Grieveson and 'Tiny' Hatcher (wounded at Dernancourt) were lieutenants, and Paddy O'Brien was a company sergeant-major and would later become the battalion RSM after Dwyer was commissioned.

In the early days of his new command, Murray sought the advice of the 13th Brigade's commander, Brigadier-General William Glasgow, and afterwards paid tribute to the valuable guidance he received from this tough soldier (who was later promoted to major-general commanding the 1st Division, and knighted). Murray would have had a number of administrative tasks to attend to, assisted by his newly appointed headquarters staff. He spent some time assessing the loss of the guns at Dernancourt, and prepared a report with several recommendations for avoiding such incidents in future. A court of enquiry was held into the conduct of the battle, and Murray's notes may have been the basis for a bulletin on 'Tactical Handling of Machine Guns in Defensive Operations' issued by the General Staff in May 1918. His primary task, however, was the responsibility of ensuring that the 4th Division's machine-guns fulfilled their tasks in battle.

The tactics for using these weapons had developed steadily during the years of the war. From being initially just a part of each infantry unit, they were now regarded as a distinct branch of the service, similar to artillery and engineers. Their primary role remained the support of the infantry, but employed according to the plans of the divisional general and under the orders of the machine-gun battalion commander. By 1918 tactics had evolved for the use of machine-guns in massed batteries to support large-scale attacks, deluging the enemy's back areas with showers of bullets and interfering with the movement of reserves and supplies — something the 4th Brigade machine-gunners had attempted at Hill 60 on Gallipoli in 1915 with the small numbers of guns available then. In a defensive situation, again it was the division that would now decide the disposition of the guns according to an integrated plan.

There remained many tactical situations where individual infantry units needed the immediate support of machine-guns in attack and defence, and sections of guns continued to be attached to battalions and brigades, while still being ultimately responsible to the machine-gun battalion commander. In these situations, the records indicate that wherever possible Murray made sure that each of his machine-gun companies continued to work with its original infantry brigade, something that was apparently not always done in the other machine-gun battalions. MG battalion colonels were faced with

Three Tasmanians of the 4th Division, April 1918.
Harry Murray, newly promoted to lieutenant-colonel, with the Maxwell brothers,
Captains Duncan (left) and Arthur. Despite his high rank, Murray is wearing a private
soldiers' jacket with a minimum of officers' accoutrements.
Duncan Maxwell was 6 ft 3 in (190 cm) tall, his brother 6 ft 5 in (195 cm).
(Australian War Memorial Neg Number E02234)

something of a balancing act to make sure their resources were properly used in the battle zone, and much attention was paid to developing close liaison between the various levels of command. Murray and his staff were also responsible for matters of transport, signals, supply, training, and promotions and discipline for the battalion as a whole.

Handling machine-guns in action was not just a matter of pointing the gun in the general direction of the enemy and blazing away; there were a number of technical issues involved, particularly with long-range barrage fire. Often a battery of guns would be firing over the heads of the infantry, the bullets following a curving trajectory to strike the target area in the enemy lines. The gun crews, particularly the section officers, needed to work out the right aiming point and elevation for their guns using maps, compasses, clinometers for measuring angles, and rangefinders. The remarkable accuracy of the Vickers gun meant that once it was set up correctly, its fire was sure to fall in the planned area even if the target was not actually visible, a situation referred to as 'indirect fire'.

Murray may have been a little rusty on the finer points of machine-gun work, and he had been scheduled during April to attend a training course in England, but these orders were soon cancelled — perhaps it was realised that there was not, after all, very much he needed to learn. In any case, he had plenty to occupy his time in France. The battered 4th Division was taken out of the front line for a welcome rest after Dernancourt, and moved into the area between Amiens and Villers-Bretonneux, although the division's infantry brigades remained separated during most of April, as did Murray's four machine-gun companies. During this period, the 24th Company ensured that it would be remembered in history for something other than the unfortunate episode at Dernancourt. One of the 24th's guns, set up for anti-aircraft work, was firing when the German ace pilot Manfred von Richthofen, the Red Baron, was shot down and killed on 21 April. Although the identity of the Baron's conqueror has been a matter of controversy ever since, the 24th's claim is the most credible.[5]

On 24 April a renewed German attack captured Villers-Bretonneux village, a key position which opened the way to the major city of Amiens. The 13th Brigade was brought up to join the 15th Brigade (5th Division) in an immediate counterattack, and the Australian force won a brilliant victory on Anzac Day 1918. Some of Murray's machine-guns from the 13th and 24th companies took part in the battle, providing fire support to the infantry in the recaptured ground. In the aftermath of the battle, the now-reunited 4th Division took over the front line around Villers-Bretonneux and began to turn the ruined village and its environs into a fortress against any further enemy attacks. Murray finally had all his sub-units together and was able to fully exert his control over the whole battalion. He took a personal role in the layout of the battalion's guns in the defensive trench lines, and particularly in siting guns in the village itself. His reports show the care he took with this exercise, and his attention to detail in selecting positions and laying out lines of fire.

Battalion headquarters was established at Glisy, a few kilometres to the rear, but Murray spent much of his time up at the line visiting his gunners in their positions. With the roads and paths in reasonable condition, he usually rode a bicycle most of the way; his old battalion, the 13th, was stationed in the sector, and Captain T A White of the 13th wrote of often seeing Murray cycling past in his shirtsleeves in the pleasant weather.[6] One young gunner, Private Jim Knight, was stationed on the railway embankment south-east of the village, from which his team was delivering harassing fire into the German lines, when Murray visited their position. Many years later, Knight recalled the incident. The gunners noticed Murray and the battalion chaplain picking their way up through the shell-holes; apparently some type of enemy fire came down in the vicinity, and Murray was among those who ducked.

> He said to me, 'Pretty warm [dangerous] up there boys?'
> And I said: 'It must be warm when a VC ducks!'
> 'Look, me boy,' he said, 'I'm no gamer than you are, only when I've got to be.'[7]

There in a nutshell was Murray's attitude to his own exploits. This exchange also shows that he took no offence at a little banter from subordinates, and that he was not as reluctant to show a natural reaction to danger as he had been in the previous year.

The Australian Corps (except for the 1st Division defending Hazebrouck in the north) was now holding the right of the British line, linking up with the French sector of the front. The troops of the 4th Division in and around Villers-Bretonneux were eager for the Germans to try another attack, confident that their defences were a hornet's nest that would beat off anything the enemy could throw at them. In this area however, the Germans confined themselves to artillery bombardments, including a high proportion of gas shells. The next big enemy assault in fact fell on the French army well to the south. Again the Allies were taken by surprise, and again the Germans achieved a spectacular breakthrough, but again they were unable to maintain the pressure and the assault eventually petered out.

The only major action around Villers-Bretonneux at this time was an unsuccessful attack by the 12th Brigade on Monument Wood to the south of the village, and the 12th Machine Gun Company provided covering fire for the infantry in this operation. Shortly afterwards, the 4th Division was relieved by the 3rd and moved to the rear for a short rest in reserve positions. Returning to the front line early in June, the division took over the sector a little to the north of Villers-Bretonneux, opposite the German-occupied village of Hamel. Murray's rank of lieutenant-colonel had been made permanent on 24 May. His activities during this period included introducing an American machine-gun officer to the front line, and enforcing discipline among the battalion's officers. The battalion diary mentions that he 'severely censured' a junior officer for misbehaviour when out of the line, and two others seem to have been court-martialled for other lapses.

A change in command of the Australian Corps had just occurred: General Birdwood had been promoted to command the Fifth Army, and the corps now had an Australian-born commander in Lieutenant-General John Monash. The new commander had overcome the handicaps of a background that was both Jewish and German, and of not being a professional career soldier, to reach this position. Monash was anxious to resume the offensive against the enemy. Since Villers-Bretonneux the Australians had been involved in a few minor actions, and all units had been chipping away at the German positions through the aggressive skirmishing that they called 'peaceful penetration'. Monash's fertile

*A post of Murray's 4th Machine Gun Battalion (24th Company) near
Villers-Bretonneux, May 1918. (The gun is covered by the tarpaulin.)*
(Australian War Memorial Neg Number E02305)

mind now formed a scheme for a larger operation to capture Hamel village and the area surrounding it; the operation would use infantry brigades from several divisions, controlled by the 4th Division staff.

The plan developed by Monash and his staff represented a significant advance in battlefield technique. For the first time, infantry, artillery, aircraft, machine-guns and tanks would work together in a fully coordinated operation. The tanks had come a long way since their disastrous performance at Bullecourt; the Australian infantry still distrusted them, but demonstrations of their improved reliability and tactics soon produced a more positive attitude. Supporting fire for the infantry attack included a large number of machine-guns, control of which would be the responsibility of the 4th Division, and hence of Harry Murray as CO of the 4th Machine Gun Battalion. Murray was briefed on the operation at a divisional conference on 25 June. His first task was to prepare an outline plan for the disposition of the guns, which would also include the 5th Machine Gun Battalion, temporarily under his control to double the available firepower. The outline was duly approved by division headquarters the next day, and Murray and his staff set to work on the detailed planning and preparation for the battle.

The plan called for the positioning of 32 machine-guns near Bouzencourt in the northern sector of the battle-line; the location of the opposing front lines meant that these guns would be able to fire 'in enfilade' along the German lines in the objective area. Murray spent most of 26 June selecting sites for these guns, and the next day conferred with the infantry brigades and Australian Corps Headquarters to firm up on details of the operation. On 27 July, he went with his transport officer to check the routes to the selected battery positions, and working parties began the necessary digging for the gun emplacements. Next day the battalion's horse-drawn limbers began moving up material and supplies. By the evening of 30 June, each gun position had been prepared for its occupants, with ammunition (half a million rounds altogether), camouflage equipment and a reserve of water for the guns.

Murray had been anxious to get this work out of the way well before the planned 'zero day' (4 July) to avoid congestion on the roads at crucial times. Aside from the new battery positions, other guns were to give covering fire from the existing front-line positions, and more would advance with the infantry units to provide direct support. Murray had been forced to make some changes to his original plans when he was informed that the 5th Machine Gun Battalion could not after all be made available. He was allotted, however, several gun sections from other battalions to make up some of the shortfall. All together, Murray would have a total of 112 machine-guns and their crews under his command for the operation. On 30 June, he attended the major conference of all commanders at Australian Corps Headquarters, where he had his first experience of one of Monash's lucid, detailed command briefings (there were 133 items on the agenda for this meeting).

Among the innovations of Monash's Hamel plan — which was something of a watershed in planning and became the model for the Allies in future battles — several affected the machine-guns: aircraft would be used to drop extra ammunition by parachute, and more ammunition and some of the forward guns would be transported by tanks. The 4th Machine Gun Battalion's final orders were issued the next day, accompanied by detailed task-maps for the subordinate commanders. Murray had spent as much time as possible during the previous few days visiting his companies in the line, ensuring everyone was kept up to date on the battle plans, and that all tasks were fully understood. He made his final rounds on the evening of 3 July, making sure all was in readiness for 'zero' — 3.10 on the following morning. The Australian Corps' policy statement on the machine-gun organisation commented that 'the machine-gun battalion commander must be a real "live" commander who makes his presence felt at all times,' and Murray was certainly living up to that requirement.

The Hamel offensive got under way on schedule, the infantry (including some American troops attached to Australian units) advancing behind a crashing artillery barrage, with Murray's machine-guns providing support with their showers of bullets. The tanks and aircraft worked together with the infantry according to plan (a few tanks carrying supplies did the work of many hundreds of soldiers), and the attack was completely successful. The Germans were overwhelmed by the rapid, coordinated advance and the Australians captured all of their objectives almost exactly according to schedule. The 4th Machine Gun Battalion played its part in the success, the barrage guns firing off 177,000 rounds into their various targets in the initial stage, and the 'forward' guns taking part in several combats as they moved up with the advancing infantry. The 4th Brigade led the infantry advance in the southern sector, and Lieutenant Rule of the 14th Battalion recorded a number of incidents showing how the forward guns were employed.[8] Concerned about a threat to the left flank of his platoon at one stage, Rule called on a Vickers gun to provide covering fire. Later, facing some resistance from a German post, he arranged for two more guns to be sent up and positioned to sweep open ground and keep the enemy's heads down (one of the gunners was killed by a sniper during this skirmish).

Following the main fighting, the captured ground was consolidated, and a number of the machine-guns were positioned to cover the new line in the captured position, opening fire several times on suspected enemy counterattacks. Apart from some skirmishing, the Battle of Hamel was over — 'the most up-to-date battle ever fought' enthused the 13th Battalion history — and the units engaged were soon rotated to the rear for a few weeks rest. Murray had done well in his first battle as a battalion commander, and he could be well satisfied with the performance of his unit; all of their tasks had been performed smoothly and effectively, at comparatively low cost in casualties — five killed and twenty-eight wounded. Murray prepared several pages of notes after the battle, highlighting a number of issues that had emerged from the experience. He took the opportunity of mentioning some items that appear to have been contentious when the battalion was first set up, in particular the centralised control of the transport facilities, the advantages of which he 'again insisted upon'.

Murray produced a number of these 'Lessons Learnt' papers after each period of intensive action.[9] Presumably distributed to the battalion officers, they contain succinct, clear statements (mainly of a technical nature) outlining those aspects of the operations that had proven particularly successful and aspects where he considered improvements or extra training were needed. He continued to spend as much time as possible with the front-line troops and officers, visiting each of the battalion's companies regularly. Although he was 'making his presence felt', Murray's reports show his satisfaction with subordinates using initiative and making their own decisions on the spot. He seems to have asserted his authority and his own ideas firmly at the beginning, then eased the pressure once he was satisfied that the battalion was responding as he wished.

During this period in reserve, Murray amused himself with some hunting to supplement the officers' mess rations. The wrecked buildings of 'Toute Suite Farm' in the Australian lines were home to hundreds of pigeons; Murray had managed to acquire a double-barrelled shotgun, and he was observed bringing down the birds two at a time. The area was under frequent German artillery fire, and he would wait until a bursting shell drove the pigeons into the air before firing. This type of activity, incidentally, had been indulged in by troops of the 13th Brigade earlier in the year, when it was regarded as a breach of discipline! It may have been at this time that Captain Cyril Longmore, former instructor sergeant-major at Blackboy Hill, called in on his star pupil. Murray introduced Longmore to the battalion officers with the words, 'Gentlemen, I heard one of you say the other night that no man had ever put the wind up your colonel. Let me introduce to you the man who put the wind up me at Blackboy Hill.'[10]

The pause in serious combat was short-lived, and the 4th Machine Gun Battalion began preparing for its part in the next round of operations, scheduled for early August. The coming battle would be among the most decisive of the war. The Allied high command, now unified under Marshal Foch, was planning a major counteroffensive against the Germans. The British part of the plan involved an advance along both sides of the Somme river, and the Commander-in-Chief, Sir Douglas Haig, chose the Australian and Canadian Corps to form the spearhead of his attack. By now all five divisions of the Australian Corps were located together, the 1st Division having finally been relieved of its tasks in the north to join the rest of the corps. The new offensive would follow the techniques developed in the action at Hamel, although this time on a much larger scale: infantry moving forward rapidly behind a sudden overwhelming artillery barrage, which would 'creep' just ahead of the infantry as they advanced; tanks and aircraft working closely with the foot soldiers; and massed machine-guns harassing the enemy's rear areas, the whole operation working to a clear, detailed plan. The days of static warfare in the dreadful squalor of the trenches were over, and the war was now becoming one of comparatively open movement. The soldiers still used picks and shovels as often as rifles, but their digging was now more to provide temporary shelter while preparing for the next advance.

The Australian Corps, as part of General Rawlinson's Fourth Army, would advance westwards in two waves with its left on the Somme. The Canadian Corps would be on the right of the Australians, with a British corps on their left, on the northern bank of the Somme. The 4th Division was in the second wave of the Australian attack; it would leapfrog the 3rd Division once the latter had secured the German front line, and push ahead to the line of the final objective, well in the enemy's rear. For the 4th Machine Gun Battalion, its tasks in this operation were mainly direct support of the 4th Division infantry brigades. Most of the machine-guns would advance with the infantry, using packhorses and limbers for transport. A number of guns would also be carried by tanks, to support the infantry pushing on to the final objective. The initial machine-gun barrage would be provided by the 3rd Division, and sixteen of Murray's guns were allocated to reinforce the 3rd's batteries for the first forty minutes of the battle, after which they would be attached to the reserve infantry.

The Battle of Amiens began at 4.30 am on 8 August 1918 when over 2000 Allied artillery pieces opened fire 'almost with a single crash' and the waiting infantrymen rose to their feet and started forward. Those troops of the 4th Division who had been members of the original 4th Brigade may well have thought back to the fighting at Gallipoli three years before to the day (indeed almost to the hour), when the sick, exhausted men had been driven back from the assault on Hill 971, and Lieutenant Black, Sergeant Murray and their comrades of the old 4th Brigade machine-gun sections had arrived in time to prevent complete disaster. The situation was very different on this 8 August, as the tough, confident, well-trained troops moved steadily into the attack, supported by the latest battlefield technology and efficient headquarters planning.

The experienced veterans in the Australian ranks had by this stage of the war developed a ruthless efficiency on the battlefield. They had the canniness and caution to make sure that it was the enemy who died rather than themselves; at the same time, they instinctively knew when the tactical situation demanded the taking of extreme personal risks to turn the scales, and they had the confidence and morale to take those risks. The Australian units were never at full strength during 1918, but their effectiveness would be out of all proportion to their numbers in battle. On this day, the German lines crumbled before the devastating assault, in what the German commander Ludendorff later called the 'black day' of his army, when whole units collapsed for the first time in the war. By sunset the attackers had penetrated fifteen kilometres into the German positions and captured thousands of prisoners and hundreds of artillery pieces.

The attack did not go entirely according to plan along the whole battle front, however, and it so happened that the 4th Brigade faced the most difficult task in the Australian Corps on 8 August. The brigade formed the extreme left of the second wave, advancing along the south bank of the Somme to penetrate deep into the German position. Of Murray's machine-gunners, sections of the 4th and 24th companies moved forward with the infantry, with other sections of the 12th Company supporting the 12th Brigade in the centre of the Australian line. More guns of all companies would come up in reserve for the final stage of the advance, some being carried by tanks. Guns of the former two companies gave covering fire for the battalions advancing on Cerisy village, which was duly captured with the aid of several tanks. On emerging beyond the village, however, the troops suddenly came under close-range fire from German artillery and machine-guns positioned on the other side of the river. The ground in this sector was supposed to have been taken by the British 58th Division, but those troops, faced with very difficult terrain, had been unable to reach their objective. As a result, the Germans occupying the high ground of Chipilly ridge and village in a loop of the river were able to fire into the flank of the 4th Brigade as it moved past them, and even into the rear of the 16th Battalion advancing to the final objective.

The Australians were also held up at this point by more German machine-guns ahead of them, but they eventually fought their way past this obstacle, again with the aid of tanks. During this phase, one of the Australian machine-guns took on the German artillery across the river, and others rushed to the front line to fire on the enemy machine-guns ahead of the advance. The fire from the Chipilly heights continued to present a serious problem to the 4th Brigade, however.

Murray had moved his headquarters forward with the advance, setting out with a few of his staff on bicycles as soon as the morning fog had cleared, and they set themselves up in some former German dugouts. Word began to come through of the difficulties on the left flank, and Murray went up to the sector to assess the situation for himself. He had already issued orders to the sixteen guns of the 13th and 24th companies, which had finished their barrage tasks, to prepare to advance at short notice. In the early afternoon these gun teams moved up to the Somme bank on the 4th Brigade's left, and with four more (probably from the 4th Company) formed a defensive line facing north, spread over 3000 metres.

From this position, the machine-guns maintained heavy fire on the German artillery and machine-guns across the river, the Australians sometimes shooting at more than 2000 metres range. Enemy shells wrecked several of the Vickers guns and killed or wounded their crews, but the machine-gunners stuck to their task. Their shooting drove many of the German artillerymen away from their weapons, and Murray later reported that his gunners had gained 'complete superiority of fire'. They covered the advance of a number of mobile field guns, brought up at the gallop to engage in a grim duel with the German artillery. Further south, the machine-guns in support of the infantry advance were frequently in action (one gun crew of the 12th Company, scrambling from a blazing knocked-out tank, set up their weapon just in time to shatter a German counterattack).

By late afternoon the fighting had died down; all objectives south of the river had been taken, and the victorious troops reorganised to hold the captured ground, with the machine-guns now setting up for defence. Chipilly on the north bank of the Somme remained a problem, with the Germans still in possession of the high ground and the village. The area was eventually captured late on the evening of the next day. The American 131st Regiment overran the northern part of the ridge in a fine effort by inexperienced troops at the end of an exhausting march, but in front of the village a battalion of the 10th London Regiment hesitated in the face of the German machine-guns. At this juncture, a patrol of only six men from the 1st Australian Battalion, which was part of the Australian reserve, crossed the river and proceeded to silence the enemy machine-gun posts one after the other. This astonishing display of audacity cleared the way for the British force, its confidence restored, to occupy the village and the remainder of the ground enclosed by the river-bend. By this time, General Monash had been given overall control of the sector on the northern bank, and he now ordered a further advance to capture the high ground in the next loop of the river, around the village of Etinehem. This task was allotted to the 13th Brigade of the 4th Division, which crossed the river on the night of 10 August, encircled the village and occupied most of the objective ground. The 13th Machine Gun Company was rushed up from its defensive line at short notice (Murray later recommended the use of motorcycle dispatch riders for transporting urgent orders) to provide supporting fire for the brigade. The company went forward with the infantry in its advance, then dug in its guns as part of the defensive lines formed to hold the captured position. The guns fired off 10,000 rounds into the German-held areas during the night, and the next morning the Australian line was pounded by enemy artillery, one of the 13th's gun crews receiving a direct hit after its fire had scattered a large party of German infantry.

The remainder of the area was cleared of enemy troops over the next few days. The 13th Company was temporarily detached from the 4th MG Battalion to continue with the operations north of the river, the other three companies pulling back with the remainder of the 4th Division for a few days in reserve. Murray's battalion had been in the forefront of the battle and the unit's casualty total of ninety was higher than all but one of the division's seven infantry battalions engaged up to 14 August.[11] The week following the attack of 8 August had not seen the same spectacular success as the first day, owing to stiffening German resistance and a decline in the level of coordination between the Australians, Canadians and British. The advance continued however, and attacks by the French and Americans further south also gained much ground; the Germans were now in retreat all along the Western Front. In their sector, the divisions of the Australian Corps alternated in leading the advance, and after taking their turn at the front, the 4th Division units enjoyed a rest of two weeks before their next major action.

During its rest period, the 4th Machine Gun Battalion carried out routine training and refitting, and on 30 August held its first formal parade as a complete unit, the 13th Company having rejoined by then. Murray conducted a formal inspection of his command in an exercise that was probably a rehearsal for another parade held the next day, when the battalion was inspected by the divisional commander, Major-General Sinclair-MacLagan. A 'Church Parade' of the full battalion on 1 September completed the formalities, and the battalion made ready for its next stint in the front line, with the rest of the 4th Division. The Australian Corps had been pushing ahead steadily and by early September was approaching the Hindenburg Line, from which the Germans had launched the great offensives of March. Along the way, the 2nd Division had brilliantly captured the 'impregnable' German position of Mont St Quentin. Now the 4th and 1st Divisions would assault the formidable line of outposts protecting the main enemy bastion of the Hindenburg Line itself.

The 'Hindenburg Outpost Line' was an extensive system of earthworks, partly based on the old British trenches which had originally been constructed to oppose the true Hindenburg Line. It was strong enough to warrant a full-scale attack, and the Australians approached the task in much the same way as they had in the battles of the previous two months, with careful planning and coordination of all arms. For this attack, the number of tanks available was less than usual, owing to heavy losses in the earlier battles. To partly compensate for this, General Monash arranged for two more machine-gun battalions to join in the opening barrages; thus all 64 of the 5th Division's guns were employed to fire the barrage in the 4th Division's sector on the right (southern) flank, leaving most of Murray's 4th MG Battalion to work in close support of the infantry advance. Some of the 4th's guns would advance with the infantry to the line of the first objective, then set up as batteries to provide a secondary barrage covering the advance to the next objective. Aside from such differences in detail, the operations of the Australian Corps had become almost routine by now. As Edgar Rule of the 14th Battalion wrote,[12] 'Today we are having real victories, not like those we used to have, which cost us just as many men as they did the Hun. Our staff work today is such that victory is almost a foregone conclusion before we go over the parapet.'

In the days leading up to the battle, Murray continued his practice of frequent visits to the companies in the line, and held discussions with his company commanders to make sure they were fully briefed. On the night before the battle, he established an advanced headquarters for the battalion in a railway cutting almost at the front line. The battle began at 5.20 am on 18 September, in driving rain, with the artillery flinging its hail of shells into the German lines and '200 machine-guns ripping out with a single roar,' as the *Official History* described it. The combined barrage crept forward through the enemy positions, with the machine-guns sweeping 150 metres ahead of the shell-bursts, and the infantry following close behind.

Working their way forward through difficult country (this was the wilderness of the old Somme battlefield), the troops rapidly overran the German positions in the first two objective lines. Capturing the third and final objective presented some problems however, the Germans resisting fiercely. In the 4th Brigade's sector, this task fell to the 14th Battalion, but it appears that something went wrong with their supporting machine-guns at this point (the *Official History* notes that supporting fire for the 14th's attack was inadequate). The 14th managed to gain a foothold in their objective against heavy fire, but further progress was stalled. The 46th Battalion's attack further south had been held up also, and the high command decided to allow a pause for reorganising, followed by a renewed assault at 11 pm. An extemporised supporting barrage from artillery and machine-guns was ordered. The 4th MG Battalion received preliminary instructions in mid-afternoon, and Murray and his staff worked quickly to have detailed orders with the selected companies (the 13th and 24th) by 5 pm. The companies had positioned themselves in the front line by 9 pm, and joined with the artillery to cover the infantry advance two hours later. This time the troops, with a supreme effort, captured the enemy position, the demoralised Germans surrendering in droves. The final task for the weary men was the consolidation of their gains, with the machine-gunners as usual setting up their posts in the defensive line.

The 1st and 4th Divisions were relieved a few days later, and the troops gratefully made their way to the rear, neither division aware that they had in fact fought their last battle of the war. Harry Murray had come ashore at Gallipoli on the first Anzac Day with the 4th Division's founding brigade, fought in all the division's main actions throughout the war, and had now taken part in its final battle as commander of the divisional machine-guns. He still had another battlefield duty to go, however. Monash had arranged for an 'Australian Mission' of 200 officers and men from the resting divisions to work as advisors with the II American Corps, which was attached to the Australians for the forthcoming assault on the main Hindenburg Line. The mission's task was to lend their experience and skills to the Americans, newcomers to the front line, and Murray was chosen as the senior machine-gun advisor. He and several of his officers and NCOs were detached for this duty on 24 September, as the remainder of the battalion began settling into its rest area. Murray was assigned to help the machine-gun units of the 27th US Division in the attack on the Hindenburg Line between 29 September and 1 October. The American command was sufficiently impressed by his energy and expertise to recommend him for their Distinguished Service Medal, although in the event the decoration was not awarded.[13]

The 27th Division was withdrawn from the battle area on 1 October, and Murray rejoined his own battalion the next day. With the 4th Division assured of a full month's rest out of the line, the battalion began a program of refitting and training, together with exercises aimed at developing its esprit de corps as a unit and maintaining the men's fitness. This mostly took the form of organised sports, together with battalion parades, church parades, and at least one route march. The battalion took on reinforcements to replace recent casualties as it was thought that the war would continue well into the next year, and the Australian units expected to be involved in further heavy fighting. At the same time, it was apparent that the end would come sooner rather than later as the German armies continued to fall back under the hammer-blows of the French and Americans in the south, and the British and Empire forces in the north, and political unrest was growing in the enemy homeland. With a view to fitting the men for their eventual return to civilian life, the AIF had recently introduced a program of education and technical training, and the 4th MG Battalion began holding classes for the troops during October. As well as these activities, the battalion caught up on its administration, and a number of promotions were made to fill vacancies. Several decorations were conferred during the month also, and among these it was announced on 6 October that the French government had awarded the Croix de Guerre to Colonel Murray for his work during the year; it was his fifth decoration of the war.

In early October the 2nd Division fought what would be the last battle of the war for the Australian infantry, at Montbrehain. Following this victorious but costly action, the 2nd was withdrawn to join the remainder of the corps in the rest areas. In this quiet time, Murray took the opportunity to proceed on a month's leave to the United Kingdom; although his itinerary is not recorded, he would almost certainly have visited Hattonburn House again. He departed from the battalion on 3 November and so was away from his unit when the Armistice was announced on 11 November. The long horror was over at last, the end coming suddenly as the fighting power of the Germans collapsed.

The part played by the AIF in the Allied victories of 1918 has been well summed up by Bill Gammage in his book *The Broken Years*.

> Since 27 March they had opposed thirty-nine enemy divisions, nineteen more than once. They defeated all, and forced six to disband. They took 29,144 prisoners, 23 per cent of the British total, 338 guns (23.5 per cent), and 40 miles of ground (21.5 per cent). They made possible much more, and weightily influenced momentous events, yet they made up less than 10 per cent of the British Army. They served King and country well, for few soldiers during that war produced a comparable record.[14]

Chapter 11

HOMECOMING

Murray returned from leave in mid-December 1918, his main duty now being to organise the gradual disbandment of his unit. The AIF had introduced a program for the repatriation to Australia of its 150,000 soldiers in Europe and Britain, regular quotas departing for home as shipping became available. While waiting for their turn, the troops were able to take advantage of an expanded educational program, which included opportunities for practical experience in selected industries. Murray became involved in such activities himself during 1919, but for the time being the battalion could look forward to a fairly leisurely period of administration after the previous eight months of heavy fighting.

Harry Murray could reflect with some satisfaction on his time as the first and only commanding officer of the 4th Australian Machine Gun Battalion. His task had required abilities quite different from those that had made him such an outstanding front-line fighting leader before 1918. This time, other people had done the actual fighting, and as their commanding officer he was responsible for ensuring his men were given the best possible conditions in which to do their jobs. At the same time, he was answerable to higher authority for the accomplishment of his unit's assignments in battle. The general instructions from above needed to be converted to detailed battle plans and maps, and written orders for the guidance of the front-line officers, and for such matters as transport, supply and movement of reserves. Added to these were the myriad, constant tasks of administration, training and discipline always present in military units. A commanding officer of course had his staff to do the detail work, and a good adjutant in particular would contribute a great deal to the smooth running of the unit, but the overall responsibility rested with the colonel.

That the commanders of the new machine-gun battalions had a particular challenge in bringing together their previously independent companies, was mentioned in Chapter Ten. For Murray the task would have been far more demanding than his short stints in command of the 13th Battalion, when he was looking after a going concern in which he had already established himself as an inspiring presence. It is apparent from the battalion records that Murray was very conscious of the potential for resentment in his sub-units, and he gave a lot of attention to that factor. He visited the officers and men of the companies in the front line frequently, making sure at the most basic level that the men knew they were now part of a battalion, and knew who their commander was. The battalion diary records many instances of activities in periods out of the line, aimed at emphasising the status of the unit as opposed to the companies. At the same time, as noted previously, he maintained the link between the companies and the infantry brigades whenever the tactical situation allowed, no doubt with the aim of building a new esprit de corps without destroying the old one.

Murray led an effective, efficient unit which contributed much to the 4th Division's victories of 1918. His personal achievements were naturally much less spectacular than previously, but his superiors were well aware of the value of his work. As well as the award of the Croix de Guerre, he was Mentioned in Dispatches twice more (31 December 1918 and 8 July 1919) making a total of four 'mentions'. His crowning honour as a commanding officer came on 3 June 1919, when he was created a Companion of the Order of St Michael and St George, one of numerous awards to servicemen in the King's birthday honours for that year. General Sinclair-MacLagan's recommendation for the CMG noted his 'conspicuous gallantry, ability, tactical knowledge and devotion to duty.' If there were any limits to Harry Murray's talents as a soldier, they were not apparent in the 1914–18 war.

Final demobilisation of the 4th Machine Gun Battalion took place early in May 1919. Murray's own movements for the next few weeks are not recorded, but he appears to have spent some time in Germany itself (he was photographed in Cologne during May),[1] before reporting to AIF Headquarters early in June. Evidently Murray had no intention of remaining in the army after the war, and he took advantage of the AIF education scheme to spend a period of four months studying stock-raising techniques in Britain and Europe. His particular interest was in sheep farming, and in addition to his own training, he led parties of soldiers in tours of farming areas. According to Captain W D Joynt, VC, who had similar duties at this time, each tour lasted about two weeks and took in a number of large and small farming properties.[2]

Murray must have spent some time in Scotland during this period (he gave a forwarding address in Glasgow), but all that can be stated with any certainty is that whatever point his relationship with Clementine Montgomery had reached, it would go no further. The tradition in the Montgomery family is that the eighteen-year-old Clementine was in love with Murray and wanted to marry him and go with him to Australia, but her parents forbade the union. She was their only child remaining at home, an older daughter having died and one son having emigrated to New Zealand; perhaps they were also concerned by the age difference, even if not aware of its full extent. Clementine never did marry, and it was speculated in the family that she never really 'got over' Murray. There appears to have been little or no animosity, however; a 1937 letter of Murray's shows that he was on cordial terms with Lady Purvis-Russell Montgomery at that time, and he remained friends with Clementine.

Murray sailed for Australia on the ship *Ormonde* in November 1919, with one of the last groups of repatriated soldiers.[3] He was in distinguished company: Lieutenant-General Sir John Monash, commanding general of the

Australian Corps, was going home on the same ship, and the Englishman General Sir William Birdwood, the AIF's long-serving overall commander, was also travelling on the *Ormonde* with his wife and daughter, to begin a tour of Australia. After an uneventful, if rough, voyage, the ship reached Fremantle on Friday 19 December; it was twelve days short of five years since the old 4th Brigade had sailed from Albany on its way to the great adventure. The *Ormonde* berthed at Victoria Quay at about 10.30 am. The return of the three distinguished officers had attracted plenty of advance publicity and thousands of people had turned up at the docks. The crowd included many returned Diggers who had come to cheer the two popular generals, but they were even more eager to welcome Harry Murray home.

For the small, isolated city of Perth, capital of what was still regarded as a 'frontier' state, the arrival of the *Ormonde* was a major event. The fact that their city was the first port of call in Australia for the famed generals was exciting enough for the populace, but in Harry Murray was the most outstanding example of those Australian fighting men who had brought the name of their young country to the notice of the world. And more than that, Murray was a 'local'. Even if he had not been born in the west — which was true of much of the population anyway — he had lived and worked there for many years and had enlisted at Blackboy Hill. The sight of the crowd spilling over the barricades on the wharf may have given Murray some inkling of what was coming, but nothing could have prepared him for the extraordinary scenes which were to occur during that tumultuous day.

Among the dignitaries present were Senator George Pearce (Minister of Defence), the Premier of Western Australia James Mitchell, and the president of the Fremantle branch of the Returned Soldiers' Association, A E Pady. Descending the gangway to the wharf, Generals Birdwood and Monash were greeted with an outburst of cheering, and Murray received an 'especially warm welcome,' according to the newspapers. After an introduction at the foot of the gangway by the RSA president, Birdwood and Monash each gave a speech, during which Murray tried to slip away, with the intention of quietly making his way to the Fremantle Town Hall where a civic reception was scheduled. At the wharf, the crowd called for Colonel

Murray, only to be told that he had already left. Before he could reach the waiting official cars however, someone spotted him and a group of Diggers hoisted him shoulder-high and carried him protesting to his car; the vehicle headed for the Town Hall with thirty men clinging to it and many others following behind. Another crowd was waiting outside the Town Hall, and the building itself was packed to overflowing. After the rest of the distinguished party had entered the hall, Murray was again raised on the shoulders of several Diggers, and carried up to the stage amid tremendous applause.

A round of speeches began. Local speakers introduced the generals and Murray ('very proud that a West Australian who went away in the ranks had come back decorated as he was')[4] to repeated cheering. General Birdwood responded first, then Monash, both generals making neat speeches of thanks to warm applause. Monash then called on Murray, 'who had come out with him as a private in the 4th Brigade and was now lieutenant-colonel commanding the smartest machine-gun battalion in the AIF.' The cheering rose to a climax again, with the crowd on its feet, and it was some time before the noise subsided enough for Murray to speak. His discomfort at being the centre of attention was apparent, but he began a brief speech by thanking the crowd for the welcome back to his homeland. At this point he was distracted by a foolish interjection of 'What about Tasmania?' when he had obviously meant Australia, but concluded by acknowledging 'the privilege and honour of commanding the most magnificent fighters in the world … the Australians.' Murray resumed his seat 'in a perfect furore of cheering and applause.'[5]

A different personality to Murray might have enjoyed this type of attention. The gregarious Birdwood appeared to take it in his stride, and Monash was not averse to a little adulation. Murray, reticent at any time, found the uncontrolled public acclaim deeply distressing, and unfortunately for him there was more to come. It is difficult to be critical of the Diggers for their reactions, however. Not long home from the war, their relief at survival, pride in their achievements, and a heartfelt patriotism seemed to find a sudden focus in Harry Murray, the local working man who had enlisted as a private soldier and survived years of mortal danger to return as a senior officer and the 'champion of decorations'. They spontaneously poured out their emotions onto a man who seemed to symbolise their whole experience of the war.

On the conclusion of the Fremantle reception, the visitors left for the next stage of their itinerary, boarding their cars to drive into Perth. Murray managed to reach his car on foot, avoiding a determined attempt to chair him again, and the motorcade set off. After a stop at Kings Park, where Sir John Monash laid the foundation stone for the Jewish war memorial, the party drove into the city. Here they were due to attend another reception organised by the RSA, at His Majesty's Theatre, before an audience of returned soldiers and their wives. All room in the theatre had been occupied within a few minutes of the doors opening, and the guests were greeted with a tremendous cheer when they arrived at about 1 pm. The function followed much the same pattern as that in Fremantle, and among the greeting party were several former 4th Brigade officers: Brigadier-General Drake-Brockman, and Colonels Pope, Peck (of the 14th Battalion) and Tilney.

Again Birdwood and Monash spoke at some length to enthusiastic applause, then Colonel Tilney took the floor to introduce Murray. He touched briefly on the first weeks at Blackboy Hill, the audience cheering at a mention of Percy Black, and called on Murray with the comment, '[You will] not see him at his best. It was behind a machine-gun that he shone out.'[6] As Murray came forward, another uproar of cheering and applause broke out, and again he had to wait for some time, 'obviously ill at ease' as a reporter observed, before he could make himself heard.

'At a time like this,' he began, 'I find that speech almost fails me. I don't mind talking to a battalion, but it is another matter to speak from a public platform.'[7] After this statement of what was certainly the simple truth, he remarked on the progress made by the Returned Soldiers' Association, thanked the Diggers for their great welcome, and sat down again. After a further round of cheering and one or two more speakers, all stood for the national anthem to conclude the reception.

Next on the agenda was lunch at Government House, and the official party left the theatre via the King Street stage door to board their vehicles. Large crowds had been gathering outside, and as Murray's car began to move off it was surrounded by scores of ex-Diggers (including 'a popular AIF padre') and forced to stop. Murray was plucked from his seat and once again hoisted shoulder high. He was carried in procession along Hay Street, the crowd increasing all the time and blocking the traffic, with many more people looking on from every window and doorway. The procession covered a city block to William Street, before the Diggers relented and allowed Murray down from his perch. Another car was commandeered for him, and with men hanging on all over it, the vehicle crawled through the streets to Government House, the crowd following along. The *West Australian* commented that it was 'such a rousing official reception as has never been accorded to another soldier in Perth.'[8]

Once inside the grounds of Government House, the frenetic atmosphere abated somewhat; there were still numerous VIPs to meet and socialise with however, and pressmen and photographers were in attendance. The local newspapers reported the visit of Birdwood, Monash and Murray at great length, the story easily overshadowing the federal election count, which was in progress at the time. The afternoon paper, the *Daily News*, gave Murray pride of place over the two generals in its edition that day, leading its story on 'The Big Three of the AIF' with several columns recounting his career. He was described as 'Murray the Marvel', 'the sleeper-cutter colonel', and 'the right marker of the AIF'. (In a military parade, the right marker occupies the position from which everyone else lines up.) The reporter assessed him as 'one of those men to whom the war brought life's great opportunity — a soldier born ... between Murray the sleeper cutter, and Murray, VC officer, there is the difference of a man who has found himself.' Predicting correctly that he would hate being feted and honoured, the story pointed out (not quite accurately) that Murray was the most highly decorated soldier, not only of the AIF, but of the whole British army.

The reporters described Murray as 'of medium height, neatly, almost slenderly built, in appearance young almost to the point of boyishness [Murray had in fact turned 39 during the voyage home], quiet yet decisive in manner, with a frank open gaze, and a smile ever ready to light up at the sight of an old comrade, or the recital of another man's gallant deed.'[9] He declined to be interviewed about himself, although 'he is not a man who can be called retiring. He is a personality. He will talk "shop," which means machine-guns and soldiering, and talk it forcibly and well. But he has nothing to say as Murray, VC.'

The two generals had further commitments during the afternoon and evening (Monash described the whole program as 'hysterical')[10] but Murray does not seem to have been involved in those events. He was scheduled to appear at several functions on the next day with Birdwood, but Monash intended to continue the voyage on the *Ormonde* to Melbourne instead, and Murray decided to join him — he would not endure a repeat of the first day's scenes. If he had ever intended to spend time visiting friends and family in Western Australia, the prospect of more public adulation was enough to change his mind. While he was perhaps not very close to his brothers, he was fond of his sister Madge Gray and his young niece, with whom he had corresponded through the war; the latter family lived in West Perth and he may have had an opportunity for a reunion during the day.

In any case, the following day found the Mayor of Perth, W F Lathlain, apologising for Lieutenant-Colonel Murray's absence from a function because he 'had decided to at once visit his mother in Tasmania.' The *Ormonde* proceeded to Melbourne (with a stop at Adelaide for a few hours), arriving on Boxing Day 1919. Melbourne was Monash's home city, and this time it was the general who was chaired through the streets in another tumultuous welcome, a procedure that he apparently enjoyed. Murray was also greeted enthusiastically, but with nothing like the pandemonium in Perth. Returned soldiers from the 4th Brigade met Murray at the Melbourne Town Hall, delivering three cheers as his car drew up, then pressing forward to shake his hand. He was evidently delighted at this greeting from old comrades, although less so 'when a lady rushed forward, and, throwing her arms around his neck, kissed him heartily. She then presented him with a box of chocolates and a rag doll[!].'[11] Murray talked with the 4th Brigade men for some time before heading off to Government House.

Government House, Perth, 19 December 1919.
Harry Murray is second from the right in the back row. In the front row are
Generals Birdwood (far right) and Monash (far left).
(Courtesy Battye Library and WA Newspapers)

Anxious to get to Tasmania, Murray found that a strike by ferry crews had halted regular sailings from Melbourne. He spent about two weeks in the Victorian capital waiting for transport to his home state, fending off further attempts by journalists to extract from him an account of his exploits. 'If you like,' he told the reporter from the *Argus*, 'I will speak of the men, without whose assistance none of the things I have done would have been possible. They were wonderful. No matter what one set them to do they would do it, and the individual was always willing to sacrifice himself for the collective good. Their discipline was perfect in that they would always accomplish their task … They never let me down.'[12] He let it be known that he was planning to 'settle in one of the northern states and take up pastoral pursuits,' once he had been discharged from the army. Murray also briefly became involved in a controversy that had broken out in the British press over Monash's writings on the campaign of 1918. Excerpts from the general's book on the Australian part in the battles of that year had been published in Britain, and his criticism of the Third Corps' effort at Chipilly in August 1918 had roused the ire of a British officer. 'We all know that the Australians and the Americans won the war,' wrote the Englishman, 'but due credit should be given to the English troops for their minor successes.'[13] Asked for his views by the press, Murray supported Monash's version of events, making what for him was an unusually long statement. He summarised the situation of the battle, and related how he had personally observed events at Chipilly on 8 and 9 August from the vantage point of the opposite bank of the Somme: 'I was an eyewitness of an attack by the American troops on the Chipilly Spur … The position from which I viewed this attack was one which enabled me to see every detail, being directly on the flank of the position attacked and not more than 1000 yards away.'[14]

He then outlined the 13th Brigade's subsequent operations on the north of the river. This part of his account may contain some errors, as it differs slightly from that in the Australian *Official History*, but it is interesting to note that he was by no means reticent in speaking about professional matters — only about himself.

Shortly before the *Ormonde* reached Melbourne, a daring aviator, Lieutenant Long, had flown a light aeroplane across Bass Strait from

Tasmania. With the ferries not running, Murray expressed the wish to go along as a passenger on Long's return flight. This was possibly a leg-pull (Murray's sense of humour tended towards teasing), but in any event the flight was delayed by damage to the aircraft, and Murray managed to obtain a passage on a small steamer crossing the strait to Burnie on the northern Tasmanian coast. From Burnie he took the train for Launceston, where his mother and sister Dot were now living.

Word of his impending arrival had reached some of his former comrades from the old days in the Launceston Volunteer Artillery, who arranged a reception for him at the Launceston railway station. 'Nothing elaborate,' they later said. The group made the mistake of telegraphing Murray to advise him of the arrangements, and his reaction was to leave the train at Spreyton and finish the journey by car, bypassing the planned reception. He rejoined his family on the evening of 7 January, seven years after his previous brief visit. No doubt it was a joyous occasion for the family, but there was deep disappointment in those gathered at the railway station when they realised that Murray would not be appearing. He made amends a few nights later, attending a function at the Launceston Hotel and speaking in reply to addresses of welcome, although he dodged other public functions during the month.

Murray was given a pre-discharge medical examination at Launceston on 9 January 1920, the doctor finding that he was generally in good health apart from a 'slight stiffness in right knee at intervals.' Murray also had a couple of 'foreign bodies' removed from his chest and left thigh — presumably he had been carrying splinters from German grenades. Later in the month, terrible news arrived from Sydney. In a tragic two-day period on Sydney beaches, four people had perished in the surf, among them Lieutenant-Colonel Douglas Marks, former commanding officer of the 13th Battalion and Murray's close friend. Marks, who had become manager of a paper company on leaving the army, was at Palm Beach with friends on 25 January when he noticed a woman in difficulties in the water. He plunged into the surf fully clothed in a rescue attempt but was caught in the rip himself and carried out to sea. Marks was drowned, as was the woman (Johanna Rogers) he had tried to rescue. His body was never recovered. A memorial service for Marks was held at St James'

Church on 8 February 1920, the congregation overflowing onto the street. The service was conducted by Canon Frederick Wray, who had been the 13th Battalion's chaplain.

It is not entirely clear from the sources whether Murray attended the service; it can be assumed, however, that if it were humanly possible, he would have been there to farewell his friend. Many years later he wrote a tribute to Marks, in which he recalled his friend's 'high indomitable spirit, his dash and daring, his million and one manly qualities … I close this appreciation through a slight mist,' he wrote, 'recognising that "Whom the Gods love, die young."'[15]

Harry Murray's army appointment was officially terminated on 9 March 1920. Later that year, he achieved his ambition of becoming the owner of a grazing property in northern Australia. He purchased 15,000 acres at Blairmack, near the hot springs town of Muckadilla in the south of Queensland, where he ran a flock of 10,000 sheep. In October he wrote to Charles Bean from Blairmack, joking that he was training the sheep to march in fours. Bean had requested some information for the Australian *Official History*, and in his reply Murray repeated the fiction that his birth-year was 1884 (rather than 1880), thereby ensuring that the wrong date would appear in the *History*; he also mentioned that he preferred to nominate Launceston as his birthplace, and that he was 'a true child of the soil and jolly glad to be back on it.'

A year later he was a married man. His wife was Constance Cameron, a descendant of John Macarthur, founder of the Australian wool industry (Macarthur had arrived in New South Wales with the Second Fleet in 1790 — as had the teenaged convict Anne White, Harry Murray's great-grandmother). Almost no details are known of the six-year marriage, except that it was unsuccessful. The events of this period are shrouded by the natural reluctance of the families concerned to talk about a painful episode, and perhaps it is best that it remains that way. Franki and Slatyer record, from Murray family sources,[16] that Constance wanted an active social life and hoped to gain advantages from marriage to a famous man; difficulties arose from Murray's preference for a quiet life in the country. Perhaps it had come as an unpleasant surprise for Constance to find that Murray really did intend to isolate himself — and her — in the outback for the rest of their lives. One wonders how they could have reached the point of marriage with such a fundamental misunderstanding of each other's aims in life.

Evidently the marriage had virtually broken down by 1925 when Murray first met his wife's twenty-three-year-old niece Ellen (Nell) Cameron (also a Macarthur descendant) in a Brisbane hotel. The circumstances are not clear, but it appears to have been arranged that he should meet her, perhaps to bring her to the property for a visit. It seems there was an immediate mutual attraction; like Clementine Montgomery, the attractive, gentle Nell Cameron was more than twenty years Murray's junior, and was also a sportswoman (she was a very good tennis player), and unlike Constance she was inclined to the rural life. Within a short time Harry and Nell had established a relationship. They left Australia for New Zealand (where Nell had been born) and spent the next two years there while the Murrays' divorce proceeded through the Queensland courts. On 11 November 1927, as announced in a brief press item the next day, a previous decree nisi was made absolute 'with costs against the defendant … on ground of desertion.'[17]

Harry Murray and Nell Cameron were now free to marry, and did so almost immediately, at the Auckland Registrar's Office on 20 November. The couple returned to Australia shortly afterwards. As they must have expected, Murray's property had gone to Constance in the aftermath of the divorce, and the newlywed couple was almost destitute. Murray's determination to succeed as a pastoralist was undiminished however, and he was strongly supported by his new wife. With moral and financial support from family and friends, the Murrays sought another property in Queensland, and found what they were looking for in the outback north-west of the state — Glenlyon station, near the township of Richmond. The Murrays took over the 74,000-acre property in April 1928 and began the task of building up a viable business from scratch. There would be some difficult years ahead, but Harry Murray came to love Glenlyon, and he would remain there for the rest of his life. At the age of 47, after many years of wandering, of deadly danger, outstanding achievement and sudden fame, he had at last found his home.

Chapter 12

THE SUNLIT PLAINS

*And the bush has friends to meet him, and their kindly voices
    greet him,
In the murmur of the breezes and the river on its bars,
And he sees the vision splendid of the sunlit plains extended,
And at night the wondrous glory of the everlasting stars.*

A B Paterson, 'Clancy of the Overflow'

The town of Richmond is situated on the south bank of the Flinders River, about 500 kilometres inland from Queensland's eastern coast, in a region of vast open grasslands. The area's settlement dates from the 1860s when parties searching for the lost Burke and Wills expedition first noted its promise as pastoral country. The tropical weather conditions produce a wet season from December to March that can result in severe floods, and a 'dry' for the rest of the year; droughts are not uncommon. Temperatures vary from 49°C in midsummer to minus 8°C in winter. A shallow inland sea once covered the area, and fossils of prehistoric animals have been found there, including a huge Kronosaurus skeleton. More recently, the Flinders River has been home to crocodiles, particularly during flood times, and even the occasional shark made its way to Richmond via flooded watercourses.

Glenlyon was situated about 80 kilometres south of the Richmond town site; the property had been established for some years, with at least two previous owners (both named Brown, although unrelated). The region was true outback country, with a population of around 1700 for the township and district combined in 1930; the first-ever call to the Flying Doctor Service was made from Julia Creek, 150 kilometres to the west, in 1928. There was no public electricity provided, even in the town itself, until 1952, and everyone made do with hurricane lanterns and kerosene refrigerators or hessian coolers. The mail run to outlying properties took place once a week only, on Sundays; Glenlyon was the central drop-off point for several surrounding properties, and Sundays would bring visits to the station from neighbours picking up their mailbags.

The Murrays took on Glenlyon without stock, and they began the slow process of building up a Merino sheep flock. Through drought, flood, financial difficulties and the Great Depression, the Glenlyon flock gradually improved in both numbers and quality until in the 1950s it comprised about 19,000 animals and was recognised as one of the finest in the district.[1] A small herd of cattle was acquired later, and Harry Murray took considerable pleasure in growing an extensive vegetable garden. Murray ran the property with only one permanent employee (station hand Jack O'Keefe, who worked at Glenlyon for thirty-five years until his death), bringing in casual labour occasionally for large tasks, and of course shearing teams in season. Many returned soldiers had found themselves at something of a loss in a civilian world that they had almost forgotten; horrible as the war had been, it had given them a high purpose and a chance for great achievements, in contrast to the monotonous everyday life that many now found in peacetime. Harry Murray, however, had given himself a huge challenge, which required planning and forethought, technical skills and the hard work that he needed to absorb his great physical energies.

The Murrays succeeded in paying off their debts by the late 1930s, and

Glenlyon steadily developed into a going concern. Life for graziers in the district was still precarious, however, with the vagaries of the climate and the price of wool. In 1939, Murray wrote in a letter, 'We are slowly but surely climbing the hill. We slipped down during the depression and drought years … one needs to study every avenue by which an out-go occurs. We Primary fools have no control of our income.' By this time, Harry and Nell Murray had become parents. Their son Douglas, named in memory of Douglas Marks, was born in 1930, and daughter Clem in 1934; the origin of her name is obvious.

Life was not all hard work. Nell Murray was an excellent tennis player, and Harry soon took up the game and become devoted to it. They laid out a tennis court at Glenlyon, and neighbours visiting for the Sunday mail run would stay for a game and a general get-together. The Murrays were early members of the Richmond tennis club, and Nell often represented the district in tournaments and helped out around the club. The Reids, long-time club stalwarts, later recalled that 'Mrs Colonel Murray' had the job of looking after the money at the clubrooms, and how 'the Colonel' would insist on his opponents rolling the ball back to him under the net rather than tossing it over (there were other, unrelated, Murrays in the district, and Harry Murray was usually referred to as 'the Colonel').[2] Aside from the tennis club, it seems that he was not particularly fond of the town itself — 'four hours twice a year does me,' he wrote in a 1939 letter.

Murray also found time for writing, and during the 1930s he contributed several pieces to the New South Wales RSL magazine, *Reveille*. The magazine began as a fairly routine publication, but quickly became a forum for soldiers' reminiscences of 1914–18. These personal insights into the AIF's experience of the war make *Reveille* a virtual treasure-trove for researchers (it is the source of much of the detail in this book). Murray's contributions began in the December 1929 issue, when part of his letter to the editor was printed. This was a tribute to Percy Black ('the most truly brave soldier and gentleman I ever knew') together with some comments on the tanks at First Bullecourt. Some short pieces relating incidents at Gallipoli followed in the next few years, then a longer account of his Bullecourt experiences appeared in April 1933. A significant article in December 1935 described the 13th Battalion's first attack at Mouquet Farm. Murray's theme was the importance of battle discipline in overcoming the natural instinct of self-preservation, and he illustrated this by writing frankly of his own fear during the battle. His candour brought appreciative comment from readers in following issues.

A year later he produced a much longer article, 'Memories of First Bullecourt',[3] which expanded considerably on his 1933 piece and ran to more than five two-column pages. Murray wrote in vivid detail of the battle from his point of view, and the article made a big impression on his readers — the next edition of *Reveille* printed three pages of letters from veterans. Among the correspondents was Newton Wanliss, the historian of the 14th Battalion, who wrote that Murray's 'epic account of First Bullecourt provides stirring reading and makes one proud to be an Australian. It is fitting, too, that the story should be told by one of the outstanding heroes of the AIF.'[4] A former 14th Battalion sergeant, D W Blackburn, who had fought alongside Murray at Bullecourt,[5] wrote that his 'reference to the tanks' "exploits" is a much fairer criticism than some of us would give, but that only shows the tact and understanding of Harry Murray.'[6] A veteran of the 4th Brigade's machine-guns at Gallipoli, Blackburn also expressed his appreciation of Murray's remarks about 'gallant Percy Black. What a soldier! What a man!'

In a 1937 article on some of the AIF's unsung heroes — the runners, signallers and cooks — Murray made a revealing comment. He was well-read on military subjects and familiar with the American Civil War, so he was probably aware of Robert E Lee's comment at the battle of Fredericksburg: 'It is well that war is so terrible — we should grow too fond of it.' Murray expressed a similar thought in his article.

> Surely there is something about that terrible thing called War, which manages to call forth all that is best and most unselfish in men. Is it not a fact that, at the bottom of our hearts, we all love it, and love the men who fought and bled with us, and afterwards even the men we have fought

against? It is the greatest and most terrible of human dramas.[7]

Murray's account of the Stormy Trench fight appeared in December 1937 (most of his longer pieces were prepared late in the year, when work on the station was not so pressing), and in this article he said virtually nothing about his own actions; his intention was to describe how well his men had fought. Perhaps he felt that his part in the battle had received enough publicity over the years; apart from numerous articles and the 13th Battalion unit history, Volume IV of the *Official History* (published in 1933) described it in some detail. The *Reveille* editor, however, printed an introduction to the article drawing attention to Murray's VC and the citation for the award. Murray was annoyed enough by this to write immediately to the editor, giving him a 'good strafe': 'Surely … you could see it was my desire not to pat my own back.' With typical affability, he then went on to congratulate the editor on the recent issue of the magazine.

Murray's last long battle piece was entitled 'The First Three Weeks on Gallipoli', a four-page article that appeared in April 1939 and was reprinted (in slightly abridged form) in April 1955. His accounts of Gallipoli, Mouquet Farm, Stormy Trench and Bullecourt are all of considerable interest. They were written in a lively style, sometimes including classical allusions (in one of his Gallipoli articles he compared Percy Black to Diomed, a hero of Homer's *Iliad*). Murray usually mentioned his own part in battles in a self-deprecating manner — his involuntary dunking coming ashore at Anzac Cove, for instance, and taking evasive action during the advance at Bullecourt. His general viewpoint may seem a little jingoistic to modern readers, but he was not alone in this, and by no means as extreme as some. As well as the articles which appeared under his name,[8] Murray contributed to other writers' work: his comments on Percy Black made up half of Cyril Longmore's feature on Black in the October 1936 *Reveille* and included a moving tribute to his old friend:

The bravest of us all, and this without disparaging the many very brave men of the AIF. He was brave to the last degree of bravery, and not because he did not know fear, but because of his complete mastery of it. He loved life, and enjoyed living it, and hoped to keep on enjoying it. He took the good things with a quiet, whole-hearted enjoyment ... Black was as gentle as a Sister of Mercy, and his sense of justice so strong that he could see the other fellow's side before his own. I never heard him speak against any man, but always found him eager to praise ...

Percy never went berserk and never sought death ... one or two of us who were his intimate friends knew he had all the natural fear of the Unknown, but never did he let it influence his actions when in danger ...

He had a wonderful personality. His level, cool, penetrating wide-spread eyes, his quiet voice and confident yet most unassuming manner, inspired confidence from the first acquaintance ...

Black was a born leader of men and a natural soldier, and his every instinct was that of a gentleman. I have always thought that had he been trained before the war, his promotions, fast as they were, would have been much faster. He could grasp a situation as quickly as if he had been a student of Stonewall Jackson and Napoleon all his life, and just as quickly form a plan to meet it. His brain was very quick, and his hands moved with his brain.[9]

This feature was part of a series in *Reveille* entitled 'Celebrities of the AIF'. Perhaps it is no surprise that the first subject of this series, in August 1930, was Lieutenant Colonel H W Murray, VC.[10] Among the most interesting items of Murray's writing during this period was not a magazine article, but a letter. In 1939, George Mitchell, a former 4th Division soldier mentioned in earlier chapters, was working on a publication about battlefield psychology, which eventually saw the light of day in the form of a small handbook, 'Soldier in Battle', published in 1940. Mitchell asked Murray for his comments on the draft, and the latter's reply included a number of revelations concerning his experiences and feelings, both before the war and in battle. In particular, he described his thoughts before the Landing at Gallipoli. These insights are available from no other source; as he wrote in his letter, 'Now I've told you a good deal I've never told anyone and never particularly written before.'[11]

These writings ensured that Murray's name and reputation were not forgotten among the brotherhood of returned soldiers, but in every other respect he kept himself out of the limelight. Although he was a member of the local RSL branch, he attended Anzac day functions on perhaps only one or two occasions in his life, apparently not prepared to risk excessive public attention. He resisted all encouragement to enter any form of public life. Invitations to attend 13th Battalion reunions were declined with regrets, often accompanied by donations to fundraising activities. There is no reason to suppose, however, that he was trying to avoid contact with former comrades; certainly running Glenlyon would have demanded a lot of his time during the 1930s, and visitors to the property were welcome. Among those who were quite aware of Harry Murray's distinction was an unidentified man from Sydney, who wrote to the Army Records Office in 1937 claiming to be Murray and requesting a copy of his discharge certificate. The bizarre incident is recorded in Murray's service file.

In the late 1930s the international situation was deteriorating rapidly, and it was apparent that the aggression of Nazi Germany, and of Japan closer to home, were likely to bring on another major war. Not before time, the Australian government began to work on expanding and modernising its military forces, which included the raising of new militia units. In June 1939 Harry Murray was invited to take command of the 26th Infantry Battalion, constituted by splitting the existing 15/26th Battalion, and oversee its recruitment and training. Murray had no hesitation in accepting the post. The new unit drew its recruits from the small towns and grazing properties around Richmond, Hughenden and Longreach in northern and central Queensland, and Murray selected his founding group of officers from the same region also. Among these was another VC holder (and machine-gunner), Edgar Towner, who later became the battalion second-in-command. The 26th began its training at Kissing Point camp near Townsville in September 1939, at the same time as Australia found itself again at war with Germany, in support of the mother country. The unit moved to Townsville itself in November, then to a camp named Miowera, near Bowen on the coast, in February 1940. Here the 26th joined with the other two battalions (the 31st and 51st) of the 11th Brigade.

In May 1940, the Miowera camp was wrecked by a cyclone, and the 26th Battalion moved back to the Townsville area, where it remained for the next year. As the senior military officer in the area, Murray was regarded as the area commander during this period. The main work of the battalion was training, and there was considerable turnover of personnel as volunteers were detached for overseas service with the Second AIF and new recruits joined to begin their training. In June 1941 the battalion was relocated again, this time to Sellheim camp near Charters Towers. The first paperwork of Murray's Second World War service appears in his file in October 1941, when he signed mobilisation papers giving his date of birth as 1 December 1885. In another document he took a further year off his true age, putting his birth-year as 1886 and thus giving an age of fifty-five when he was in fact sixty years old.

With the outbreak of war with Japan in December 1941, the now-mobilised citizen forces in northern Australia were given some operational tasks in addition to training, being deployed several times to defend against rumoured invasions. These proved to be false alarms, but it was apparent that active duty would come sooner or later, and Murray was keen to take part. One of his officers, Alexander Stewart, recorded in his memoirs an assessment of Murray as a commander: 'He was a proven leader who expounded the principles of leadership to his officers, and who put those principles into daily practice. He was also a modest man, and one of great dignity. In addition, he was a man of absolute integrity who had a very high sense of justice and of discipline.'[12]

That Murray's sense of discipline remained focused on the battlefield rather than the parade ground is shown by a couple of pleasant stories from a former soldier. Henry Eather remembered that the colonel, as a VC holder and camp commandant, was entitled to have the camp guard squad turn out and formally present arms whenever he passed the guardhouse. Murray had no wish to be the object of this ceremonial, and as a former private himself was no doubt sympathetic to the men on guard. He let it be known that if he was using a track behind the guardhouse rather than the main road into camp, he could be safely ignored. On the odd occasion when he found it necessary to use the road, he would send word ahead to give the guard warning of his arrival.[13] Another recollection of Mr Eather appears in the 26th Battalion history. On this occasion Murray had been playing tennis and, dressed anonymously in his tennis gear, walked past some recruits. 'One of the new arrivals called out, "Hey mate, what are they doing with an old bastard like you in the army?" Colonel Murray assured the man there was a place for old blokes in the army. When the CO came out next day with all his glory the rookie was speechless!'[14] Former servicemen may wonder how many officers of their acquaintance would have reacted like that in similar circumstances.

On another occasion, Murray was again attired for tennis in shorts, singlet and sandshoes, when he visited an anti-tank unit that had just arrived at Sellheim Camp. He had a casual conversation with the unit's battery sergeant-major, Mark Barnett,[15] who at first took him for a civilian hygiene labourer, then, when the man drove off in a staff car, decided he must be an old soldier acting as the camp commandant's driver. It was only when Murray appeared that evening in his shirt bearing the rank badges of a Lieutenant-Colonel that Barnett realised who he was. Another instance of Murray's informality was illustrated when a young private asked if he might see his VC medal. When the private and his mates returned to their tent after their day's work, they found a wooden box on one of the camp-stretchers. This proved to contain all of Murray's medals. When the men got around to returning the medals some weeks later, it was to the relief of their CO, who had forgotten what he had done with them!

The 26th Battalion continued with routine duties and exercises through the first months of 1942, relocating to several different camps. The time was approaching when the battalion would be posted for active service overseas, but to his bitter disappointment, Murray was not to be part of this. The army was going through a process, driven by the new commander-in-chief, General Blamey, of replacing older officers with younger men. Already in the 26th Battalion, Major Towner, VC, who was ten years younger than Murray, had been compulsorily retired, and in August 1942 Murray was abruptly told (apparently by Blamey in person) that he was relieved of his command. There is no reason to suppose that there was any animosity on Blamey's part, or any factors involved other than Murray's age; the same thing was happening to many senior officers at this time, regardless of fine records. There were a number of cases earlier in the war of older officers suffering in health under the strain of combat,[16] so perhaps Blamey's approach was correct on general principles. Murray's effectiveness in the training of his unit could not have been in question; the 26th fought well in the south-west Pacific later in the war, and Murray's period of command had laid the foundations for that performance. He had also been responsible for the initial training of many soldiers who passed through the 26th before joining units of the Second AIF.

His military service was not over yet, however: offered command of the 23rd Regiment, Volunteer Defence Corps, he swallowed his disappointment and accepted this task, in which he retained his rank of lieutenant-colonel. The VDC was an Australian version of the British Home Guard, a part-time force formed from men too young or too old for regular service, or who were working in reserved occupations (work considered necessary for the support of the fighting forces). The 23rd Regiment's particular focus was to form a guerrilla force in the event of a successful Japanese invasion of northern Australia, to harass the enemy's communications and hamper their access to local food supplies. Murray's responsibility was to enlist, train and command the new unit. With the assistance of a few officers detached from the 26th Battalion, he toured the outback areas north to the Gulf of Carpentaria, recruiting men from the pastoral properties and bush towns. After several months, about 200 recruits had been enlisted and formed into sub-units. The men were given as much training as possible in weapons and ambush tactics, and instructed in carrying out surveillance and coast-watching as part of their usual work on the cattle properties in the area. VDC Headquarters apparently referred to the 23rd Regiment as 'Murray's Marauders', although this was not known to the unit itself; 'Never at any time during my service with the unit did we see or were visited by any officer of [the VDC's] administrative personnel,'[17] wrote Captain A C Stewart, who was one of Murray's small full-time staff.

Their surveillance activities continued into 1944, by which time the Japanese had been driven back at all points and any danger of them invading Australia had disappeared. Murray was now over 63, and suffering intermittent poor health, having been hospitalised several times with cellulitis (a potentially dangerous skin infection) in an arm and a leg. He was discharged from the service in February 1944, and the 23rd Regiment was disbanded later in the year. Murray returned quietly to his civilian life at Glenlyon; very likely he would have wished to end his military service for his country in less mundane fashion, but it was not to be.

The post-war years were prosperous ones for Glenlyon on the whole. Wool prices were good, and although the cycle of drought and flood continued, the highs more than compensated for the lows. Murray had taught himself the elements of finance, and his wise investments in the good years provided a hedge against the poor ones. The mid-1950s also saw Harry Murray emerge occasionally into the limelight. Travelling to Adelaide with the rest of the family in 1953 for his daughter Clem's wedding, he attended a reunion dinner held by South Australian members of the original 16th Battalion. In 1954, the recently crowned Queen Elizabeth visited Australia with the Duke of Edinburgh, and Colonel and Mrs Murray were among the distinguished citizens invited to meet the royal couple during the Queensland leg of their tour.

The 1954 wet season in north-eastern Australia was one of severe floods, which were at their height at the time of the royal visit to North Queensland in March. The Queen's itinerary had Townsville as the main venue for this part of the country, but the floods seriously interfered with travel for guests from the inland districts. Harry and Nell Murray were only able to attend the function with the assistance of friends who owned private aircraft and presumably had some dry ground on their properties. 'I could not even drive my car out of the backyard,' Murray told a journalist later,[18] but he and Nell were able to board the plane owned by their neighbour Bill Anning. He got the Murrays to nearby Ennis Downs station, from where Mrs Hazel Roberts flew them to Townsville in her Beechcraft. A crowd of 50,000 was in the city on 12 March for the occasion. When Harry Murray was presented to the Queen, she asked the distinguished soldier, 'What do you do now?'

'In between wars, I grow wool,' was the reply.

The Queen laughed and asked Murray to repeat the remark to the Duke, who was equally amused.[19]

In 1956 celebrations were held in London to mark the centenary of the institution of the Victoria Cross, and invitations were extended throughout the British Commonwealth for all Victoria Cross winners and their wives to attend. Having avoided public events for nearly forty years, Harry Murray had no intention of going. But pressure from the RSL, combined with the realisation that this was something that Nell wanted to do, eventually overcame his reluctance. In Sydney on 10 June 1956 on the way to London,[20] Murray attended a special reunion of former 13th Battalion members, the first time he had ever been to one of their functions. He gave every sign of delight at meeting men whom he had not seen since the war, and his old comrades responded with equal pleasure. It was inevitable that Murray would be the centre of attention; the 13th's former commander, J M A Durrant (by then retired as a major-general) was there, and he gave a speech focusing on the Stormy Trench fight. This was followed by the proposing of a toast to Murray, and it was in responding to this that he spoke of his doubts about whether he had fully deserved his first decoration, the DCM at Gallipoli. As to his attitude to fame, Murray said, 'I had never sought, nor had I taken part in any affairs in life after the war which would attract attention to me because I felt that a medal, once

The lion in old age. Harry Murray, aged about eighty,
reluctantly displays his medals for a family camera at Glenlyon.
(Courtesy C Sutherland)

bestowed, and recognition once given, was sufficient, and it was not right to refer to it constantly. The act had been done and the award had been given. One should not seek more.'21

The centenary celebrations began with a thanksgiving service at Westminster Abbey on 25 June, where the Archbishop of Canterbury gave the address. A week of various functions and meetings with dignitaries followed; the VC winners paraded in Hyde Park for a review by the Queen, and with their wives attended a garden party at Marlborough House, where the Murrays had the pleasure of meeting the Queen Mother. After the centenary events, a group of fifty Australians, VC winners with wives and relatives, travelled to France and Belgium for a tour of the Western Front battlefields and war graves. Harry Murray did not join this expedition, however. The old hero of Mouquet Farm, Stormy Trench and Bullecourt had no desire to revisit the scenes of his personal triumphs, for they were also the places where so many friends had died. 'There was nothing I wanted less than to go over the battlefields,' he said later. 'That would have been an unnecessary raking up of very sad memories, of comrades who never returned.'22

Instead the Murrays took the opportunity for a three-month holiday (their son Douglas was managing Glenlyon), beginning with a tour of England and Scotland by car, and a week at the Wimbledon championships. They visited Paris and Switzerland, took a flight over the North Pole and returned home via Hawaii, completing their world trip in time for the shearing. Both were interviewed by the press on their return, and there are signs that Murray was beginning to mellow a little as far as publicity was concerned, for he spoke at some length to a *Reveille* writer, although he would not expand on his feelings about the old battlefields. He had returned home to what must have been a good life for him after his early struggles: a loving wife and family, a degree of prosperity, and a home that he loved and where he could enjoy both the companionship of friends and neighbours and the privacy his temperament required.

The subsequent years were uneventful ones beyond the normal ups and downs of pastoral life, but Murray's health steadily declined with advancing

Harry Murray's funeral, Brisbane, 14 January 1966.
(Courtesy Queensland Newspapers Pty Ltd)

age. He was increasingly affected by arthritis and heart trouble, and he had suffered several injuries while working on the property; the old Gallipoli wound in his right knee continued to trouble him also. Murray turned 85 on 1 December 1965, and shortly afterwards one of his Tasmanian cousins, H F Littler of New Town, was surprised to receive a letter from him mentioning this milestone — for once, Harry Murray put his true age on paper. Mr Littler, who had served in the 12th Battalion, had last seen his cousin shortly before the Gallipoli Landing.

In the new year of 1966, Harry and Nell Murray set out on a 1500 kilometre drive to the Gold Coast for a holiday. Towards evening on 6 January they were near the town of Miles when one of their Valiant's tyres blew out; Nell, who was driving, was unable to control the vehicle and it overturned. A nearby resident heard the crash and hurried to the scene where he found the wrecked car, with its occupants shocked and with minor injuries. Harry Murray was still in the car, held by his seat belt; he had suffered broken ribs, broken bones in one hand, and several cuts and bruises. Nell Murray had been thrown out of the vehicle when it rolled, injuring her chest, back and arm.[23] Ambulances were called, and the Murrays were taken to the Miles District Hospital for treatment. Nell later made a full recovery, but although Harry Murray's injuries were not serious in themselves, the shock proved to be too much for his ageing frame, and some time after midnight that great heart stopped beating.

At first Murray's family intended to hold a private funeral, but this was reconsidered, and the old warrior was given a full military funeral in Brisbane on 14 January 1966. Three hundred people attended the service in St Andrew's Presbyterian Church. The pallbearers, who included six lieutenant-colonels and two majors, carried the flag-draped coffin from the church, and another major followed carrying Murray's decorations. With an escort of 150 soldiers, the coffin was transported on a gun-carriage through the streets of Brisbane to the Mount Thompson crematorium. There a volley was fired, a bugler played the *Last Post* and *Reveille*, and Harry Murray's body was cremated. It was the end of a journey that had begun in the outback districts of Australia and had taken a decisive turn at

Blackboy Hill in 1914, when Private Murray and Private Black had discovered a mutual interest in machine-guns and duty, and those ordinary men of extraordinary qualities had gone on to create their own personal part of the Anzac legend.

Chapter 13

GREAT-HEARTED MEN

At the beginning of his article on First Bullecourt in the December 1936 *Reveille*, Harry Murray warned that an account by one participant, 'may give the impression that his unit was the only one there.' Similarly, in assessing the importance of Percy Black and Harry Murray in the story of Australia in the 1914–18 war, one must be careful not to imply that they won the war by themselves. Their significance lies in how they illustrate the particular character of the Australian contribution to that dreadful conflict, and in the qualities they possessed as individuals. As soldiers, both men showed supreme gifts as combat leaders, with qualities of personality that inspired the admiration and affection of their colleagues. Both had all the instincts of the natural soldier — that instant judgement of the right thing to do in the most stressful of situations, with the risk of death or disablement at any moment, deafening noise all around, and bearing the responsibility for other men's lives. Both were also very effective at the most basic of military tasks — killing the enemy or otherwise putting him out of action. As leaders and officers, even above their own lives and those of their men, it was their responsibility to see that the instructions of higher commanders were carried out as far as possible.

More details are known of Harry Murray's exploits in action than those of Percy Black, partly for the obvious reason that Murray survived the war and was able to record some of his experiences. Although he tended to downplay his own deeds, his writings encouraged other people to fill in some of the details in their own writings. As well, the 13th Battalion's history focused on many of Murray's personal exploits — he was a key figure in all the unit's most dramatic and desperate battles up to March 1918. The 16th Battalion, with which Percy Black spent all his army service, seems not to have produced any long memoirs from individuals that might have given close views of Black in action, and the battalion history lacks detail in some areas. In contrast to Murray, any assessment of Black as a military man has to be more generalised, particularly for the war in France. What may be said of both of them is that no major infantry attack led by Harry Murray or Percy Black failed to take its objective. In several of those combats, the support that was essential to holding a captured position in the conditions of the Western Front did not materialise for one reason or another (a very common occurrence in this war), and the gains had to be given up in the end, but this does not diminish the original achievements. In the 16th Battalion's attack on the Mouquet Farm position, the troops were driven back only after Black had been put out of action, although it is difficult to see what any leader could have done when counterattacked from behind by superior numbers.

Harry Murray seems to have possessed almost unerring judgement of when to hold his ground and when to retreat. As long as there was any chance of success, he hung on and inspired his men to do the same in spite of casualties; the moment he became convinced that there was nothing more to be done, he turned all his energies to extricating his men safely. At Stormy Trench, under furious counterattacks, he knew that he could hold on, and he was proved right. Possibly he delayed a little too long at Bullecourt before withdrawing, but he must have found it difficult to believe that the artillery would continue to ignore his repeated calls for assistance. 'With artillery support we can keep the position till the cows come home,' said his message, and the events of Second Bullecourt support his judgement. Combining amazing personal daring with realistic assessment of situations, he had the steely mental control to maintain an overview of the battlefield while fighting for his life in personal combat.

Both Murray and Black possessed the knack of natural leadership, that indefinable quality that ensures other people will obey them willingly, without the need of intimidation or bluster. Accounts of them in action give the impression of differing leadership styles — Black seeming to lead by calming everyone down, Murray by firing them up — reflecting their differences in temperament. Both approaches (assuming this assessment is correct) were equally effective, and their men were devoted to them, not least because of the care they took with their troops. A recent article on Murray includes quotes from several interviews with men who served under him in the 13th Battalion. One of these mentions that when on the march, Murray would never ride the horse allocated to him as the company commander, instead using it to carry 'somebody who was half-lame with foot trouble ... Murray would always walk. He always thought of his men.'[1] Another of these interviews does, however, contain an implied criticism, suggesting that Murray was overly quick to volunteer 'A' Company for every hazardous duty that came up. If so, no-one else seems to have complained of this, and it may be that a wrong impression was gained because the company was often selected for such tasks by the battalion commander, because of his confidence in Murray. Colonel Durrant's recommendation for Murray's VC includes the statement 'I placed him on the right flank because it was the most dangerous and critical.'

Murray firmly believed in the value of discipline in motivating men in battle, and he was at pains to point out in his writings that it was the overcoming of the self-preservation instinct through discipline and training that was the basis of the AIF's combat effectiveness. He meant the discipline of the battlefield, and although he does not seem to have offered a definition of this, he would probably have agreed with the one favoured by General Gellibrand and quoted in the *Official History*: 'reliability at all times and under all conditions given appropriate leading.'[2]

Harry Murray had no particular interest in the spit-and-polish type of discipline, and he had something of a reputation for being careless about his own uniform. There are indications that he could be severe on any misconduct away from the front line — for being detrimental to Australia's reputation — but bending of the regulations for the common good did not bother him. Captain T A White had a story of an 'A' Company soldier organising the pilfering of coal from a British dump to heat the 13th Battalion's billets. The soldier was eventually found out, arrested and referred to his unit for punishment, but 'as Captain Harry Murray is OC of the man under arrest, he will probably be exonerated and get similar jobs in the future.'[3]

Murray was one of the very few First AIF soldiers to rise from private to lieutenant-colonel, proving himself just as capable at the level of unit command as he had been in all his other postings. It is probable that Percy Black would have reached that level too, had he survived Bullecourt. At the time of Black's death, several contemporaries commented that he was about to be given command of a battalion. These assertions are unsubstantiated, but at least one professional military historian accepts this as a reasonable assumption.[4] As it happened, there was such an opportunity in the 4th Brigade shortly after Bullecourt, when the 14th Battalion's popular commander, Lieutenant Colonel J H Peck, was transferred to a headquarters staff job. Peck was a regular officer with pre-war training. As such he had probably been earmarked for the staff for some time, and if so his successor would have been chosen in advance. Word may have leaked out that Black was being considered, hence the confident statements after his death.

Black was not the senior major in the brigade, but he had been promoted over seniors before. In the 16th Battalion he was junior to Major Margolin, and in the event it was Margolin who initially succeeded Peck, although the appointment was not a success. Apart from his tremendous reputation in the brigade, Black's Victorian birth would have been an advantage from the start as a potential CO of the 14th; moreover (to carry this line of speculation one final step) he may well have been the right man to handle the volatile Albert Jacka. To rise in rank and honours as rapidly as they did, both Black and Murray would have possessed a considerable degree of ambition as well as ability — not that form of ambition that is no more than a crass craving for power and prestige, but rather the desire to use their abilities to the full for the benefit of their cause.

Official recognition of Black's and Murray's deeds came in the form of the decorations awarded to them. Percy Black won his DCM for an episode of individual courage, but it is noteworthy that the other awards won by both men recognised performance over an extended period or leadership in action, as well as plain bravery. Murray won his VC and two DSOs commanding company-sized forces in desperate combat; at Bullecourt he was effectively leading an entire brigade. Harry Murray's six awards make him the most decorated of all Australian servicemen, and he is usually considered to have also been the most highly decorated infantryman of the entire British and Empire armies in 1914–18.[5]

Both Percy Black and Harry Murray received publicity at home (particularly in Western Australia) during the war, to a level unusual for individual soldiers other than generals. Although press dispatches from the various war correspondents generally avoided using names, enough feature articles appeared on both men to ensure that the exploits of both were known to the public at the time, although not always with accuracy. There was a tendency to credit Percy Black with more decorations than he had actually won, and this has crept into some modern accounts (one recent publication even refers to 'Major Black, VC'). At the time, the two men formed points of focus for Australian national pride, as the young nation's soldiers caught the imagination of the world and, as many thought at the time, laid 'the foundations of her national history.'[6]

On the surface, the stories of Percy Black and Harry Murray epitomise the Anzac legend; they are almost the legend made flesh, the blokes from the bush joining up for a bit of an adventure and showing the regulars what to do. There was of course rather more to the nature of Australian troops in 1914–18, just as there was more that was demonstrated by the careers of Black and Murray. One historian in Western Australia went as far as to treat Harry Murray's life as an allegory for the overall Australian contribution to the war: 'Colonel Murray's counterpart was the country with whom and for whom he fought … at Gallipoli did not Australia distinguish itself as a nation, and win a commission for gallantry? At the end of three and a half years was that nation not covered with fighting decorations … ?'[7]

C E W Bean deplored the superficial version of the Anzac legend, which he characterised as the 'slouching "dag", intent only on beer, thieving, "skirts" and scoring off nincompoop officers.'[8] That might describe a minuscule proportion of the First AIF, but the majority were 'keen men, under strong leaders.'[9] The true nature of the force was reflected in the degree of professionalism and expertise it developed as the war went on, achieving by 1918 'an astonishing mastery of the soldier's craft,' as Bean put it. The underlying paradox of the First AIF is that it reached the height of professional skill from an almost entirely amateur basis and from a nation with scarcely any military traditions of its own. Their temporary job done at the Armistice, nearly all of the force's members (from Sir John Monash down) returned to their civilian pursuits as soon as they could.

An important factor in the AIF's success was very likely the absence of deep social distinctions in Australian society (at least by comparison with the ingrained situation in Britain at the time), which meant that there were few barriers to the available talent being employed to the full. The significance of the practice of selecting most officers from the ranks, for instance, was not so much that it was done for the sake of lofty egalitarian principles, but because it was the most efficient way — it produced the most effective results. The soldiers themselves tended to deflect attention away from their own skills by the typically Australian habit of displaying a casual attitude on the surface while taking the business at hand very seriously indeed. At the same time, the men of the First AIF did not suffer from any false modesty about their worth as soldiers, although it would be wrong to say that they all thought they were the best. A 57th Battalion infantryman, W H Downing, wrote in *To the Last Ridge* that he put the French Canadians first, with his own AIF next and equal with the Scots and the English-speaking Canadians. F M Cutlack, the Australian war correspondent and author, rated the New Zealand Division as the best all-round formation in the British Army.[10] Of those contemporary observers who put the AIF as the foremost fighters of the war, the words of Newton Wanliss in the 14th Battalion's history are worth quoting.

[Australia's] representatives were throughout dominated by an exceptionally high sense of duty and patriotism … [the First AIF] was comprised almost entirely of civilians, without any knowledge or thought of war. When the war terminated fifty-one months later, these raw civilians had established a reputation as fighting men that has rarely been equalled. It would be absolutely incorrect … to say that the Anzacs won the war, but it would not, perhaps, be an exaggeration to say that … they were the finest soldiers on either side who took part in the greatest war in history.[11]

To be outstanding in such company takes exceptional personal qualities. Harry Murray and Percy Black were both described as supermen by fellow soldiers, and were widely admired almost to the point of hero-worship, something rarely bestowed by Australians, and then usually only to sports champions. These were Cyril Longmore's comments on Black:

Percy Black was one of these super-men … With no experience of the profession of arms he brought with him into the army a wide knowledge of men and the initiative and energy which are always parts of the personal equipment of the pioneer … he was a rock to lean upon in those stirring first days on Gallipoli … When he fell across the German wire at Bullecourt in April 1917, there was a widespread feeling of sorrow throughout the whole AIF that was not often shown in those days when casualties were so numerous.[12]

Harry Murray was summed up by T A White in the 13th Battalion history in these terms:

[Murray's] work throughout the war was that of a superman — a superman in heroism, energy, spirit and self-sacrifice, resourcefulness and devotion to duty … Not only was the 13th proud of him but the whole brigade was, from General to Digger. And his unconscious modesty won him still greater admiration … Murray's courage was not a reckless exposure to danger … [it] was a deliberately formed quality derived from a fervent loyalty, an earnest sense of duty, a thorough confidence in himself and his men, and a firm belief in the justice of his cause.

Some VC winners aimed at death; Murray always at victory. The knowledge that death was a probability never deterred nor held him from his main aim.[13]

With their 'bush' backgrounds, their patriotism and sense of duty, and the supreme expertise they developed so quickly in wartime, the two men could be said to represent the ultimate 'Digger'. Black's death in 1917 prevented the complete fulfilment of his potential (which can of course be said of countless others) but his reputation at that time stood extremely high. Writing many years after the war, Bean bracketed him with Murray, Jacka and Bill Lynas of the 16th Battalion as the most notable leaders of the 4th Brigade.[14] Bean also noted in the *Official History*[15] that many people regarded Black as the bravest man in the AIF. Such a distinction is of course impossible to prove, but one who had a firm view on that point was Lawrence McCarthy, VC, another of the 16th Battalion's notable personalities.

I have fought alongside VC winners — Murray, Jacka, Axford, Hamilton, Carroll and O'M[e]ara, and I make bold to say we all take our hats off to Percy Black as a brave soldier and leader in battle. It may be asked what particular formula can be used in allocating degrees of bravery. This question would trick me, but in spite of it I again assert that Percy Black is the bravest man I have known.[16]

Harry Murray, whose survival of so many attempts by numerous Turks and Germans to kill him was little short of miraculous, was described by Bean as 'the most distinguished fighting officer in the AIF'.[17] A good case has been made for that distinction to be applied to Albert Jacka instead,[18] but trying to make comparisons between those two great soldiers would be tiresome and pointless. The focus on the 4th Brigade could also be questioned. There were of course fourteen other infantry brigades in the First AIF, each with its quota of heroes: some names have already been mentioned in this book, and others who come to mind are Wally Hallahan (11th Battalion, 3rd Brigade) and Joe Maxwell, VC (18th Battalion, 5th Brigade). Nonetheless, any attempt to identify the greatest individual fighting soldier in the First AIF would have to include both Murray and Black in the shortest of short lists. It is extraordinary, that out of over 300,000 enlistees, these two men should be close mates who happened to begin their careers in the same small sub-unit and were in the same machine-gun crew at Gallipoli.

Public commemoration of Percy Black and Harry Murray has not been extensive by any means, but there are (or have been) a number of reminders of the impact they had in their time. The *Official History* recorded both men's deeds in some detail, in the context of the battles in which they took part, and they are also mentioned in more recent works of Australian military history. The first full biography of Harry Murray (*Mad Harry* by George Franki and Clyde Slatyer) was published in 2003. In the same year an Australian war memorial was opened in London, and in a speech by the Australian Prime Minister John Howard at Australia House prior to the ceremony, Harry Murray was one of only two Australian soldiers mentioned in detail (the other was General Sir John Monash).

Percy Black's immediate family preserved his memory in several direct ways. His brother Sam was in charge of the police station at Queenscliff, Victoria, in the 1920s, and he kept a large photograph of Percy, facing the public entrance — visitors frequently mistook the portrait for one of Lord Kitchener.[19] One of Percy's nephews, a son of his sister Jessie, was named Major Percy Black Adamson, and was usually known as Percy (Percy Adamson was the father of the former Collingwood footballer Lee Adamson). On the Yilgarn goldfields, Black's friend and business partner, J G Hughes, donated a handsome timber and silver shield for competition between the rifle clubs of the district. The Major Percy

Black Memorial Shield, which has a silver central boss engraved with a summary of his military record, was contested between 1918 and 1920, and presently hangs in the Moorine Rock Hotel near Southern Cross.

Cyril Longmore's history of the 16th Battalion, *The Old Sixteenth*, was published in 1929, and the book's dedication is to 'the memory of Percy Black and those other gallant men of the 16th Battalion, AIF, who gave their lives for Australia, 1914–18.' The frontispiece of the book is a full-page photograph of Black in officer's uniform. This and the dedication are unusual for AIF unit histories, in that he was neither a former commanding officer nor a VC winner (and the 16th boasted three of the latter), and shows Percy Black's great standing in the 16th's traditions. He was also mentioned by name in the histories of the other 4th Brigade battalions (as were Murray and Jacka) as well as in the 28th Battalion history; this again was unusual, as the somewhat parochial AIF unit histories rarely name anyone from outside the unit, apart from generals.

Percy Black's memory remained immediate with his wartime comrades. In 1933 a former 4th Brigade officer, visiting Perth from interstate, was scheduled to give a speech at the Soldiers' Institute; unexpectedly finding himself standing near the Institute's picture of Black, the visitor was overcome with emotion. 'Just behind me,' he said, 'is the photograph of one of the greatest soldiers and finest gentlemen I ever met.' He then broke down in tears and could not continue.[20]

As one of the nearly 60,000 Australian servicemen who lost their lives on active service during the Great War, the name of Percy Black appears on several official war memorials. In France, he is among the many thousands with no known grave who are listed on the Australian memorial at Villers-Bretonneux, and information about him is displayed in the local museum at Bullecourt. As well as the national roll of honour at the Australian War Memorial in Canberra, and the Western Australian state memorial in Kings Park, he also appears on the local memorial at Southern Cross. Also in Southern Cross, the Yilgarn History Museum has a small display on Black, and St George's Cathedral in Perth still houses the memorial plaque installed there in 1917 by returned 16th Battalion men.

Harry Murray, as a result of that wild night at Stormy Trench in 1917, will be remembered for as long as people remain interested in things military. The 1300 or so men who have been awarded the Victoria Cross are the elite warriors of the British and Commonwealth services, the bravest of the brave, and the prestige of the decoration is almost as high outside the Commonwealth. Accounts of Murray's exploits appear in numerous publications on VC winners. He is recognised in other ways too, particularly in Western Australia and Tasmania. Part of the original area of the Blackboy Hill training camp in suburban Perth has been set aside as a reserve, with a memorial which features plaques commemorating all the VC winners who trained there, including of course Harry Murray. The wards of Hollywood Private Hospital, Perth's facility for treatment of veterans, are named after Western Australian winners of the VC and the George Cross, and one of these is the Henry Murray Ward.

In 1979, on the occasion of the 150th anniversary of the foundation of Western Australia, a number of large, bronze-inlaid paving tiles were permanently set into the footpath of St Georges Terrace in Perth, showing the names of distinguished citizens in the state's history. Among these is Captain H W Murray, VC, described in a publication on the plaques as 'the archetypal defiant tenacious bushman-soldier, rising through the ranks.'[21]

The timber town of Dwellingup in the south-west has a display on Murray in its History and Visitor Information Centre, and his name and decorations are engraved on an honour board in the Town Hall at Menzies in the goldfields, the main township of the district where Murray had cut wood for his brother's business before the war. Another honour board on which his name appeared was in the Perth Trades Hall, recording union members who had attained distinction in the war (this board disappeared when Trades Hall was relocated).

Harry Murray is not included, however, in the commemorative plaques of Western Australian VC and GC winners in the precincts of the State War Memorial, as he does not meet the criteria for inclusion.[22] At Evandale in Tasmania, where the younger Kennedy Murray's house — Prosperous, later renamed Fallgrove — is still standing, the Evandale History Society has established a Murray Memorial Room at the town's tourism centre, with a display that includes a reproduction set of his decorations and medals. At the time of writing, the History Society was in the process of raising funds to erect a statue of Harry Murray.[23] At the site of the Cenotaph in Hobart, a memorial commemorating VC winners born or enlisted in Tasmania was opened in 2003, and Harry Murray's details are recorded on this structure.

In addition to its huge archive of general unit records and other historical documents, the Research Centre of the Australian War Memorial in Canberra has files of documents and newspaper clippings on both Murray and Black as individuals, as well as a number of photographs. In the AWM Museum there is a diorama of the First Battle of Bullecourt, and the accompanying panel mentions Percy Black's part in the battle. The AWM possesses the painting 'Death of Major Black' by Charles Wheeler, but this was not on display at the time of writing. Similarly, the Memorial's portrait of Harry Murray by George Bell, previously hung for many years, is currently in storage. At the time of writing, the national war museum's public display material on Lieutenant Colonel H W Murray, VC, CMG, DSO and bar, DCM, Croix de Guerre — the most decorated serviceman in Australian history — consists of a single photograph, approximately nine by seven centimetres, forming part of a montage of all Australian VC winners.

Many of the West Australian goldfields towns and minesites where Harry Murray carted supplies, carried the mail or cut wood have declined, and some have vanished altogether, like Comet Vale and Linden. In the south-west, the timber town of Holyoake where Murray worked in 1914 was destroyed by bushfire in 1960. Nearby Dwellingup was badly damaged in the same fires, but was rebuilt and is now adjusting its commerce to changes in the timber industry. The centre of Harry Murray's later life in Queensland, Glenlyon Station, was run by his family for many years after his death, but was sold recently. His widow Nell Murray remarried, was again widowed, and passed away in 2000. The towns and diggings in the Murchison and Yilgarn districts of Western Australia where Percy Black searched for gold have also declined since their glory days, as the gold ran out and other minerals assumed greater importance. The Black family still farms the property at Beremboke in Victoria, although the little school was closed in 1949.

For an ostensibly peace-loving society, it is something of a paradox that Anzac Day is the most important anniversary in the Australian calendar. Volumes have been written on this topic, and it has become something of a cliche that 1914–18 marked Australia's coming of age as a nation. The thought is not less valid by being a commonplace however, and reflects what people felt at the time, as well as later assessments. The war was a disastrous, nightmarish slaughter of the flower of a generation of young men, but most of the volunteers believed, with good reason, that they were fighting for the survival of democratic principles against a ruthless militarism. The fact that the thirteen-year-old nation of Australia played an outstanding part in the struggle was a revelation to its people that their country was indeed an entity separate from its imperial origins, with its own special characteristics, worthy to take its place among the rest of the world's nations.

The 14th Battalion historian Newton Wanliss said this in 1929 about the significance of Australia's Great War servicemen:

> … their exploits will always be Australia's great epic, whilst her war heroes will be her national heroes, when her politicians and millionaires are forgotten. Their victories won, their hardships endured, their heroism displayed, have set a standard for all time …[24]

Wanliss was both right and wrong. In the general sense, the Digger has remained a national symbol, the casually heroic fellow in the slouch hat. On the other hand, little is known, outside families and specialist groups, about the individuals who made special contributions to the tradition. In some ways this may be a good thing, but in the present age, where the main motivation of many prominent people seems to be personal aggrandisement, perhaps the country needs some individual heroes and role models.

The full picture of the personalities of Harry Murray and Percy Black remains elusive. Before the crisis of war brought them to prominence, very little was recorded about them, and it was only their very considerable virtues that were noted during the war. Harry Murray enjoyed a long life after the war, and showed himself (notwithstanding what may have happened in his failed first marriage) to be an upright citizen, a good husband and father and a pillar of his community. He revealed little of his attitude to the war itself, appearing to take an 'ours not to reason why' approach to the mistakes of higher authority, at least on the surface. There are some hints in his writings, and in his refusal to visit the old battlefields in 1956, that his private opinions may have been a little different, but he generally kept them to himself. Percy Black's letters home show only a conventional optimism about the war, although this may be just to avoid alarming his family and friends; his death in action meant he had no opportunity to reveal his true thoughts on the conduct of the war.

Everyone has some negative aspects to their characters, but whatever these might have been in Murray and Black, they were not apparent to their contemporaries. What was apparent was their unshakeable integrity, honesty, courage under fire and natural leadership ability. The Australian official historian, Dr C E W Bean, knew both men personally and had the greatest admiration for them. At one time, Bean was of the firm opinion that men from the bush made the best soldiers; he later reconsidered this view, but he would no doubt have found strong evidence for his original opinion through his contact with Murray and Black.

Charles Bean spent most of the war in or close to the front line, observing and recording the deeds of the men of the First AIF, and he dedicated his life to telling their story and preserving their heritage. The final paragraph of Bean's six lengthy volumes on the First AIF at Gallipoli and in France is probably the most quoted of his work; it is his closing comment on the force as a whole, but the paragraph can be applied equally to groups and individuals. The words seem very appropriate to Harry Murray and Percy Black:

What these men did nothing can alter now. The good and the bad, the greatness and smallness of their story will stand. Whatever of glory it contains nothing now can lessen. It rises, as it will always rise, above the mists of ages, a monument to great-hearted men; and for their nation, a possession forever.

Appendix
A Note on Decorations

With the recommendations for decorations awarded to
Harry Murray and Percy Black

With the notable exception of the Victoria Cross, the decorations for gallantry awarded to British Empire servicemen differed depending on whether the soldier was an officer or 'other rank'. Thus a particular deed could bring an award of the Military Cross (MC) to an officer, but a comparable effort by a ranker would be rewarded by the Military Medal (MM). Those two decorations ranked below the Distinguished Service Order (DSO) for officers and the Distinguished Conduct Medal (DCM) for others. However, in listing a soldier's decorations after his name, the 'officer' award would take precedence over the 'others'. Hence if Private Smith won a DCM, was subsequently commissioned and then won an MC, he would be referred to as Lieutenant Smith, MC, DCM.

The DSO was an unusual award in that it began as a minor order of knighthood (the full title was 'Companion of the Distinguished Service Order') but soon evolved into a true decoration, and could be won more than once. DSOs could be awarded to senior officers for outstanding performance as commanders on active service, and also to junior officers for gallantry in actual combat. Thus Harry Murray won the DSO twice while at the rank of captain. Such multiple awards of decorations are known as 'bars'. On the full medal, this is indicated by a metal bar across the ribbon, and by a metal rosette if the soldier is wearing just a ribbon strip. The expression 'MC and two bars', for instance, means that the soldier has been awarded the Military Cross three times (bars are often not mentioned in the most formal listings of names with post-nominal letters). Senior officers could also be appointed to minor orders of knighthood, as in Harry

Murray's Companion of the Order of St Michael and St George (CMG).

The Victoria Cross, of course, takes precedence over all other awards and makes no distinction of rank. The discussion that follows uses the expressions 'highly decorated' and 'most decorated' with reference to the 'value' of the awards won. A soldier with the VC and no other decoration would be considered as more decorated than one with, say, four other awards but not the VC.

Harry Murray is regarded as the most highly decorated infantryman of the entire British and Empire armies in 1914–18. The occasional descriptions of Murray as the most decorated Empire *soldier* are incorrect; the distinction of 'infantryman' is necessary because there were men in other branches of the services who were awarded even higher honours. A British medical officer (Captain N G Chavasse) won the VC twice, for instance, and the leading aviators of the Royal Flying Corps tended to be very highly decorated. Brigadier-General F W Lumsden of the Royal Marine Artillery was awarded the VC, CB (Companion of the Bath), DSO and three bars and the Belgian Croix de Guerre during the war. Lumsden, who also held several infantry appointments, was killed in 1918.

Harry Murray does have a rival for his title as the most decorated infantryman of the war in the English-born New Zealander Bernard Freyberg. Freyberg won the VC, CMG and three DSOs in 1914–18, the same level of awards as Murray (counting a DCM as the equivalent of a DSO) in terms of British decorations. Murray was also awarded the Croix de Guerre by France, but some sources state that Freyberg also won the Croix de Guerre.[1] Freyberg was an infantry officer throughout the war; although he initially held naval rank, this was as an officer of the Royal Naval Division, which was an infantry formation. Freyberg, who seems to have been as close to truly fearless as a sane person can be, became a professional soldier and went on to very high honours in the Second World War and after.

When it was felt that a soldier had earned a decoration, his commanding officer prepared a recommendation to higher authority. If the award was approved, the recommendation would be abridged into a citation, which could be printed in official publications such as the regular government gazettes. The recommendations for Percy Black's and Harry Murray's decorations are reproduced below. These generally provided more information than the equivalent citations, although they could still be quite brief early in the war, as seen by the one for Black's DCM. The inclusion of extra detail in later years was perhaps due to a greater need for commanding officers to 'make a case'. Certainly Colonel Durrant, Harry Murray's CO in the 13th Battalion, went to some length in preparing his recommendations.

Recommendations for Awards [2]

Percy Black

i. Distinguished Conduct Medal 22 May 1915 (rank of Lance-Corporal)

On night May 2/3rd during operations near Gaba Tepe: For exceptional gallantry; after all his comrades in his machine-gun section had been killed or wounded, although surrounded by the enemy, he fired all available ammunition and finally brought the gun out of action.

ii. Distinguished Service Order 13 August 1916 (rank of Major)

For very gallant leadership on the night of 9/10th August 1916, when he led his company over 'No Man's Land' in a charge against a German strong point; this charge was in addition to being a very gallant action a very difficult event, as it necessitated a change of direction, after passing one German strong point under very heavy artillery and machine-gun fire. Subsequently supervising the work of consolidation not merely on the frontage of his own company, but the consolidation of the frontage of two other companies, and subsequently on the night of the 10/11th August for seizing, under a very heavy barrage of artillery fire, with the assistance of the battalion bombing platoon, a further strong point some 200 yards further in advance of the firing line. The officer displayed great gallantry and marked powers of leadership during the operation on 9/12th August 1916 and is strongly recommended for a higher distinction.

Major Black's previous record is a very fine one — Private in the beginning of the war, promotion to NCO and commissioned at Anzac [from] NCO.

Harry Murray

i. Distinguished Conduct Medal undated — late May/early June, 1915 (rank of Lance-Corporal)

At Monash Valley, this NCO has been reported on in the very highest terms by the CO Battalion, Machine Gun Officer of the battalion and the Brigade Machine Gun Officer.

Although this NCO has been twice wounded in action, he has returned to duty at the earliest possible moment, being absent only long enough to have his wounds dressed. He has been most resourceful and energetic, in looking out for suitable targets and in finding concealed positions for his guns, and has repeatedly done most capable and meritorious work, under difficult circumstances, and in dangerous positions.

The efficiency of this non-commissioned officer has undoubtedly resulted in the infliction of serious losses upon the enemy.

The above services cover the period May 5th to May 31st.

ii. Distinguished Service Order 3 September 1916 (rank of Captain)

On 29th August during the attack at Mouquet Farm, this officer commanded the left flank Coy [company] of the 13th Battalion front line which was heavily shelled from daylight until dark. By his personal example he inspired confidence and resolution into his men throughout the day so that at 11 pm when the assault was delivered they moved steadily forward to the attack. Despite extremely heavy rifle and machine-gun fire and bombing, the objective was taken but the Coy was then so weakened by the losses that there was a tendency to give way before the strong counterattack which the enemy immediately made. By the fine example set by Capt Murray they beat off this attack and three subsequent attacks. Rifles were useless owing to the mud but Capt Murray extemporised a system of bomb supply and the fight continued for one hour during which he was twice wounded (since evacuated) but continued fighting. At one period an enemy bullet started a man's equipment exploding whereupon Capt Murray rushed to the man and tore his equipment off him thus saving the man's life at great personal risk. Realising that it was useless to remain longer in the German trenches Capt Murray then arranged the retirement of the remains of his Coy in the coolest possible manner although he had just previously shot two Germans in [a] hand-to-hand encounter. He continued on duty until all was safe on the morning of the 30th when, fainting from loss of blood, he was compelled to hand over his Coy. For coolness, bravery and soldierlike qualities this officer ranks among the best in the Australian Forces and is recommended for very high distinction.

iii. Victoria Cross 7 February 1917 (rank of Captain)

Captain Murray commanded the right flank Coy in the attack by the 13th Battn on Stormy Trench, NE of Gueudecourt on night of 4–5/2/17.

I placed him on the right flank because it was the most dangerous and critical. He led his Coy to the assault with great skill and courage and the position was quickly captured. Then followed the severest fighting in the history of the 13th Battn and I am sure that the position could not have been held and our efforts crowned by victory but for the wonderful work of this Officer. His Coy beat off one counterattack after another, three big attacks in all, although one of these consisted of no less than five separate bombing attacks. All through the night the enemy concentrated the fire of many 4.2s and 5.9s [artillery guns] on the sector of trench held by this Coy, and in 24 hours the fighting strength dwindled steadily from 140 to 48 i.e. 92 casualties including 1 officer killed and 2 officers wounded. On one occasion the men gave ground for 20 yards but Capt Murray rushed to the front and rallied them by sheer valour. With his revolver in one hand and a bomb in the other, he was ubiquitous, cheering his men, heading bombing parties, leading bayonet charges or carrying wounded from the dangerously shelled areas, with unequalled bravery. So great was his power of inspiration, so great his example, that not a single man in his Coy reported himself shell shocked although the shelling was frightful and the trench at times was a shambles that beggars description. His Coy would follow him anywhere and die for him to a man.

He won the DCM at Anzac and the DSO at Mouquet Farm in France.

I most strongly recommend Capt Murray for the Victoria Cross.

iv. Bar to the Distinguished Service Order 16 April 1917 (rank of Captain)

He rendered conspicuous service in the attack near Bullecourt on 11/4/17. He led his Coy with great courage and skill through 1200 yards of shell and machine-gun fire and he and his Coy still kept on although they lost 75% of their strength before reaching the 2nd Objective. Capt Murray being the senior Officer of the 4th Brigade in the 1st and 2nd Objectives went along the whole frontage [of] 900 yards organising and directing the defence, always encouraging the men of all units by his cheerfulness and bravery and always moving to the points of danger.

When the bomb supply was running out and the men gave ground, he rallied them time after time and fought back the Germans over and over again. When there was no alternative but to surrender or withdraw through the heavy machine-gun fire, Capt Murray was the last to leave the position. He is not only brave and daring but a skilful soldier possessing tactical instinct of the highest order. He has already been awarded VC, DSO, DCM.

v. Companion of the Order of St Michael and St George undated 1919
(rank of Lieutenant-Colonel)

This officer has commanded the Machine Gun Battalion of the [4th] Division since its inception on the 15th March 1918. His work has been marked by conspicuous gallantry, ability, tactical knowledge and devotion to duty. During the period 18th September to 11th November he commanded the machine-guns of the division (and those of an attached Machine Gun Battalion) with marked success in the operations which resulted in the capture of the Hindenburg Outpost Line. He also, as Liaison Machine Gun Officer with the 2nd American Corps, largely contributed to the successful work of the machine-guns of that Corps in the operations resulting in the breaking of the main Hindenburg Line near Bellenglise.

He is recommended for high distinction.

Bibliography

Archives and Original Documents

Australian War Memorial

War Diaries:
   13th Infantry Battalion
   16th Infantry Battalion
   4th Machine Gun Battalion
   12th Machine Gun Company
   24th Machine Gun Company
   4th Australian Division

The 'Bean Papers' — diaries, notebooks and correspondence of C E W Bean — Australian Archives papers held at the AWM (Series 3DRL8042 and 3DRL606).

Papers of Lieutenant G McDowell, 13th Battalion.

Document files and newspaper clippings relating to Lt Col H W Murray, VC, and Maj P C H Black (including Murray's letter to G Mitchell dated 5 June 1939).

Battye Library, Perth
Letters of H W Murray to C A Longmore, dated 26 April 1917 and 3 February 1918, in the 'Longmore Collection'.

Others
Army Service Records (Australian Archives) of:
   H W Murray
   P C H Black
   G Demel
   H George

Notes on Percy Black compiled by his nephew, the late Mr Ian Black, including several personal letters of Major Black. Copy in the Army Museum of Western Australia, and copy supplied to the author by Mr Black's widow, Mrs Beryl Black.

Diary of Lt Col D G Marks (extracts made available by George Franki).

Notes on Kennedy Murray (senior) and Anne White, compiled by June Dark.

Interview notes, made available to the author by Mr G Franki:

Mrs E Waugh (formerly Murray) interviewed by D Chalk

Mr Douglas Murray, interviewed by Mr Franki

Mr Joseph Cocker, interviewed by Mr Franki

Newspapers

Argus (Melbourne)

Black Range Courier

Brisbane Courier, and *Courier Mail*

Chinchilla News

Daily News (Perth)

Daily Telegraph (Sydney)

Herald (Melbourne)

Hobart Mercury

Kalgoorlie Miner

Launceston Examiner

Southern Cross Times

Sunday Times (Perth)

Sydney Morning Herald

The Times (London)

Weekly Courier (Launceston)

West Australian

Western Mail (Perth)

Westralian Worker

Books and Publications

Australian Dictionary of Biography, Melbourne, 1979 and 1986 (articles on P C H Black by C H Ducker, and on H W Murray by Merrilyn Lincoln).

Authurs, J. *From Wyangarie to Richmond: An Historic Record of the Richmond District of North West Queensland,* Richmond Shire Council, 1995.

Ballan Shire Historical Society. *A Pictorial History of the Shire of Ballan,* Ballan, Victoria, 1989.

—— *Brief History of Ballan & Surrounding Districts,* Ballan, 1981.

Bean, C E W. *Anzac to Amiens,* Australian War Memorial, Canberra, 1946.

—— *Gallipoli Mission,* Australian War Memorial, Canberra, 1948.

—— *Official History of Australia in the War of 1914–18, Vols I–VI,* Angus & Robertson, Sydney, 1929–1942 (also University of Queensland Press edition, St Lucia, 1983).

Belford, W C. *Legs-Eleven* (history of 11th Battalion), Perth, 1940.

Bunbury, B. *Timber for Gold,* Fremantle Arts Centre Press, Fremantle, 1997.

Burke's Peerage and Baronetage, 106th edition, London, 1999.

Carne, W A. *In Good Company* (history of 6th Machine Gun Company), Melbourne, 1937.

Charlton, P. *Pozieres: Australians on the Somme*, Methuen Haynes, Sydney, 1986.

Chataway, T P. *History of the Fifteenth Battalion*, Brisbane, 1948.

Collett, H B. *The 28th: A Record of War Service with the Australian Imperial Force, Vol I*, Perth, 1922.

Coppard, G. *With a Machine Gun to Cambrai*, Imperial War Museum, London, 1980.

Cutlack, F M. *The Australians: Their Final Campaign, 1918*, Sampson Low Marston, London, 1918.

de Havelland, D W. *Gold and Ghosts, Vol I*, Hesperian Press, Carlisle, WA, 1985.

Dennis, P, Grey, J, Morris, E and Prior, R (eds). *The Oxford Companion to Australian Military History*, Oxford University Press, Melbourne, 1995.

Doneley, R. *Black over Blue: The 25th Battalion A.I.F. at War, 1915–1918*, USQ Press, Darling Heights, Qld, 1997.

Ellis, J. *Eye-Deep in Hell*, Penguin Books, London, 2002.

Ford, R. *The Grim Reaper: The Machine-Gun and Machine-Gunners*, Sidgewick & Jackson, London, 1996.

Franki, G and Slatyer, C. *Mad Harry*, Kangaroo Press, Sydney, 2003.

Gammage, W L. *The Broken Years*, Australian National University Press, Canberra, 1974.

Grant, I. *Jacka, VC*, Macmillan, Melbourne, 1989.

Grey, J. *The Australian Centenary History of Defence, Volume I: The Australian Army*, Oxford University Press, Melbourne, 2001.

Gunzburg, A and Austin, J. *Rails through the Bush*, Light Railway Research Society of Australia, Melbourne, 1997.

Haythornthwaite, P. *The World War I Source Book*, Arms & Armour, London, 1992.

Hughes, R. *The Fatal Shore*, Collins Harvill, London, 1987.

Hunt, L (ed.). *Yilgarn: Good Country for Hardy People*, Yilgarn Shire, Southern Cross WA, 1988.

Joynt, W D. *Breaking the Road for the Rest*, Hyland Press, Melbourne, 1979.

Kennedy, L and Ollerenshaw, P. *An Economic History of Ulster*, Manchester University Press, Manchester, 1985.

Longmore, C A. *Carry On: The Traditions of the A.I.F.*, Perth, 1940.

—— *The Old Sixteenth*, 16th Battalion Association, Perth, 1929.

Maddock, M J. *Murray VC CMG DSO & bar DCM Croix de Guerre*, Evandale History Society, Tasmania, 1998.

Middlebrook, M. *The First Day on the Somme*, Allen Lane, London, 1971.

—— *The Kaiser's Battle*, Allen Lane, London, 1978.

Mills, J. *The Timber People*, Bunnings Ltd, Perth, 1986.

Mitchell, G D. *Backs to the Wall*, Angus & Robertson, Sydney, 1937.

—— *Soldier in Battle*, Angus & Robertson, Sydney, 1940.

Richards, R. *Murray and Mandurah: A Sequel History of the Old Murray District of Western Australia*, Shire of Murray and City of Mandurah, Pinjarra WA, 1993.

Rodgers, P and Rodgers, B. *No Sign of the Times: A Collection of Stories of the Menzies District*, Hesperian Press, Carlisle, WA, 1992.

Rule, E J. *Jacka's Mob*, Angus & Robertson, Sydney, 1933.

Senior, S L. *Sandstone*, Shire of Sandstone, WA, 1995.

Serle, G. *John Monash*, Melbourne University Press, Melbourne, 1982.

Stewart, A C. *Service on Land and Water 1939–46*, J C & M Stewart, Brisbane, 1995.

Thompson, J. *Machine Guns*, Greenhill, London, 1990.

Turrell, A N. *Never Unprepared: A History of the 26th Australian Infantry Battalion (AIF)*, *1939–1946*, 26th Battalion Reunion Association, Wynnum, Qld, 1992.

Von Stieglitz, K. *A History of Evandale*, Evandale History Society, Tasmania, 1992.

Wanliss, N. *The History of the Fourteenth Battalion*, 14th Battalion Association, Melbourne, 1929.

War Office, *Machine Gun Training*, HMSO, London, 1925.

Welborn, S. *Bush Heroes*, Fremantle Arts Centre Press, Fremantle, 1982.

White, T A. *Diggers Abroad*, Angus & Robertson, Sydney, 1920.

—— *The Fighting Thirteenth*, Tyrells Ltd, Sydney, 1924.

Wilson, P (ed.). *So Far from Home* (diaries of Eric Evans), Kangaroo Press, Sydney, 2002.

Wood, I S (ed.). *Scotland and Ulster*, Mercat Press, Edinburgh, 1994.

Journal Articles

Reveille

(Anon.) 'Harry Murray VC Home Again', October 1956, p. 4.

(Anon.) 'War Hero Guest at Reunion', July 1956, pp. 6–7.

Aarons, D. 'Terrible Tragedy: 16th Bn's Black Day', April 1933, pp. 24–5.

'A.W.B.' 'Major Percy Black: His War Career', January 1930, pp. 2–3.

Blackburn, D. 'Tank Opens Fire: Shock for 14th Battalion', April 1933, pp. 42, 60.

—— letter in January 1937 issue, p. 16.

Brand, C. 'Who Broke the Hindenburg Line?', April 1933, pp. 7, 61.

Herring, S. 'Three Waves: Dash for Hill 60', August 1932, pp. 54–5.

Knowles, B. 'Bullecourt Tragedy: Retrospect', April 1931, pp. 15, 26.

Longmore, C. (with comments by H W Murray). 'Major Percy Black', October 1936, p. 6.

Loughran, S. 'Hill 60: 4th Brigade Attacks', August 1933, pp. 36, 52–3.

Mitchell, G. letter in January 1937 issue, p. 15.

Murray, H W. 'Bravest Man in the AIF', December 1929, p. 8.

—— 'Capture of Stormy Trench', December 1937, pp. 10–11, 62–5.

—— 'Experimental Stage: Tanks at Bullecourt', April 1933, p. 10.

—— 'First Three Weeks on Gallipoli', April 1939, pp. 10–11, 60–2.

—— 'Get Through at Any Cost', April 1937, pp. 6, 52.

—— 'Grave and Gay: VC's Reflections', August 1932, p. 13.

—— 'His Hardest Battle', December 1935, pp. 33, 48.

—— 'Memories of First Bullecourt', December 1936, pp. 4, 56–9, 63–5.

—— 'Training Juniors: Field Ranks', June 1933, p. 2.

Wells, T. 'First Stunt: Vivid Impressions', August 1932, p. 34.

Winn, R. 'Stormy Trench', February 1938, p. 7.

Other Journals

(Anon.) 'Beremboke School', *The Settler* (newsletter of the Ballan Shire Historical Society), September 1988, pp. 6–7.

Baker, H. 'Australian Defence', *Early Days* (journal of the Royal Western Australian Historical Society), Vol 3, Pt 3, December 1941, pp. 43–4.

Bean, C E W. 'Percy Black', *The Link* (journal of the Toc H Society), January 1927, p. 6.

Chalk, D. 'The Great Harry Murray', *Wartime: Official Magazine of the Australian War Memorial*, No 8, 1999, pp. 28–33.

McCarthy, L. 'Our Bravest Fighter', *The Listening Post* (journal of the WA Branch, RSL), September 1924, p. 12.

Williams, J. 'The Death of Major Percy Black', *The Settler*, July 1991, pp. 6–7.

Notes

Chapter 1: Colonists and Convicts

1   Black and Longmore are both Scottish names. Percy Black gave his religious denomination as Presbyterian on his army enlistment papers, and was described as 'Scotch' and a 'Highlander' in later writings of his friend Harry Murray.

2   A school record shows the eldest as William John *Longmore*, suggesting that William Black was not his natural father (the similar Christian names may be coincidental).

3   Figures from S Welborn, *Bush Heroes*, pp. 25–6.

4   One source gives Hughes' first name as Thomas. There is no Thomas Hughes on the local electoral roll around this time, however, and Black was certainly closely associated with a John Griffin Hughes on the goldfields.

5   C E W Bean, 'Percy Black', *The Link*, 1 January 1927, p. 6.

6   In *The Fatal Shore*, 1987.

7   By coincidence, the Von Stieglitz family that had pioneered the Ballan district in Victoria were also prominent in the history of Evandale.

8   The author is grateful to Mrs Ruby Murray for information about her late father-in-law Charles Francis Murray (1870–1943).

9   This distance (210 miles) is stated in Murray's letters to G D Mitchell dated 5 June 1939. The Linden gold mine has been researched recently by Mr Alex Palmer, who has advised the author that the distance mentioned is too far for the shortest practicable round trip on the tracks between Kookynie and Linden. Murray may have simply been mistaken, or else his courier route covered a wider area.

10 It is equally likely that the courier run was Harry Murray's first job in WA, and his work in his brother's businesses was continuous.

11 From Bill Bunbury, *Timber for Gold*, 1997, p. 81.

12 An excellent account of the sleeper hewers' life in those days can be found in R Richards, *Murray and Mandurah: A Sequel History of the Old Murray District of Western Australia*, 1993. See also J Mills, *The Timber People*, 1986.

13 See Franki and Slatyer, *Mad Harry*, p. 7.

14 See C E W Bean, *Official History*, Vol. I, pp. 11–14.

Chapter 2: Blackboy Hill to Cairo

1   Winifred May, quoted in W Belford, *Legs-Eleven*, 1940.

2   C Longmore, *The Old Sixteenth*, 1929.

3   Based on C Longmore, *The Old Sixteenth*.

4   Enlistment forms did not ask for date of birth, just age in years and months.

5   Well-known as 'Non-com' in the *Western Mail*.

6   *The Old Sixteenth*, p. 8.

7   *Gallipoli Mission*, 1948, p. 46.

8   As stated in *The Old Sixteenth*. This time seems to include setting the sights and firing; 'Action' in the 1925 manual means the drill of setting up the gun and loading it, with a required time of 25 seconds. One of Harry Murray's letters indicates that the times achieved by the 16th's section did include sighting and firing.

9   H L Sykes ('Number One' on the second gun at this time), in the *Western Mail*, 29 November 1934.

10   T A White, *The Fighting Thirteenth*, p. 11.

11   Quoted in D Chalk, 'The Great Harry Murray', *Wartime*, No. 8.

12   *Official History*, Vol. I, p. 125.

13   G Mitchell *Soldier in Battle*, 1940, p. 126.

Chapter 3: Distinguished Conduct

1   Letter, H W Murray to G Mitchell, 5 June 1939, AWM Library.

2   C Longmore, 'Major Percy Black', *Reveille*, October 1936, p. 6.

3   H W Murray, 'The First Three Weeks', *Reveille*, April 1939, p. 61.

4   Described in Franki and Slatyer, pp. 20–21.

5   It is not clear from his account whether he had been hit during this action or his wound from 26 April was troubling him. Another of the machine-gunners, H L Sykes, later recalled that Murray had been 'hit under the left arm on [the] second day, in the head and through the finger' during the first weeks on Gallipoli (*Western Mail*, 15 August 1929). The head wound, presumably superficial, could also have been the one mentioned on page 80.

6   H W Murray, 'The First Three Weeks', *Reveille*, April 1939, p. 62.

7   With new units or large contingents of reinforcements, officers could be selected from the ranks during training.

8   The day before, Demel had been informed that he was to be commissioned as a lieutenant, but the army would not confirm this after his death, despite strong representations by his family. Murray and Black both wrote to the Demel family in support of their case. Copies of their letters are in Demel's Service Record.

9   E J Rule, *Jacka's Mob*, pp. 82–3.

10   ibid. The officer was Captain Albert Jacka, VC.

11   In *Backs to the Wall* (1937), pp. 109–11.

12   To G Mitchell, 5 June 1939, AWM Library.

13   Copy of original memo provided by Mr G Franki.

14   Anon, 'War Hero Guest at Reunion', *Reveille*, July 1956, p. 7.

Chapter 4: Officers and Gentlemen

1   When Murray first recorded this story, in a *Reveille* article, he wrote as if he had been watching the experience of another Australian. In his private memoirs, however, he affirmed that the soldier involved had been himself.

2   *Official History*, Vol. II, p. 662.

3   Letter in the 'Bean Papers', AWM 3DRL8042/23.

4   From an anonymous letter in the *Western Mail*, 8 April 1937. The correspondent was not specific about the date and location, and Murray may have been hit before the machine-guns moved up to cover the retreat.

5   Quoted in the Perth *Daily News*, 19 December 1919.

6   This incident is described in detail in the 16th Battalion history, *The Old Sixteenth*, but is dated 27 August, in accordance with Colonel Pope's notes. This appears to be an error (see the *Official History*, Vol. II, p. 736), although it is possible that similar actions occurred on both 21 and 27 August.

7   The *Sunday Times*, 27 May 1917.

8   From Capt Loughran's account in the Bean Papers (AWM 38 3DRL8042/21).

9   S Loughran, 'Hill 60', *Reveille*, August 1933, p. 53.

10   White, *The Fighting Thirteenth*, p. 51.

11   'Training Juniors — Field Ranks', *Reveille*, June 1933, p. 2.

12   Letter quoted in Franki and Slatyer, p. 39, and in D Chalk, 'The Great Harry Murray', *Wartime*, Issue 8, 1999.

13   The *Sunday Times*, 15 April 1917.

14   H B Collett, *The 28th. A record of war service with the Australian Imperial Force*, 1922. Black's service record says that he was attached to the 25th Battalion at this time; either this is an error, or he worked with both units during this period. The 25th was also in the line near the Apex.

15   Killed in action at Gallipoli in September, he was the 28th Battalion's first fatality of the campaign.

16   See, for example, the 12th Battalion history, L Newton, *The Story of the Twelfth*, Hobart, 1925.

17   White, *The Fighting Thirteenth*, p. 55.

18   E J Rule, *Jacka's Mob*, p. 28.

19   Quoted in Gammage, *The Broken Years*, p. 84; see also *Official History*, Vol. VI, pp. 1094–5.

Chapter 5: Western Front

1 This incident is recorded only in the *Official History* (Vol. III, p. 73n). Murray himself seems never to have mentioned it in any of his own writings. The *History* refers to 'Lieutenant Murray' although he had been a captain since March; it is just possible that the officer involved was Lieut *Harold* Murray.

2 In *Backs to the Wall* (1937) and *Soldier in Battle* (1940).

3 Quoted in the introduction to the UQP edition of the *Official History,* Vol. III.

4 In *Jacka's Mob*, also quoted in the *Official History*, Vol. III, p. 599.

Chapter 6: Mouquet Farm

1 According to the *Official History*. The 15th Battalion history says the attack was launched at 8 pm, and the history of the 13th (which was in support) says 1 am on 10 August.

2 From the battalion War Diary. (The *Official History* says thirty prisoners.)

3 C A Longmore, 'Major Percy Black', *Reveille*, October 1936, p. 7.

4 For his courage in carrying water and supplies up to the line and evacuating the wounded, Private Martin O'Meara (like Murray a former timber worker) was awarded the Victoria Cross.

5 C A Longmore, 'Major Percy Black', *Reveille*, October 1936, p.6.

6 The incident described here is based on an extract from the soldier's memoirs, and is among the papers on Percy Black compiled by his nephew, the late Mr Ian Black. Unfortunately, the author has been unable to identify the man.

7 At one point both units had to occupy the same narrow trenches while the changeover was taking place.

8 'His Hardest Battle', *Reveille*, December 1935, p. 33.

9 Peter Charlton, in *Pozieres: Australians on the Somme*, 1986, p. 236.

10 Lieutenant Henderson, for one, would appear to have earned a decoration.

11 There is a misconception that Black was awarded the DSO for this action. In fact, as the recommendation makes clear, the award was for his work on 9–12 August (see p. 122).

12 This is recorded only in the recommendation Colonel Durrant prepared a few days later; he must have heard the story from one of Murray's company.

13 *The Fighting Thirteenth*, p. 75.

14 'Major Percy Black', *Reveille*, October 1936.

15 Black apparently knew her and her family before she was married, but her maiden name is not known.

16 Letter in possession of Ian Black.

Chapter 7: 'Sheer Valour' at Stormy Trench

1   The 13th's MO, Captain Shierlaw, was on leave.

2   From R Winn, 'Stormy Trench', *Reveille*, February 1938, p. 7.

3   *The Fighting Thirteenth*, p. 85.

4   It was later said that one, Private V L Harris, was only thirteen years old (*Western Mail*, 29 December 1932).

5   The descriptions of 'A' Company's battle in Stormy Trench in the various sources differ in some respects, particularly in the sequence of events. The most detailed account is Murray's in *Reveille* of December 1937; with his usual modesty and to the dismay of potential biographers, however, he set out to describe the deeds of his men rather than his own. While I used Murray's version for the sequence of the various incidents, details of his personal actions are taken from the other sources. The combat which White's *Fighting Thirteenth* describes (Chapter XIX) as during the initial assault seems more likely to have occurred during the first counterattack. The two accounts written by Bean (*Official History*, Vol. IV, pp. 32–7, and his article in the *Western Mail*, 27 April 1917) tend to support this, although again there are some differences in detail (even between those two accounts themselves). Bean implies that the third German counterattack was a half-hearted affair, but other accounts describe a very serious attack which was only repelled with difficulty; Murray called it 'the most determined attempt of the night.'

6   He also included the map reference for his right flank.

7   H W Murray, 'Capture of Stormy Trench', *Reveille*, December 1937.

8   Colonel Durrant's report gives 'A' Company's total killed and wounded as 92, which would leave 57 unhurt.

9   'Capture of Stormy Trench', *Reveille*, December 1937.

10 In the 16th Battalion there was an officer named Ahrens and another called Aarons. Ahrens later changed his name to Ahearn.

11 *The Fighting Thirteenth*, p. 89.

12 The Battalion War Diary initially recorded 43 killed and 18 'missing' as well as 172 wounded.

13 The full text of the recommendation is in the Appendix.

14 *Official History*, Vol. IV, p. 35.

Chapter 8: Death in the Wire

1   A re-entrant is a 'dent' in the line, so to speak, where part of the line is further away from the opposing troops than the main portion of it, so that an attacking force would have to advance between enemies on either flank to reach their objective; it is the opposite to a salient.

2   As if this was not enough, yet another objective was originally proposed: to then sweep eastwards a further 3000 metres across the rear of the Hindenburg Line to confront the switch trench at close range. Fortunately this part of the plan was abandoned. Bean commented that 'victory might have been sought almost as reasonably by a plan to capture the moon.'

3   Reinforced by the report of a reconnaissance patrol led by Captain Jacka of the 14th, which confirmed that the enemy trenches were held in strength and the wire was still largely intact.

4   Harry Murray's comments in C Longmore, 'Major Percy Black', *Reveille*, October 1936, p. 7. Murray also recorded a slightly different version: 'Well, Harry, we have been in a few stunts together, but this is my last. I'll have that Hun front line first.' (*Reveille*, December 1929, p. 8).

5   *The Fighting Thirteenth*, p. 93.

6   Sergeant D Blackburn of the 14th Battalion, writing in *Reveille* many years later, expressed the situation succinctly: 'It certainly put Fritz wise to our little game.'

7   *The Fighting Thirteenth*, p. 93.

8   *Official History*, Vol. IV, p. 295.

9   B Knowles, 'Bullecourt Tragedy', *Reveille*, April 1931, p. 15.

10   ibid.

11   H Murray, 'Memories of First Bullecourt', *Reveille*, December 1936, p. 56.

12   There is a question as to whether Harry Murray saw Percy Black die. The sources are about evenly divided on this point, and Murray's own writings — his battlefield message at Bullecourt and his *Reveille* articles — also do not make it completely clear. The relevant battalion histories, for instance, say either that 'Murray saw him dying' (*The Fighting Thirteenth*, p. 95) or that he only saw the body afterwards (*The Old Sixteenth*, p. 135). C E W Bean's writings, however, consistently have Murray not actually witnessing Black's death. The *Official History* (Vol. IV, p. 302) says that Murray 'made an impassioned search for the body of Major Black, his old comrade,' and Bean took a similar line in his article on Black in *The Link* magazine (January 1927, p. 6). The question is probably settled by an entry in Bean's notes on First Bullecourt (AWM 3DRL1722/21): 'M[urray] wouldn't be satisfied till he saw him lying there.' It was Bean's practice to interview survivors after a battle, and he may well have got this comment from Murray himself.

13   Quoted in the *Official History*, Vol. IV, p. 317.

14   ibid.

15   The 48th Battalion was isolated in the German trenches and finally pulled back in good order an hour after the rest of the troops.

16   Blackburn and eight of his section (four wounded) got back to the Australian lines. (D Blackburn, 'Tank Opens Fire', *Reveille*, April 1933, p. 60.)

17   *Official History*, Vol. IV, pp. 349, 354.

18   C H Brand, 'Who Broke the Hindenburg Line?' *Reveille*, April 1933, p. 7.

19   N Wanliss, *The History of the Fourteenth Battalion*, p. 209.

20   D Aarons, 'Terrible Tragedy: 16th Battalion's Black Day', *Reveille*, April 1933, p. 25.

21   C Longmore, 'Major Percy Black', *Reveille*, October 1936, p. 6.

22   She was granted a bereavement payment of four pounds nine shillings per fortnight.

23   Letter in the possession of Mr Ian Black.

24   The original telegram form still exists.

25   *Sunday Times*, 27 May 1917. The comment on Black's promotion is not strictly correct: in fact he went straight from lance-corporal to second-lieutenant.

26   *Southern Cross Times*, 23 June 1917.

27   ibid., 30 June 1917.

28   *West Australian*, 25 June 1917.

29   The picture's present whereabouts are not known.

Chapter 9: The Path of Duty

1   In the 14th Battalion, Lieutenant Rule wrote (in *Jacka's Mob*) that his platoon 'seemed to be composed of school-children.'

2   In *Backs to the Wall*, 1937, p. 113.

3   *The Times*, 4 June 1917.

4   There were twelve nurses among the award recipients.

5   In fact, Murray was technically not entitled to the rank of major at the time of the investiture; his service record was endorsed on 22 May to the effect that he was required to relinquish his temporary major's rank as from 30 April, on the return to duty of Major Twynam, an original 13th Battalion officer rejoining the unit after a long absence.

6   The author is indebted to Sir David Montgomery of Kinross-shire (nephew of Clementine) for information about his family.

7   Letter in McDowell's papers, held by the Australian War Memorial Research Centre (AWM PR 00 276).

8   Diary published as *So Far from Home* in 2002.

9   Holmes said that Monash had 'abruptly interposed' himself and 'without my permission or consent, presented two of my officers' to HRH the Duke. Monash maintained that General Godley, the corps commander, had called him forward to make the presentations. (Serle, *John Monash*, p. 283.)

10   *So Far from Home*, p. 90.

11   As recorded in C E W Bean's diary on 25 August 1917 (AWM 3DRL606/132).

12   ibid.

13   Recorded in Lieut McDowell's letter of 20 June 1917, among his papers in the Australian War Memorial.

14   *Daily News*, 19 December 1919.

15   *The Fighting Thirteenth*, p. 126.

16   Later the 13th Battalion historian.

17   In *Diggers Abroad*, p. 119.

Chapter 10: Commanding Officer

1 Another instance in the 4th Division, John Corrigan, was a miner before the war, although a posting as a battalion adjutant suggests that he had a good formal education.

2 See the Bean Papers (AWM38 3DRL606/106).

3 *Sydney Morning Herald*, 9 April 1918.

4 W A Carne, *In Good Company* (1937).

5 See the *Official History*, Vol. V, Appendix 4.

6 In *Diggers Abroad* (p. 164) and *The Fighting Thirteenth* (p. 136).

7 Quoted in T Matthews, *Crosses*, 1987, p. 122.

8 In *Jacka's Mob*, p. 133.

9 Copies can be found in the unit War Diary, AWM Research Centre.

10 *Western Mail*, 22 December 1932.

11 Shortage of reinforcements had forced the reduction of the 12th Brigade to three battalions.

12 *Jacka's Mob*, p. 127.

13 The full text of the recommendation is given in Franki and Slatyer, pp. 143–4.

14 Gammage, *The Broken Years*, p. 204.

Chapter 11: Homecoming

1 See *Reveille*, 1 December 1939.

2 Described in Joynt's book, *Breaking the Road for the Rest*, 1979.

3 The *Ormonde* left England on 15 November, but Murray seems to have joined it at Toulon on 19 November.

4 *West Australian*, 20 December 1919.

5 ibid.

6 *Daily News*, 19 December 1919.

7 ibid.

8 Jacka's welcome in Melbourne a few months earlier was comparable.

9 *West Australian*, 20 December 1919.

10 Geoffrey Serle, *John Monash*, p. 422.

11 *Argus*, 27 December 1919.

12 ibid.

13 *Argus*, 30 December 1919.

14 ibid.

15 In T Wells, 'Lieut-Col D G Marks', *Reveille*, November 1936, p. 7.

16 *Mad Harry*, Ch. 9.

17 *Brisbane Courier*, 12 November 1927.

Chapter 12: The Sunlit Plains

1 *Sydney Morning Herald,* 12 June 1956; *From Wyangarie to Richmond,* p. 59.

2 *From Wyangarie to Richmond,* p. 158, and conversation with the author, 2003.

3 *Reveille,* December 1936.

4 *Reveille,* January 1937, p. 15.

5 See Chapter 8, page 170.

6 *Reveille,* January 1937, p. 15.

7 'Get Through at Any Cost', *Reveille,* April 1937, p. 52.

8 Murray's *Reveille* articles are reproduced in full as an appendix in Franki and Slatyer, *Mad Harry.*

9 'Major Percy Black', *Reveille,* October 1936, pp. 6–7.

10 *Reveille* did point out, however, that the order of selection was random and was not intended to indicate comparative merit.

11 A copy of this letter is held in the AWM Library.

12 *Service on Land and Water,* 1995. The author is grateful to Mr George Franki for extracts from this book.

13 In *From Wyangarie to Richmond,* p. 289.

14 A N Turrell, *Never Unprepared,* 1992, p. 12.

15 Later lieutenant-colonel. The author is indebted to Barnett's son, Mr Joel Barnett, for this story and the following one, which appeared in Mr Barnett's letter to *Defender* magazine, Spring 2003.

16 See J Grey, *The Australian Army* (Vol. 1 of *The Australian Centenary History of Defence*), Ch. 4.

17 *Service on Land and Water,* p. 68.

18 *Sydney Morning Herald,* 13 March 1954.

19 The alternative version of this story has Murray making the remark to the Duke and repeating it to the Queen.

20 They travelled by air (a four day trip in those days), in order to be in time for the first centenary event on 25 June. Most of the Australians attending the celebrations had left by ship in May, but the Murrays had been delayed at Glenlyon.

21 *Reveille,* July 1956, p. 7.

22 *Reveille,* October 1956, p. 4.

23 *Chinchilla News,* 13 January 1966.

Chapter 13: Great-hearted Men

1 David Chalk, 'The Great Harry Murray', *Wartime,* No 8, 1999, p. 32.

2 Bean, *Official History,* Vol. VI, p. 1083.

3 White, *Diggers Abroad,* p. 23.

4 Grey, *The Australian Army,* p. 61.

5 This point is discussed further in the Appendix.

6 Cutlack, *The Australians: Their Final Campaigns, 1918*, p. 13.

7 H W Baker, 'Australian Defence', *Early Days* (Journal of the Royal Western Australian Historical Society), December 1941, p. 44.

8 Bean, *Official History*, Vol. VI, p. 1085n.

9 ibid.

10 Cutlack, *The Australians: Their Final Campaign, 1918*, p. 18.

11 Wanliss, *History of the Fourteenth Battalion*, p. 354.

12 Longmore, *The Old Sixteenth*, pp. 1–2.

13 White, *The Fighting Thirteenth*, p. 90.

14 *Official History*, Vol. VI, p. 589.

15 Vol. IV, p. 293.

16 Letter in *The Listening Post* (journal of the RSL of WA), September 1924, p. 12.

17 *Official History*, Vol. I, p. 500.

18 See I Grant, *Jacka VC*, 1989.

19 Melbourne *Herald*, 30 April 1924. Samuel Black retired from the Victoria Police in 1926. The location of the picture is not known.

20 *Western Mail*, 16 February 1933.

21 WAY 79 Commerce Committee, *A Walk through the History of Western Australia*, 1979.

22 These criteria are: the recipient should have been born in Western Australia, or served in a West Australian-raised unit, or have lived most of their lives in Western Australia. The state of enlistment is not a factor. Murray was born in Tasmania, was serving with a New South Wales unit when he won the VC and moved to Queensland after the war. The latter point explains why John Carroll is included — although he was born in Queensland and won the VC with the 33rd (NSW) Battalion, he remained in Western Australia after the war. Only two of Western Australia's Great War VCs were actually born in the state. The author is grateful to Captain Wayne Gardiner RFD, curator of the Army Museum of Western Australia, for clarifying this matter.

There is an anomaly here, however. The memorial undercroft forms the state roll of honour, with the names of those killed or who died on active service engraved on the walls. RSL Trustee Mr Bob Mercer has advised the author that to be included here, the deceased individual need only to have enlisted in Western Australia. The implication of this is that, had Murray been killed after winning his VC (or in the process of winning it), his name would appear on the state's roll of honour, but not among its VC winners.

23 As of May 2005, there were strong indications that the Federal Government would be making a substantial grant of funds for the statue. It appears that the noted sculptor Peter Corlett will be undertaking the work.

24 *History of the Fourteenth Battalion*, p. 355.

Appendix

1   P Singleton-Gates, *General Lord Freyberg VC*, Michael Joseph, London, 1963, p. 84; and the article on Freyberg in Sir O Creagh and E M Humphries (eds), *The VC and DSO*, Vol. I, Standard Art Books, London, 1924. Debrett's Peerage, Baronetage, Knightage and Companionage (1923), p. 1552 also credits Freyberg with the Croix de Guerre.

2   A few minor alterations to spelling and punctuation have been made to the original documents.

Index

Contents

List of Maps

No Ordinary DETERMINATION

Percy Black and Harry Murray were extraordinary men who each made an enormous contribution to the Anzac tradition, yet these two great soldiers of the First AIF are largely unknown in the public sphere today. Both were workingmen in the West Australian bush when they joined up as privates in 1914; in their mid-thirties, they were older than the average enlisted man. Starting as the crew of a machine-gun at Gallipoli, their courage and natural abilities took them to high rank and earned them many awards for gallantry. Harry Murray finished the war as the most decorated infantryman in the British Empire and Percy Black, who lost his life on the barbed wire of the Western Front, was considered by many contemporaries to have been the bravest man in the AIF.

Jeff Hatwell has lived in Western Australia most of his life. He served in Vietnam as an infantryman in 1971 and now works in the public service. He completed a degree in economics and history at the University of Western Australia and has a deep interest in military history. *No Ordinary Determination* is his first book.

No Ordinary
DETERMINATION
Percy Black and Harry Murray of the First AIF

JEFF HATWELL

Fremantle Arts Centre Press

Australia's finest small publisher

First published 2005 by
FREMANTLE ARTS CENTRE PRESS
25 Quarry Street, Fremantle
(PO Box 158, North Fremantle 6159)
Western Australia.
www.facp.iinet.net.au

Consultant Editor Janet Blagg
Cover Designer Adrienne Zuvela

Cover photographs: *Lieutenant-Colonel H W Murray* (Government Printing Office,
State Library of NSW); *Major P C H Black* (Courtesy L Chamberlain); *Mouquet
Farm* (Australian War Memorial Neg Number E00005). The 'Rising Sun' emblem
is reproduced throughout with the permission of the Australian Army.

Typeset by Fremantle Arts Centre Press
and printed by Griffin Press.

National Library of Australia
Cataloguing-in-publication data

Hatwell, Jeffrey Edwin, 1949-
No ordinary determination.

Bibliography.
Includes index.
ISBN 1 920731 41 5.

1. Black, Percy, 1877-1917. 2. Murray, Harry, 1880-1966. 3. Australia. Army.
Australian Imperial Force (1914-1921) - History - World War, 1914-1918. 4.
Soldiers - Australia - Biography. 5. World War, 1914-1918 - Campaigns - Turkey
- Gallipoli Peninsula. 6. Australia - History, Military - 1901-1922. I. Title.

940.394

The 16th Battalion machine-guns were in [the] charge of men of no ordinary determination. 'Number one' in one of the gun's crews was Lance-Corporal Percy Black ... 'Number two' beside him was Private Harry Murray ...

C E W Bean

Lieutenant-Colonel H W Murray
VC, CMG, DSO and Bar, DCM, Croix de Guerre.
(Government Printing Office, State Library of NSW)

Major P C H Black
DSO, DCM, Croix de Guerre.
(Courtesy L Chamberlain)

Acknowledgements

The author is very grateful to the following people who provided information, assistance and encouragement in the writing of this book:

Bernard Arrantash, Joel Barnett, Beryl Black, Lorna Chamberlain, Des Colevas, John Cox, June Dark, Jessie Dehnert, Mitchell Evans, George Franki, Wayne Gardiner, Bev Harvey, Coral and Len Langford, M J Maddock, Bob Mercer, Sir David Montgomery, Douglas Murray, Ruby Murray, Dorothy Payne, 'Mum' Reid, Clyde Slatyer, Clem Sutherland and Alf Worth. Steve Fraser and Joan and John Munckton read the early drafts and made many useful suggestions. Special thanks are owed to my editor Janet Blagg, and to the people at Fremantle Arts Centre Press for their faith in a first-time author. Finally, my deepest gratitude to Elspeth Langford, whose unflagging confidence and enthusiasm ensured that an idea became a reality.

Maps were drawn by Colin Criddle, adapted from originals as follows: pages 57 and 77: L Carlyon, *Gallipoli*, Pan Macmillan Australia, 2001; page 100: J Laffin, *Australians at War: Western Front 1916–17*, Time-Life Books, 1987; page 111: R Doneley, *Black Over Blue: The 25th Battalion A.I.F. at War, 1915–1918*, USQ Press, 1997; pages 118, 124, 125, 128, 129 and 159: C E W Bean, *Official History of Australia in the War of 1914–18*, Vols III and IV; page 194: R R Sellman, *A Historical Atlas 1789–1962*, Edward Arnold, 1962; page 200: G Serle, *John Monash*, Melbourne University Press, 1982. The diagrams on pages 102 and 104 were adapted by Colin Criddle from those in J Ellis, *Eye Deep In Hell*, Penguin, 2002.

For Connie and Jessie